Matinee Melodrama

Matinee Melodrama

· ·

Playing with Formula in the Sound Serial

SCOTT HIGGINS

Rutgers University Press

New Brunswick, New Jersey, and London

Library of Congress Cataloging-in-Publication Data
Higgins, Scott, 1968–
    Matinee melodrama : playing with formula in the sound serial / Scott Higgins.
        pages cm
    Includes bibliographical references and index.
    ISBN 978–0–8135–6329–9 (hardcover : alk. paper)—ISBN 978–0–8135–6328–2 (pbk. :
alk. paper)—ISBN 978–0–8135–6330–5 (e-book (web pdf))—ISBN 978–0–8135–7396–0
(e-book (epub))
    1. Film serials—United States—History and criticism. 2. Motion picture plays,
American—History and criticism. I. Title.
    PN1995.9.S3H54 2016
    791.43'616—dc23
    2015012448

A British Cataloging-in-Publication record for this book is available from the British Library.

Visit our website: http://rutgerspress.rutgers.edu

Manufactured in the United States of America

For Jack, Bess, and Sam
Adventurers!

Contents

	Acknowledgments	ix
1	Serials, Melodrama, and Play: Why Study Serials?	1
2	Storytelling on a Schedule: Narrative Form in the Sound Serial	27
3	The Serial World	49
4	Cliffhanging	72
5	Narrative and the Art of Formula	98
6	Film Style and the Art of Formula	125
7	Cliffhanger Legacies	156
8	Conclusion	178
	Appendix: Some Sources for Sound Serials	185
	Notes	189
	Selected Bibliography	201
	Filmography, 1930–1956	205
	Index	211

Acknowledgments

I cannot name, much less repay, all the colleagues, teachers, students, and friends who made this book possible, but I will try. Jeanine Basinger, a woman who has more ideas in a day than the rest of us have in a year, first suggested that sound serials might merit a book of their own, and she remained a keen adviser and advocate throughout. Sara Ross kept my work honest with her incisive observations about plotting, melodrama, and character. Steve Collins and Marc Longenecker challenged me to articulate what I found cinematic and reminded me to meet these films on their own terms. Lea Carlson somehow created time for me to write every week, while keeping everything else from falling apart. I count myself as terribly fortunate to have such very smart and tolerant people in my daily life.

Chris Holmlund and Eric Lichtenfeld were unstinting comrades in action, their erudition matched only by their generosity and humor. David Schwartz shared resources from the Museum of the Moving Image and had the good sense to anticipate my research by recording panel discussions years before I started thinking about serials. Members of the Popular Seriality Research Unit opened my eyes to new conceptual possibilities and welcomed me into their conversation. Frank Kelleter, Ruth Mayer, Ika Brasch, Jason Mittell, and Shane Denson breathed intellectual life into this project when it was most needed. Phyll Smith joined the effort, pointing me in the direction of new research and clarifying historiographical questions. Dara Jaffe pored over archival documents and served as an all-around research henchwoman.

This book has its origins in the Cinema of Adventure and Action course that I teach at Wesleyan. Without my students (many of whom have long since become colleagues), these ideas would never have taken form. Among them, Matt Connolly, Jeremiah Friedman, Katie Walsh, Thad Ruzicka, Logan Ludwig, David Kongstvedt, Maegan Houang, Gabriel Urbina, and Ethan Young reminded me of "mindless" action's cinematic merit and helped me find the words to describe it.

Wesleyan University provided financial support in the form of a Project Grant to defray expenses of my research. Leslie Mitchner at Rutgers University Press was the epitome of both patience and rigor. India Cooper saved me from grammatical embarrassment and helped match words to meaning. All those I fail to name will, I hope, forgive the limits of my memory in the wee hours before a looming deadline. I promise to return the countless favors whenever and wherever. Finally, none of this could have been thought or written without the financial, spatial, temporal, emotional, figurative, and literal support of the inhabitants of 8 Belvidere Terrace. Sally, Jack, Bess, and Sam are my fighting legion.

Matinee Melodrama

1

Serials, Melodrama, and Play

● ● ● ● ● ● ● ● ● ● ● ● ● ● ● ● ● ● ● ●

Why Study Serials?

The opening chapter of *The Phantom Empire* (Brower and Eason, 1935) boils with cockeyed vitality. Gene Autry's "gang" robs a stagecoach of musical instruments. Back at their "Radio Ranch" they launch into the speedy patter song "Uncle Noah's Ark," part of their weekly broadcast. Frankie and Betsy (Frankie Darro and Betsy King Ross), the young "president and vice-president of the National Thunder Riders Club," step to the microphone and invite the radio audience to join their organization. To explain its name, the two kids introduce a flashback in which legions of caped and helmeted horsemen bolt across the landscape. Frankie, still within the flashback, looks directly into the camera and announces: "That's how we came to call our club the Thunder Riders." Without delay, Autry narrates the next installment of the Thunder Riders' Radio Play, enacted before the camera by members of his band. Bandits batter at a cabin door held tight only by the brave homesteader's arm in place of the bar lock. Autry announces, "It seems but a moment before his bruised and tired arm would break," and then asks: "Will the Thunder Riders get there in time?"

All of this is mere prelude to the introduction of the villainous Professor Beetson (Frank Glendon), who has his sights set on the lode of radium hidden beneath Radio Ranch, and the spectacular revelation of the (miniature) underground "scientific city" of Murania, ruled by Queen Tika (Dorothy

Christy), who monitors the primitive surface civilization on her giant television. In less than ten minutes, we are asked to enjoy the show, encouraged to acknowledge its silliness, and invited to play in and with this world. Bizarre juxtapositions, direct address, suspenseful interruption, and the mandate to employ any cheaply available means for a thrill are the serial's indispensable resources. *The Phantom Empire* is part of a rich tradition that thrived at the very margins of studio-era Hollywood: a tradition of creative ridiculousness, visual brio, and distinctively outlandish storytelling (see figure 1).

The founding premise of this book is that sound serials are intrinsically interesting; they demand our film-historical attention simply because they exist. These films, over two hundred of which were produced between 1930 and 1956, also merit study because they have been influential and because they are relevant to contemporary media scholarship. Two generations after the last American serial was produced, they continue to inspire dedicated fan communities and to reverberate in our media culture, from the costumed attendees

FIGURE 1 Promotional art for *The Phantom Empire* (1935). Author's collection.

of Comic-Con to contemporary action film franchises. Researchers in the burgeoning field of seriality studies consider continuing narrative "a defining feature of popular aesthetics."[1] In comparison to work on television, comics, and silent film, however, academics have been surprisingly slow to take up the sound serial. The present volume addresses the serial's influence and participates in scholarly discourse, but it originates in the observation that these films are deeply engaging, powerfully entertaining, and infinitely watchable.

They are also quick, dirty, and unabashedly formulaic. By the standards of most feature films, sound serials can appear cheaply melodramatic and devoid of psychology, subtlety, or elegance. But this is not their failing. The serial's strengths aren't the classical feature's dramatic unity, coherence, or even continuity but strongly drawn situations, starkly physical characters, and predictable, inhabitable worlds. Indeed, the case of sound serials helps demonstrate how selective and narrow our conception of studio-era cinema might be. Our aim here is to meet these films on their own terms by dwelling within the form. Sound serials deliver direct, visceral, and extended narrative experiences that reassure us in the face of risk, beckon our return, and, above all, invite us to play.

Generally, this book follows the "poetics" model of film scholarship described by David Bordwell, an approach that privileges formal concerns while rooting analysis in proximate aesthetic, economic, technological, and cultural contexts. Bordwell frames the analytical and historical questions of poetics this way: "What are the principles according to which films are constructed and through which they achieve particular ends? . . . How and why have these principles arisen and changed in particular empirical circumstances?"[2] In the case of serials, this means closely examining their sounds, images, and stories, attending to the craft practices of filmmakers, and reconstructing the constraints that shaped the filmmakers' choices. The form's regular rhythm of action, cliffhangers, Rube Goldberg logic, and confident implausibility was the result of artistic problem solving, carried out in peculiar institutional contexts. This methodology emphasizes analyzing film form and narrative in detail and carefully taking stock of story structures, editing patterns, cinematography, and staging.

Such tactics, at home in a study of *Citizen Kane* (Orson Welles, 1941) or *Vertigo* (Alfred Hitchcock, 1958), may seem out of place in a book about routine formula films. Why should we devote energy and time to analyzing apparently simple movies? One reason is that we know so little about them. Serials are deceptively familiar. Their basic conventions and components are identifiable after two or three episodes, and this can give historians a false sense of mastery. To paraphrase Viktor Shklovsky, serials swiftly cover themselves in "the glassy armour of familiarity" and "cease to be seen and begin to be recognized."[3] That armor has tended to deflect scholarly inquiry, consigning sound serials to the province of passionate fans who are not so easily dissuaded from "seeing." The majority of writing on sound serials consists of large-scale tax-onomies of genre types and studio outputs, or exhaustive catalogs of chapters, performers, production staff, repeated footage, and the like.[4] Genre guides and episode-by-episode commentaries, many of them sharply observed, provide an overview of conventions, some evaluative guidelines, and even a rough canon. They tend not to explore serials' film-historical specificity, their distinctive relationship to Hollywood aesthetics, or the precise methods by which they organize viewer experience. In contrast to the fans' often obsessive attention to interesting minutiae, the best scholarly work on sound serials has, so far, focused on context rather than the films themselves. Recently, Guy Barefoot has undertaken a meticulous and illuminating study of sound-serial distribution and exhibition during the 1930s, and Rafael Vela has written extensively about the form's economic and cultural circumstances.[5] Both works provide an invaluable background to the present volume, even as they highlight our need for an account of storytelling and style.

Another reason for analyzing sound serials is the insight they can offer into cinematic storytelling in general and Hollywood filmmaking in particular. Because they are so bare-bones, sound serials are virtual laboratories for suspense and action. If Hitchcock built cathedrals of suspense from fine brick-work of intersecting subjectivities and formal manipulations, sound serials used Tinkertoys. Because of this, we can plainly see narrative armatures and variations. Where Hollywood features provide motivations, psychologies, and complex style to naturalize and efface the telling of the tale, sound serials reach back to more rudimentary but nonetheless graceful practices of silent one-reel films made before 1912. Cliffhangers that remain riveting despite shopworn gimmicks shed light on the basic processes behind, and the limits of, cinematic suspense.

Finally, though marginal, sound serials are firmly rooted in the studio era, often referred to as the period of Hollywood classicism. Debates about the explanatory value of classicism have raged since the term was first formalized in Bordwell, Janet Staiger, and Kristin Thompson's tome *The Classical Hollywood Cinema: Film Style and Mode of Production to 1960*, published in 1985. Without detouring through those debates, we might safely note that sound serials challenge some principles of classicism, like unity of time and compre-hensibility, while obeying others, like goal orientation and continuity editing. In broadening our view of Hollywood beyond feature films, serials can deepen our grasp of studio-era norms, classical or otherwise.

Serials also deserve our time because they are only apparently simple. As we will see, basic principles yield sophisticated variation. With a tight set of con-ventions in place, like an episode's five-part structure, or the regular and timely interruption of catastrophe, serial filmmakers experimented to hold their audiences and keep things fresh. Constraints set clear limits, encouraged proficiency, and enabled innovation. Stunt crews at Republic, for instance, refined action choreography in fight routines that breathe with kineticism, while editors at Universal excelled in building new sequences out of stock footage. Our detailed look at *Daredevils of the Red Circle* (Witney and English, 1939) and *Perils of Nyoka* (Witney, 1942) will show how screenwriters and directors distinguished their work by adjusting the regular alternation of exposition and action scenes. Moving directly from a fight through a chase and into an entrapment might create a continuous chain of action, but it also required methods for shoehorning exposition in along the way. Balancing action against plot constituted an art among serial creators. Alternatively, screenwriters might outdo one another in frantic absurdity by packing ideas together, speedily introducing and resolving situations, as in the opening of *The Phantom Empire*. Like a game of few rules that generates complex play, serials are easily learned but offer opportunities for masterful variation. By studying them, we can observe filmmakers' ingenuity in handling a narrative blueprint, solving creative problems, and recombining standard parts. They testify to the constructive advantages and artistic possibilities of formula.

Art at the Margins: A Historical Overview

This is a work of poetics rather than straight history. However, an overview of the production, critical reception, and intended audience of the sound serial will help situate the analyses that follow. Sound serials had a good run. Columbia, Universal, Republic, and tiny houses like Mascot, Regal, and Principle Pictures produced over two hundred twelve-to-fifteen-part chapterplays between 1930 and 1956. During the 1940s the three largest producers each released about four serials a year, enough to supply independent neighborhood and rural theaters with an episode a week.[6] They represent a minor but remarkably sturdy production trend that did consistently solid business on tightly controlled budgets. *Variety* explained, "Turning out serials is a tough grind that permits neither wasted time nor motion. . . . They are a studio's big sales lever with the smaller showshops and in the sticks. The back country exhibs don't object to the 'A' product but they require serials and westerns."[7] At its height in the late 1930s and early 1940s, the form rated serious attention from the Hollywood industry amid a drop in attendance and disaffection with double bills. In March of 1940, *Variety* reported that "a rapidly increasing number of houses have added cliffhangers to their Saturday matinee shows during the past two years" and credited presold properties from radio and comics for the "skyrocketing" business.[8] In November, the trade paper reported that the big five studios (Warner Bros., MGM, Paramount, RKO, and 20th Century Fox) were "gazing at the . . . cliffhanger takes with envious eyes" and predicted that they would "take a flier into the serial field within the next year" to get in on the "secure profit-grabbing possibilities of the chapter films" with their "fixed market."[9] The serials' ascendance was brief, and these films rarely registered on *Variety*'s radar during the remainder of the decade. Still, the form persisted at the margins of the industry until the 1950s, when its target audience of eight-to-sixteen-year-olds migrated to television and the studio system was finally dismantled.[10]

By all accounts, making a sound serial was an arduous but efficient affair. Budgets were miserly, with Republic and Columbia spending between $140,000 and $180,000 per series on average and Universal between $175,000 and $250,000.[11] This was roughly equivalent to a stand-alone programmer from the respective studios, but stretched across triple the running time. Titles were set and publicized to exhibitors in advance, leaving the production staff to envision a story that could support such an outsized project.[12] Teams of writers penned phonebook-sized screenplays that ran to several hundred pages. Republic's pressbook for *The Lone Ranger* (Witney and English, 1938), for example, brags that the final film contains some 1,800 scenes, as compared to 400 to 500 in a regular feature.[13] The cutting continuity, a detailed log of every shot in the film, for the twelve-chapter *Ghost of Zorro* (Brannon, 1949) lists a staggering 2,657 shots.[14] Producing a narrative at this scale demanded rigorous proficiency. Assistant directors broke the shooting down by location and actor on production boards, which would serve as daily schedules.[15] Two directors routinely shared filming, alternating preproduction and shooting day to day. Neither would have time to screen rushes, and so depended on the money-minded producers to check their work. Shooting out of continuity was the Hollywood norm, and serials pushed it to an extreme. Recalling his work at Republic, William Witney described shooting master shots for six different chapters from a single camera position on a recurring set in one day, and then moving in to mediums and close-ups.[16]

Studios allotted a mere four to six weeks for shooting, which translated to sixteen-hour workdays for the crew.[17] To handle inevitable delays due to weather, serial units shot exteriors first, keeping a cover set available in case of rain. This usually meant that stunt and action scenes would be finished first, using doubles, and the principals' interior scenes were scheduled later. Filmmaking ingenuity helped make the most of tight schedules and budgets. Witney reports having made the twelve-chapter *King of the Mounties* (1942) in only twenty-two days, shooting locations with the leading man and a small troupe of doubles standing in for the rest of the cast. He filmed quickly and without sound, and then brought the principals in to film dialogue on a soundstage, standing before projections of still photographs shot on location.[18] Witney pushed the serial mode of production to its limits, but his choices typify priorities and production practices: action first, dialogue and story second.

The editorial staff went to work before the shooting stopped, logging footage according to scene and episode each day, so that they could begin final cutting immediately after production wrapped.[19] Jack Mathis, discussing Republic, estimates that each episode took one week to edit and postproduce (including music, sound effects, etc.). The unrelenting rush continued into the serial's distribution, as studios released chapters as soon as half of the episodes were complete. While the first installment was playing a matinee, the seventh was still being cut and scored.[20]

Those involved in this breakneck creation made no pretense of artistry, and few film critics deigned to comment on serials' aesthetic merits. Only the *Motion Picture Exhibitor*, a small trade paper aimed at independent theaters, consistently reviewed serials, and it provides an invaluable view of the form's shifting qualities during the studio era. Each of the 214 short reviews published between 1934 and 1958 (including reissues) indicates the serial's likely market and concludes with a rating, usually "fair," "good," or "excellent." Above all, the *Exhibitor* critic valued speed, originality, production value, and the potential for adult appeal. Juveniles were assumed to be the core viewership, but orbiting around them were "serial fans," "parents," "addicts," and "initiates." A film pitched straight to the youngster trade might receive praise, as *White Eagle* (Horne, 1941) does: "It'll have the kids sitting on edge and that's what serials are for. EXCELLENT."[21] Generally, though, acclaim was reserved for films with cross-generational appeal, defined variously in terms of pace, action, suspense, budget, and eclecticism. *Drums of Fu Manchu* (Witney and English, 1940) reached "excellent" because "its action-bent and suspenseful end makes top serial entertainment." The critic concludes, "Kids and their parents will be coming back for more."[22] Universal's casting of Dick Foran in the relatively high-budget *Riders of Death Valley* (Beebe and Taylor, 1941) led the critic to predict that it would "please the serial-addicts as well as the initiates who are lured into the theatre by the names on the marquee. . . . Excellent."[23] *The Phantom Empire* "set a new mark for serials" by mixing an ancient civilization, "the natural western atmosphere," a villainous professor, and "plenty of electrical apparatus and some swell advanced ideas in what Murania looks like." For the critic, the bizarre juxtaposition "provides plenty of selling angles," earning *The Phantom Empire* a "Top Notch" ranking and the singular approbation "New Serial Peak."[24]

Lesser serials showed budget consciousness, were derivative, and were primarily suited to the youth trade. *Overland Mail* (Beebe and Rawlins, 1942) receives a cautious "good" on this basis: "The episodes noted contained plenty of stock shots, but they're matched well. All in all, this should satisfy the kids, even though it sticks to the regular routine of this type of serial."[25] At the low end of the scale were "fairs" like *The Invisible Monster* (Brannon, 1950), judged a "slam bang meller . . . for the kids and undiscriminating serial followers," and

The Lost Planet (Bennet, 1953), which trotted out "such up-to-date things as astra radio, hypnotic ray, cosmojet, flying saucers, fluoro-ray, stellar-scope, cosmic cannon, sonic vibrator, mind monitor, thermic disintegrator, degravitizer, prysmic catapult, solar thermo furnace, etc." The *Exhibitor* concluded that it "should attract kids and serial fans" but was "pretty far-fetched, hard-to-believe stuff, even for the non-discriminating."[26] Behind the *Exhibitor's* succinct judgments was an appreciation of originality and variation within the formula. *The Phantom Empire* is certainly no more believable than *The Lost Planet*, but where the former experimented with fresh combinations, the latter reheated gimmicks in a single genre that by 1953 had lost its novelty.

Because of the paper's consistent standards, its reviews offer a gauge of the form's creative health across its history. They suggest a brief heyday for sound serials in the late 1930s and early 1940s, followed by extended decline. The eleven reviews from 1934 through 1935 are generally positive, deeming two titles "Top Notch" (*Young Eagles* [Laurier and Moore, 1934], and *The Phantom Empire*), one "Roaring" (*Burn 'Em Up Barns* [Clark and Schaefer, *1934*]), one "Excellent" (*The Miracle Rider* [Eason and Schaefer, 1935)]), and one "Swell" (*The Fighting Marines* [Eason and Kane, 1935]). Beginning in 1936, the critical vocabulary stabilized, and "very good" to "excellent" ratings began to rise. Thirty-one serials merited "excellent" between 1936 (the release of *Flash Gordon* [Stephani and Taylor]) and 1942, with extended runs of high ratings between late 1937 and early 1938, and between late 1939 and early 1941. After a small burst of five "excellent" ratings in 1942, evaluations dipped. Only two new productions were judged "excellent" from 1943 to 1958. Meanwhile, the paper had issued only nine "fairs" before 1943, but seventeen during the remainder of the decade and another twenty-five during the 1950s. By the time of the *Lost Planet* review quoted above, the *Exhibitor's* estimation of serials bottomed out. *The Great Adventures of Captain Kidd* (Abrahams and Gould, 1953), reviewed in September of 1953, was the very last serial to rate a "good." Serial fans consider the late 1930s through the early 1940s the "golden age" of sound serials, and the *Exhibitor* appears to support this.[27] During this period all three producers were delivering full slates, comic and radio adaptations were in high gear, and, as *Variety* noted above, an increasing number of exhibitors added matinees.

The *Exhibitor* also provides insight into the sound serial's mixed viewership. Children who populated Saturday matinees were the base audience, but adults, who might sneak in to early shows or see serials attached to a feature program on Friday night, also counted. This book assumes that the youth audience defined the sound-serial form and structured its appeals, but not exclusively so. Merchandising and promotional strategies sought to embed serials in children's culture by borrowing youth club campaigns associated with radio and comic strip properties.[28] *Flash Gordon* and *The Lone Ranger*, in particular, were heavily merchandised to promote dress-up play and mimicry. Even so, producers claimed that their films could spur wider interest. Universal's promotional "text book" of the late silent era, entitled *How to Make Money with Serials*, recommends exhibitors "make FRIDAY NIGHT the serial night for older folks," and advises, "Once you get the kids coming they drag the older folks along. It never fails."[29] Not all serials could hope to entice these older folks. Narrowly juvenile efforts like *Scouts to the Rescue* (Taylor and James, 1938) and *Junior G-Men* (Beebe and Rawlins, 1940) play directly to youngsters, and the *Exhibitor* predicted success for them on this basis. The reviewers proclaim, "The kiddie matinees are in for a corking treat" with *Scouts*, and "It's a cinch the kids are going to flock" to *Junior G-Men*, prospects that earned each an "excellent" rating.[30] On the other hand, serials like *Holt of the Secret Service* (Horne, 1941) and *Brenda Starr, Reporter* (Fox, 1945) resemble adult crime programmers, complete with casinos, nightclubs, and snappy dialogue. *Holt*, in fact, draws comedy from scenes of marital argument that might actually discourage younger viewers.

Scouts and *Holt* represent opposite ends of a spectrum of films that centered their address on children but did not exclude adults. The *Exhibitor*'s attention to cross-generational appeal as an evaluative criterion should dissuade us from imagining a strict age limit on the audience. Similarly, in his study of serial promotion and reception in the 1930s, Guy Barefoot offers ample evidence that they sought and found success beyond the Saturday matinee, especially in rural America: "[Sound serials were not] only made with children in mind or only watched by children. They came to be identified as appealing to children, more specifically rowdy children, but 'children' may stand in here for those lacking cultural capital, whether because of age, race, or because they didn't live in a big city."[31]

Since they were booked into unaffiliated houses that dominated in rural areas, serials and B films generally represented a higher proportion of that market, meaning that more adults might attend. For neighborhood theater owners confined to subsequent runs, they were also an inexpensive option for filling out schedules with new product. For these reasons, producers could not have constrained the serial audience if they had wanted to. In part, this book argues that sound serials manufacture fantasies especially relevant to children, but their appeal was necessarily inclusive. They offer immediacy of engagement, clarity of purpose, continuing suspense, comforting familiarity, and uninhibited preposterousness, all generally compelling qualities that often distinguish them from mainstream features. Moreover, the serial world's juvenile pleasures are built on the far-reaching and enduring appeals of melodrama and play, which transcend generational borders.

Sound serials are a seldom-traveled path into questions about cinematic storytelling, the craft of popular filmmaking, and the nature of spectator engagement. They are also unique, a particular inflection of film's potentials. Throughout this book, two frameworks will help us zero in on the sound serial's distinctive character: melodrama and play. Both are much larger fields in their own rights, with intellectual, material, and cultural histories that reach far beyond the present study. Together, they provide us with a background of concepts and lines of inquiry. Viewing sound serials as an intersection of melodrama and play, as a mode of storytelling and a kind of game, connects them to traditions that lie beyond classical Hollywood as it is commonly conceived. These frameworks can also reveal new connections between serials and more recent media forms, from action films to digital games.

Melodrama at the Matinee

Melodrama is a loaded term in film studies. On one hand, it has been associated with a specific studio-era genre typified by the emotionally and sexually charged domestic dramas directed by Douglas Sirk, Nicholas Ray, and Vincente Minnelli in the 1950s. On the other, in the sense invoked here, melodrama refers to a tradition of spectacular theater that predates cinema and, in important ways, runs counter to studio-era feature films. In his study of the Hollywood trade press, Steve Neale finds that terms like *melodrama, melodramatic,* and *meller* meant "crime, guns, and violence . . . heroines in peril . . . action, tension, and suspense." Tracing the term back to its theatrical origins in the late eighteenth century, Neale specifies a basic set of melodramatic qualities:

> (1) An unequivocal dramatic conflict between good and evil; (2) the eventual triumph of the former over the latter; (3) three principal character-types or functions: hero, heroine and villain; (4) a demonstrative and often hyperbolic aesthetic by means of which characters were typed, dramatic conflict was established and developed, and motive, emotion, and passion were laid bare; (5) an often highly episodic, formulaic, and action-packed plot, normally initiated and often driven by the villain . . . ; and (6) the generation of what were called "situations."

Such are the common components of "blood and thunder." By the late nineteenth century, Neale notes, a modified melodrama had emerged, which softened the extravagance and stock characterizations for middle-class patrons. Blood and thunder, though critically disparaged, continued in the inexpensive "ten-twenty-thirty"-cent circuits popular among working-class audiences.[32] The line of heredity with serials appears strikingly direct. In his study of silent serials produced between 1913 and 1918, Ben Singer describes them as more or less immediate descendants of popular melodrama. For Singer, serials like

Adventures of Kathlyn (Grandon, 1913) and *Perils of Pauline* (Gasnier and MacKenzie, 1914) adopted the stage tradition's central features of pathos, emotional intensification, moral polarization, sensationalism, and "nonclassical narrative structure."[33]

Historians agree that melodrama is an important progenitor to film storytelling, but the extent of its influence on studio-era norms has been contested. Hollywood classicists hold that melodrama's openness to implausibility and unmotivated action does not fit with character-centered causality, a norm since 1917. In *Classical Hollywood Cinema*, Bordwell explains that "coincidence and haphazardly linked events are believed to flaw the film's unity" and quotes the director Frank Borzage's 1922 claim that "today . . . we have the old melodramatic situations fitted out decently with true characterizations."[34] Others have seized on melodramatic qualities in feature films to question the classical model. Rick Altman, for instance, cites "coincidental or only minimally motivated" moments in *Casablanca* (Michael Curtiz, 1942) to argue that the film is a typical "amalgam of deformed, embedded melodramatic material and carefully elaborated narrative classicism." Altman views Bordwell's emphasis on causality as the "repression of popular theater" that effectively denies Hollywood cinema "its fundamental connection to popular traditions and to their characteristic forms of spectacle and narrative."[35] In drawing on melodrama, our study necessarily shares in these debates, but in a circumscribed way. Sound serials occupy the periphery of studio-era storytelling, a zone in which melodrama's influence may be more keenly felt.

Specifically, melodrama provides insight into serial plot construction, which routinely features outlandish contrivances and reversals. Singer's "nonclassical narrative structure" and Neale's reference to "situations" point to a storytelling practice unconcerned with character-centered unity and balance. Serial plots are founded on situational dramaturgy, a kind of plot construction rooted in blood and thunder. The concept is explained in Ben Brewster and Lea Jacobs's study of preclassical filmmaking in the teens, *From Theater to Cinema*. Brewster and Jacobs chart the close relationship between nineteenth- and early twentieth-century stage melodrama and the development of the feature film. Theatrical melodrama, a form they describe as "dominated by the aesthetics of spectacle," provided a model for early filmmakers, which was characterized by pictorial, sensational moments, or situations. Situational dramaturgy, according to Brewster and Jacobs, was a critically disreputable but extremely popular and practical way of generating plots from stock elements. Situations tend to be discrete moments, often of suspense or deadlock, when characters are arranged in seemingly inescapable dilemmas. It is the melodramatist's charge to arrange, motivate, and resolve stock situations, and this yields plots of loose plausibility and with broad latitude for coincidence.[36]

Situational playwriting manuals from the era provide evidence of this method for constructing plots. Perhaps the most influential and certainly the most accessible is Georges Polti's 1895 book *The Thirty-six Dramatic Situations*. Polti hopes to challenge playwrights to construct more original plots, a project he undertakes not by stressing creation of original scenarios but by laying out a taxonomy of situations to support the "Art of Combination." Polti lists general situations and specific variations that dramatists could link or embed. For example, under situation 36, entitled "Loss of Loved Ones," he offers variation A1, "Witnessing the Slaying of Kinsmen while Powerless to Prevent It," which might well lead to situation 3, "Crime Pursued by Vengeance," or situation 2, "Deliverance subset A, the Appearance of a Rescuer to the Condemned." Or the slaying of kinsmen might be interrupted by situation 6, "Disaster, a Natural Catastrophe." Situations can lead into one another successively, be presented as two options in a dilemma, be deployed among different groups of characters, or be set one within another. In all, Polti confidently declares that there are 1,332 possible combinations.[37]

Because character centeredness was an important standard of quality in studio-era feature films, situational moments might appear as obstacles in a larger, psychologically motivated quest. In their pure melodramatic form, though, situations were not subordinated to a higher unity. Brewster and Jacobs differentiate the situational approach thusly: "An obstacle is precisely understood in relation to the hero's goals and narrative trajectory and is therefore clearly bound to the sequential logic of the plot. To think of a story in terms of situations, as opposed to a series of obstacles, grants a certain autonomy to each discrete state of affairs. Situations can be thought of independently of the particular plots and characters which motivate them. . . . A weakening or even disregard of narrative continuity and logic is thus implicit in the concept."[38] Situational and causal dramaturgies offer two distinct conceptions of story. Stage melodrama, early feature films, and, this book suggests, sound serials, are first and foremost conglomerations of vivid, powerful moments, whereas classical narratives appear to trace chains of cause and effect emanating from characters. For viewers, this means navigating from incident to incident, each one exciting on its own, rather than investing in a character's struggle and growth.

Situations are building blocks of plot and occasions for spectacle. In nineteenth-century melodrama, situations, which tended to be laid at the end of an act, were vehicles for elaborate stage effects depicting burning buildings, train crashes, horse races, earthquakes, and floods. Two of the best-known examples cited by Brewster and Jacobs include a scene from the 1867 play *Under the Gaslight* in which the hero, bound to railroad tracks by the villain, is threatened by an approaching locomotive, and the sequence from *Uncle Tom's Cabin* (1853) that features the raging snowstorm and treacherous ice floes that prevent Eliza and little Harry from crossing the Ohio River to safety as they are pursued by slave catchers. By the end of the nineteenth century, the emphasis on sensation was such that plays would be built around the effects a theater could stage. A new method for mimicking an earthquake might occasion the development of a plot that featured a natural catastrophe.

This book contends that sound-serial plots involve a similar inversion of dramatic priorities; action sequences, set pieces, and thrilling escapes exist independently of, and take precedence over, character and story. Scholars commonly oppose spectacle to narrative, seeing the former as disruptive to the latter. In the serial, though, it appears that the two work hand in hand. Brewster and Jacobs explain: "Situation should not be assimilated to either narrative or spectacle as these concepts are currently invoked. Rather the term crosses this divide."[39] They are preexisting, visually sensational story elements, proven with audiences and combined into new plots. Part of *The Phantom Empire*'s inventiveness lies in manufacturing a rationale, however flimsy, for piling a stagecoach robbery, an alien encounter, and a home invasion into so short a time span. The melodramatist Georges Polti's proclamation that "the Dramatic" was "a language not of words but of thrills" applies equally well to the sound serial.[40] Thrills don't just dominate the story; they constitute it.

Placing sound serials on the melodramatic spectrum should not suggest that they simply reproduce their nineteenth-century forebear. Where Polti's dictionary covers a wealth of emotions and dramatic tones such as those conjured by Adultery, Mistaken Jealousy, and Falling Prey to Cruelty or Misfortune, serials almost invariably favor suspense in the face of physical danger. They refine and repeat a narrow set of melodramatic possibilities, most of them based on fundamental structures that were already well developed in the one-reel era. The chief serial situations include the taking and freeing of hostages, the standoff, the chase, and the race to the rescue. These, in turn, are filled in from a menu of concrete options: the time bombs, car chases, sieges, and gunfights that populate the serial world. The combinatory logic of situational melodrama helped producers churn out week after week of vivid thrills. We might conceive of the serial chapter as a framework into which filmmakers plugged modular actions and events, many of them ready-made, to deliver regular measures of sensation and excitement.

This commitment to sensation, and to eliciting powerful responses from its audience, may be melodrama's defining quality. Blood and thunder for the youngster trade, sound serials are engineered to grip and thrill with visceral force. An interoffice memo in the Production Code Administration file on William Witney and John English's *The Fighting Devil Dogs* (1938) confirms the effect serials could have on their intended audience. On August 8, the office received a complaint from Miss Henington of the Fox West Coast Public Relations Department that the serial was "too strenuous; that at times the children were so terrified that they wouldn't stay in their seats and either ran out or were found hiding behind curtains."[41] The film, which had not been submitted to the Breen Office for review, was subsequently removed from Fox West Coast theaters. Though easily disregarded as absurd from the vantage of adulthood, serials were intended to pack a punch. Witney recalled that the motto around the Republic studio was "a pair of wet panties for every little kiddie."[42]

On its surface, the appeal of melodrama seems curious: Why should audiences so desire the charged emotions and traumatic situations on offer? Peter Brooks, in his seminal literary study *The Melodramatic Imagination*, proposes that the form's appeal centers on its Manichaeism. In the wake of "desacralization" wrought by the Enlightenment and the French Revolution, Brooks argues, melodrama emerged as a means of depicting and demonstrating moral certainty: "The polarization of good and evil works toward revealing their presence and operation as real forces in the world. . . . The spectacular enactments of melodrama seek constantly to express these forces and imperatives, to bring them to striking revelation, to impose their evidence." For Brooks, melodrama fills a void left by the decline of the sacred, functioning as a "drama of morality" that articulates "the existence of a moral universe which, though put into question, masked by villainy and perversions of judgment, does exist and can be made to assert its presence and its categorical force among men."[43]

More recently, in adapting Brooks's approach to explore cinema and contemporary media, the film scholar Linda Williams identifies the crosscut race-to-the-rescue sequence as "the spectacular essence of melodrama." Parallel editing between victim and rescuer has been a cinematic staple since 1908, most often with alternation between lines of action accelerating as they converge. For Williams, these scenes pull viewers between the pathos of unwinnable situations and the action that might nonetheless forestall disaster until the last minute, when "'in the nick of time' defies 'too late.'" Precisely metered close calls and narrow misses wind viewers up in the play of tension and release; the more visibly inevitable the doom, the higher the anxiety, the greater the relief. Williams argues that through them and other cinematic means, melodrama elicits "sympathy for the virtues of beset victims" and rehearses the "retrieval and staging of virtue through adversity and suffering."[44] We can find evidence of the race to the rescue's emotional impact as early as 1909, when the critic for *Moving Picture World* reported that the audience members "were in a state of intense excitement" such that "the house literally 'rose'" when the heroine was rescued in the conclusion of D. W. Griffith's *The Lonely Villa* (1909).[45] The technique's ubiquity ever since suggests to Williams that it fulfills a fundamental desire: the emotional recognition of moral good "in a world where virtue has become hard to read."[46]

Sound serials, with their weekly cliffhangers, are exercises in emotionalizing time and space; they thrive on the tension between "in the nick of time" and "too late." Whether or not the loss of religious certainty was at issue for the target audience, serials traffic in moral legibility and the reassuring rescue of virtue from the jaws of villainy. Brooks declares that melodrama "starts from and expresses the anxiety brought by a frightening new world in which the traditional patterns of moral order no longer provide the necessary social glue. It plays out the force of that anxiety with the apparent triumph of villainy, and dissipates it with the eventual victory of virtue."[47]

Play and the Serial's Ludic Potential

Our second framework, the study of play, lies further afield from film studies and has only recently entered critical discussion of popular narrative. The burst of interest in new media that began in the late 1990s led some scholars to investigate intersections of gameplay and storytelling. Janet Murray, for example, coined the term *cyberdrama* to capture the possibilities of interactive, computer-based narrative. Stories and games, she argues, share common structures including the contest, or "the meeting of opponents in pursuit of mutually exclusive aims," and the puzzle, which "can also be seen as a contest between the reader/player and the author/game-designer."[48] From Murray's perspective, these correspondences create the possibility of new media forms, but we might also see them as revealing linkages that have long existed between story and play.

Early scholarly discussions of videogames were marked by disagreement over appropriate conceptual backgrounds and analytical models. Shane Denson and Andreas Jahn-Sudmann summarize the debate as between "narratological" and "ludological" approaches: "Against the narratologists' implicit claim that the telling of stories is one of the central functions of digital games, the ludologists . . . argue that narrative elements are only marginal or secondary with respect to the primary 'core' of gameplay, which involves the player in negotiations not with stories but with formal rule-sets."[49] As Denson and Jahn-Sudmann point out, the very existence of the debate brought into relief the common territory over which both camps did battle. The case of new media has helped promote a "ludic" understanding of stories.

The term *ludology*, popularized by Gonzalo Frasca in a 1999 essay on videogames, derives from the Dutch historian Johan Huizinga's foundational inquiry, *Homo Ludens: The Study of the Play Element of Culture*, originally published in 1938.[50] Huizinga proposed adding the term *Homo ludens*, or "man the player," to the titles *Homo faber* and *Homo sapiens*: "There is a third function . . . applicable to both humans and animal life, and just as important as reasoning and making—namely playing." Play, in his account, is impractical, circumscribed, self-aware, and pleasurable; it is "a voluntary activity or occupation executed within certain fixed limits of time and place according to rules freely accepted but absolutely binding, having its aim in itself and accompanied by a feeling of tension, joy, and consciousness that it is 'different' from 'ordinary life.'" Associated with risk, danger, and rapid movement, play occurs on a "playground . . . isolated, hedged round, hallowed, within which special rules obtain," and which gives rise to "play communities."[51]

Huizinga's capacious definition permits him to trace ritual, religion, law, and war to humans' propensity for play. Our interest in the concept is more specific. As a framework for studying serials, play highlights their potential to structure active engagement beyond following story. Film's impact on children's play emerged as a point of concern for sociologists and reformers shortly before the advent of sound serials. In her pioneering work *Children and Movies*, published in 1929, Alice Miller Mitchell describes the phenomenon of "playing movies": "The movie has become a new back yard for the after-school-hours child. . . . Not only is it a better and a more interesting playground to the child, but it makes more attractive to him his own playland, for when he returns from the movie to his 'back-yard' he has new ideas of what to play and how to play it. He and his little companions congregate and begin to re-enact the film they have seen." Mitchell's survey of ten thousand Chicago-area schoolchildren revealed a clear set of expectations: "A movie must have in it a hero, a villain, and 'plenty of action.'" Young boys, and many girls, regardless of class or home environment, relished physical conflict on-screen. When asked the type of movie he preferred, a typical "delinquent" responded: "I like to see somebody get killed. I like to see someone getting robbed. I like to see the police trying to catch somebody." The Boy Scouts Mitchell surveyed were equally straightforward in their tastes. One wrote that he wanted "Lots of fighting, Lots of shooting, Lots of riding."[52] Much to reformers' chagrin, genre films fed the fantasies of young people, and serials specialized in the action they desired.

Unfortunately, we have few accounts of how the target audience engaged with sound serials in the studio era, though reform-oriented literature of the late 1920s and early 1930s provides a tantalizing glimpse. Sociologists like Mitchell documented and quantified cinema's effects amid public concern over Hollywood's influence. The most famous of these efforts were the Payne Fund Studies on Motion Pictures and Youth, conducted between 1929 and 1932. The twelve publications that resulted are largely concerned with feature films, but Herbert Blumer's *Movies and Conduct* touches on serials as well. Blumer, a University of Chicago sociology professor, interviewed and solicited "motion picture autobiographies" from college, high school, and grade-school students. His attention to the serial centers on their cliff-hanger endings:

Instead of leading the excited feelings of the child to a state of quiescence of satisfaction, the serial ends at the point where they are keyed up to the highest pitch. The result is to put the youthful spectator under the spell of suspense, sometimes of frenzy or panic, which persists for a week, only to be renewed at the next installment. . . . Some of the less ultimate effects on the mind are obvious, such as the preoccupation of the child with the precarious situation in which his favorites have been left at the end of an installment; his anxiety over their safety; his curiosity and reflection as to how they will escape; his excited conversation during the week with his companions on how the escape will occur—in short the difficulty he has of freeing his mind from the thoughts of the picture.

Blumer, who uses the term *emotional possession* to describe viewer response, observes that during a serial matinee "one gets undisguised expressions of intense emotions, requiring no refined instruments for their detection." Because they deny closure, he believes that cliffhangers amplify and extend "collective excitement."

As evidence, Blumer offers the personal recollections of young people who frequented serials in the 1920s. One subject, identified as "male, 20, white, college sophomore," recalls:

Perhaps the earliest type of motion picture I can remember is the serial. . . . All the children of the district used to attend and then followed one glorious week during which each scene of the episode was enacted in our backyards. We had grand times playing "lion men" and Tarzans. During the showing of the picture itself we used to be worked up to a terrific high state of emotion, yelling at the hero when danger was near, hissing at the villain, and heaving sighs of relief when the danger was past. The serial was nearly the sole object for going to the movies for me and most of the children in the good old days when I was seven or eight years old.

Another boy recalls his friends fashioning blow darts from needles in imitation of the Hooded Terror from *The House of Hate* (George Seitz, 1918), and another remembers playing "natives of Africa" in an overgrown prairie, using "wash-boiler tops for shields, and sticks for spears," based on a serial he followed one summer.

Blumer's generalizations about film and play call serials to mind. He contends that "the most casual survey of the form and content of childhood play reveals motion pictures as a very important source" and specifies that "common to all groups of children regardless of social status is the fascination of combat and mystery themes" which appear in "most of the patterns of play taken from the movies." The sound serial's formula of regular combat embedded in an overarching mystery would seem tailored to children's prefer-ences, perhaps because they occupy story and play's shared territory of contest and the puzzle.[53]

American interest in exposing the serial's pernicious effects declined after the major studios implemented the Production Code Administration in 1934, making firsthand accounts of audience behavior rare. In England, however, reformers renewed the controversy with vigor in the 1940s and 1950s. The journalist and political philosopher Jacob Peter Mayer called for the termina-tion of commercial children's cinema clubs (which showed American serials) in his book *Sociology of Film*, published in 1946. Alarmed by his visits to the Odeon and Gaumont British Children's Cinema Clubs, where he witnessed *Don Winslow of the Navy* (Beebe and Taylor, 1941) and other titles, Mayer declared serials "pernicious in their psychological effects, leaving children at a high pitch of expectation for the next week's show, poisoning their daydreams and, by an utterly artificial unreality, influencing their play." Mayer concludes from his observations of matinee audiences giving "expression to their over stimulated feelings by shouts and cries" that serials leave them "keyed up dur-ing the whole of the subsequent week" in a "perpetual state of suspense."[54]

Our concern is not with documenting child's play during the studio era, or with discourse about that play, but with thinking about sound serials' ludic potential. Mitchell, Blumer, and Mayer were alarmed that films should linger in children's minds, a source of "persistent," "perpetual," and "collective" excite-ment. Using play as a framework highlights the ways serials channeled this energy, mirroring the playground on-screen and modeling activity between matinees. In Huizinga's terms, we might ask how serials could abet play com-munities by defining tensions and fixing limits, that is, how they could encour-age games. In theorizing the role of stories in digital games, Henry Jenkins and Jesper Juul provide two apposite, if distinct, conceptual structures that seem useful for studying serials. Jenkins suggests that games can embody stories in spaces explored by players, what he calls narrative architecture. Juul conceives of fiction as an optional adjunct to a game's rules of play. Both ideas pry the fic-tional world apart from the linear experience of narrative. They help us think about how serials might lay the groundwork for play.

Jenkins suggests that we examine role-playing computer games "less as stories than as spaces ripe with narrative possibility." For Jenkins, "game designers don't simply tell stories; they design worlds and sculpt spaces." The concept of narrative architecture connects games, stories, and spaces in mul-tiple ways. Spaces might evoke stories with which we are already familiar. Vid-eogames based on movies, for instance, work by "translating events in the film into environments within the game," giving "concrete shape to our memories and imaginings of the storyworld, creating an immersive environment we can wander through and interact with." Other times, a game designer might build "spatial stories," which are highly episodic, "privilege spatial exploration over plot development," and "are held together by broadly defined goals and conflicts pushed forward by the character's movement across the map." Moving through space might reveal a prearranged narrative, or designers might set rules for items and actors within a space so that narratives appear to emerge from the player's interaction with them.[55]

The idea of narrative architecture is pertinent to the sound serial's ongoing cinematic world. In an era when feature films disappeared from the neighborhood theater within a week, the twelve-to-fifteen-chapter format guaranteed an extended stay, a chance for viewers to revisit the characters, spaces, challenges, and spectacles over a three-month period. Sound serials used this time to build procedural worlds with physically demarcated obstacles and goals. Like Jenkins's "spatial stories," they generate engaging maps and recycle ritualized settings in which characters and viewers can anticipate and discover narrative situations. Serials rarely reward attention to the grand story; instead they proceed moment by moment, drawing one spatially delimited challenge at a time like levels in a computer game. Cliffhangers in particular resemble narrative architectures. Serial screenwriting teams began their work by laying out the devices and snares that would climax each chapter, a method that privileged design as a component of storytelling. Rope bridges, fiery pits, buzz saws, crushing rooms, flooding shafts, and sacrificial altars are physical traps with clear operational boundaries: story potential is embedded within concrete space. The best cliffhangers achieved such visual and spatial clarity that viewers might feel something like the game player's sense of agency, tracing out potential outcomes, or playing through the puzzle in the intervening week.

Cliffhangers illustrate another playlike quality of serials: the disjunction between story and formula. As we will see, when heroes fall into an inescapable deathtrap at chapter's end, we often witness their demise. Convention requires, however, that heroes endure, and the story must reverse itself to accommodate. The rule of survival entails arbitrary, sometimes incoherent, fiction. In his theory of videogames, Juul draws a useful distinction between *fiction* and *rule*. He notes: "Games have their roots in rules and play time, and this allows them to define their worlds much more loosely and less coherently than we would accept in most other cultural forms." For Juul, fiction is an optional component of gaming that tends to be created in a "tentative and flickering way: the hero dies and is respawned moments later; . . . the player dies and loads a *save game* in order to continue just before he or she died."[56] Narrative is more fundamental to the sound serial than to the videogame as Juul describes it, but they both bend story to ensure that play will continue. Film conventions differ from game rules in that they tend to be noncompulsory rather than constitutive. Because it is profoundly formulaic, however, the sound serial narrows this gap. The hero's survival across a cliffhanger amounts to an extrinsic prerequisite, and like a game's rules, it enables viewers to accept, or at least overlook, reversals in the story. Our engagement appears rooted in something other than causal logic and internal consistency: something similar to the pleasure of play.

Juul's distinction bears on the sound serial in a more general way as well. Casting narrative as separable from the rules suggests why fictional worlds can travel between cinema and playground. Videogames, Juul argues, cue players to construct fictions around the rules. Items like game boxes and manuals facilitate "projection of the game world." The title *Space Invaders*, he explains, "is by itself sufficient to describe a science fiction with battling spaceships."[57] This process is abundantly clear in early home videogames with severely limited graphics. The instruction booklet for Imagic's 1982 Atari 2600 game cartridge *Demon Attack*, for instance, features a picture of silver space lizards zooming around with rockets strapped to their backs and a brief description: "Marooned on the ice planet Krybor, you watch legions of eerie creatures scream overhead. They hover ominously. They give you no quarter. Attack and destroy them—or be destroyed! Armed with your Laser Cannon, you confront the ultimate challenge: Survive!" The game itself, a scaled-down imitation of the arcade hit *Galaxian*, is a representationally impoverished shoot-'em-up in which the "ice planet Krybor" appears as a blue bar at the bottom of the screen. Players familiar with *Space Invaders* and *Galaxian* can immediately enjoy *Demon Attack* without reference to its fictional world, just as children can play tag without pretending they are cops or robbers. The manual's evocative graphic and sketchy dramatic situation encourage players to project a full-scale demonic onslaught onto the screen's field of flickering pixels, to imagine the fight for survival while engaging in a simple game constructed around a few well-defined rules and affordances.

Serials resemble textually rich, multipurpose game manuals: they furnish worlds that could be projected onto the playground. As one of Blumer's subjects recalled, backyard games would change with the neighborhood marquee: "Our play was always influenced by the current type of serial we were inhaling. If it had to do with cowboys and Indians we played cowboy and Indian, if it had to do with cops and robbers then we played cop and robber."[58] "Cowboy and Indian" and "cop and robber" imply very general worlds, which players might fit around almost any physical contest. Serials make use of these broad categories but also provide an array of concrete playable roles and scenarios. If, as Juul suggests, minimal cues can launch a game's world, serials are cornucopias of fictional possibilities. Adventure stories, radio dramas, and comics surely furnished projectable worlds as well, but only the sound serial combined cinematic storytelling and long-term engagement. In following familiar characters and types through weekly chases, fights, and entrapments, viewers could quickly gain fluency in the world's procedures, anticipate its permutations, and apply them to an extensive range of established games. Formulaic repetition, a production necessity, helps serials merge with the routines of child's play. Moreover, serial action often mimicked schoolyard activity. As our discussion of *Daredevils of the Red Circle* in chapter 6 illustrates, scenes of pursuit and evasion resemble elaborate sessions of tag, base games, and hide-and-seek. This shared ground, and the ease of learning serial conventions, made them ripe for playful appropriation.

Recent theoretical work in film phenomenology offers another way to conceptualize the overlap between serials and physical play. Phenomenology considers film viewing a physically engaged, embodied activity. Vivian Sobchack, one of the founders of this approach, argues that "film experience is meaningful . . . *because of our bodies*" and that the spectator "fills in the gap in its sensual grasp of the figural world onscreen . . . to reciprocally (albeit not sufficiently) 'flesh it out' into literal physicalized sense."[59] Theorists claim that all films elicit embodied engagement, but action genres provide the most compelling examples. In the case of sound serials, we might consider how they encourage physical reactions. The matinee audience that Mayer witnessed certainly displayed embodied response: "In the two serial pictures, the booing of the villain reached an almost hysterical pitch, and catching of breaths was audible during situations of tension, also exclamations of 'Oh!' when some ill had befallen the hero."[60] On a more abstract level, serials' physically defined problems and solutions involve viewers in a corporeal understanding of their worlds.

Jennifer Barker describes the viewer's relationship to action films as one of "muscular empathy." At its most affective, Barker observes, "the empathy between the film's and viewer's bodies goes so deeply that we can feel the film's body, live vicariously through it, and experience its movements to such an extent that we ourselves become momentarily as graceful or powerful as the film's body, and we leave the theater feeling invigorated or exhausted, though we ourselves have hardly moved a muscle."[61]

As the most incessantly physical of all studio-era genres, sound serials involve the viewer in following, anticipating, contemplating, and perhaps imitating action. Similarities between the on-screen exploits and backyard play likely intensified muscular empathy for young spectators. Characters navigate the serial world by running, climbing, tumbling, and fighting, all familiar sensations that were within reach just outside the theater.

One of the serial world's enduring charms is that enemies are conquered and obstacles surmounted via the resources of physical play. Lisa Purse identifies a similar attraction in one of the serial's descendants, the contemporary Hollywood action film. Drawing on phenomenology, she connects the popularity of action to our desire to transcend material restrictions in a "physicalised narrative of becoming." Each action movie we see, according to Purse, returns us to an ongoing fantasy of physical mastery:

> Action bodies, with their capacity to escape physical constraints . . . offer fantasies of empowerment that allow us to rehearse our own dreamed-of escapes, our own becoming-masterful, in a fantasy context, allow us to "feel" this mastery for ourselves through our sensorial connection with the body of the hero. . . . Where action narratives come and go, end and begin again, the fantasy of overcoming . . . can exist in perpetuity . . . always present in action cinema's fictional universe, waiting to be accessed and experienced once more.[62]

This characterization suits the serial well. Audiences, child and adult, return each week to rehearse scenarios of empowerment and escape, which have as much to do with bodily experience as with following a story. By emphasizing the physical aspects of film spectatorship, phenomenology makes visible the continuities between watching and playing. The serial world was compatible with the spaces and practices of children's play; it could be "fleshed out" with sensations of play and then projected back onto the schoolyard. Cliffhangers halt the hero but incite the "keyed up" viewer to carry on the combat, contests, and puzzles.

As conceptual sets, melodrama and play operate in the background of the analyses that follow, throwing light on the structure and allure of a too-often dismissed form of cinema. They also lead us to a hypothesis about sound serials' central appeal: the fantasy of reassurance in the face of catastrophe. Both melodrama and play draw excitement from uncertainty and the risk of failure but tend to affirm the inevitability of order and success. For Brooks and Williams, virtue gains emotional strength because it has been threatened. Melodrama wields the pathos of "too late," of overwhelming adversity, to achieve moral clarity "in the nick of time." Serial cliffhangers press melodramatic reversals into a reassuring pattern even more predictable than their theatrical predecessors: villainy guarantees righteous victory. Play is more amorphous than melodrama, but it, too, rewards struggle with mastery. The play scholar Brian Sutton-Smith concludes his book *The Ambiguity of Play* with a speculation about its nature and appeal: "The primary motive of players is the stylized performance of existential themes that mimic or mock the uncertainties and risks of survival and, in so doing, engage . . . in exciting forms of arousal." He continues that play might be viewed "as a lifelong simulation of the key neonatal characteristics of unrealistic optimism, egocentricity, and reactivity, all of which are guarantors of persistence in the face of adversity."[63] Serials, like games, model perseverance in the face of unremitting difficulties and answer risk with optimism. As a condensation of melodrama and play, serials held this appeal for all audiences, but for young viewers they also offered access to the mysterious and uncertain sphere of grown-up life. Saturday matinee melodramas afforded a fantasy of adulthood as a kinetic, anxiety-saturated, and basically absurd world where moral good is achieved, problems are solved, and catastrophes surmounted, even reversed, through physical action. This book is devoted to understanding that world.

The Way Ahead

This book begins by tracing out key elements of the sound serial's formula and moves to a close consideration of how particular films enact and vary that body of conventions. Chapter 2 focuses on the serial's distinctive narrative procedures, which involve strict pacing of action within episodes but a looser, easily extensible storyline across chapters. Screenwriters built serial chapters on a five-part armature that regularly alternates scenes of physical action and narrative exposition. The structure directs attention and energy inward toward the frantic present moment. Rather than develop a single, rising dramatic arc, as in their historical predecessor the one-reel melodrama, chapters required three bursts of action. This imposes a unique narrative rhythm independent of causal logic or character motivation. The formula guarantees a basic, if routine, level of speed and excitement, and some filmmakers achieved virtuosity by expanding, compressing, eliding, or combining the five parts. The large-scale multiepisode stories, on the other hand, could be devoid of forward momentum, spinning their wheels and avoiding progress toward closure. *Zorro's Fighting Legion* (Witney and English, 1939) illustrates the meandering path that leads from enigmas and goals set out in first chapters to sudden alignments and revelations in the last. In striking contrast to the feature film's unity and efficiency, sound serials are profoundly situational, endlessly generating spectacular circumstances around more or less static characters. A serial's overarching story sets out stable parameters within which to replay a frenetic game.

These sturdy and predictable narrative structures support and shape the sound serial world, a conglomeration of character types, customs, and locations. Chapter 3 explores a few of the key elements that fill in the story. Instantly identifiable heroes and villains need little motivation and follow melodramatic protocol by unambiguously announcing their values. The rituals and procedures of heroism and villainy are far more important than the reasoning behind them. Villains set the game in motion, constructing weekly labyrinths to challenge the heroes. Usually, the two sides vie over possession of an object, "the weenie," which casts moral conflict as pursuit of a tangible item. Weenies and other serial mechanisms (secret weapons, radios, televisions, complicated deathtraps) exhibit what Neil Harris calls the operational aesthetic: a fascination with seeing systems at work, which can obtain outside of narrative.[64] Thus, chapters expend time depicting visually compelling processes and dwelling on physical chains of cause and effect. A similar logic defines the world as a whole; its problems and solutions can be laid out in schematic terms. This, combined with repeated spaces and motifs, promotes quick familiarity that allows viewers to see around the serial world, to anticipate action and ingest its conventions. Pathos, so central to other forms of melodrama, is tempered in this gamelike procedural environment. Serials that present death and loss rarely linger on it, channeling emotional potential directly into concrete plans of action. The serial world, though fraught with peril, is ultimately and comfortingly knowable, a visually legible play space of material, surmountable challenges.

Chapter 4 concentrates on the cliffhanger. A testing ground for methods of suspense, cliffhangers distinguish serials from all other studio-era production. One-reel melodramas, which preceded the development of features, provided serials with a well-stocked reservoir of suspenseful situations and cinematic techniques. Rather than drive toward last-minute resolutions, however, serial chapters proffer cataclysmic interruptions. The cliffhanger's obvious commercial logic masks sophisticated narration; they entice viewers to entertain the prospect of uncertainty despite the hero's virtually assured success. Chapter 6 of *The Three Musketeers* (Schaefer and Clark, 1933) exemplifies how rhythm, vividness, and schematic clarity can generate compelling suspense around a convincingly irreversible trap. Carrying the action through to its tragic culmination makes for a strong "curtain" but also challenges screenwriters and directors to fashion plausible reversals the following week. As we will see, cliffhanger "take-outs" (the term used by screenwriters for the resolution that takes the hero out of an apparently inescapable situation) received less attention than setups, and the five-part structure prevented characters and viewers from lingering over incoherence. Far more important, interruption at the height of tension converts the story into a puzzle, a problem space for the viewer to explore, contemplate, and inhabit. Cliffhangers connect narrative and play, priming viewers to extend their engagement with the serial after the screen goes dark, and to take up the mantles of character and narrator.

The next two chapters consider films that achieved virtuosity within the formula. *Daredevils of the Red Circle* and *Perils of Nyoka*, two Republic productions representing the sound serial's creative height, illustrate the potentials and pleasures of the serial world. More significantly, close analysis uncovers how formal and narrative constraints encouraged creative problem solving. Chapter 5 focuses on how serials employ storytelling conventions for creative ends. Columbia's Batman serials occasionally develop cliffhangers that emphasize plot revision, for instance. *Daredevils* and *Nyoka* merit extended attention for the way they fill out standard narrative structures. Both offer unusually well constructed variations of stock plots and achieve forward momentum. *Daredevils* takes the form of a villain-driven labyrinth, extending the story through repeated confrontations with a game-playing, trap-setting mastermind. *Nyoka*, on the other hand, follows a spatial itinerary as heroes and villains engage in a particularly elaborate hunt for the prized Tablets of Hippocrates.

In each, screenwriters manipulate the five-part format to extend action while maintaining exposition. Rather than simply mark time, these films create situational overabundance by feathering exposition and action together, linking perils, and implying off-screen developments. Along the way, the two serials showcase compelling procedures and creative imperilments, which distinguish the genre.

Chapter 6 investigates matters of film form. Given their budgets and production schedules, sound serials tended toward undistinguished stylistics. Filmmakers stuck close to a bare-bones version of studio-era form, which achieves minimal standards of continuity and narrative articulation. The regular pressure to produce vivid action, however, encouraged experimentation and innovation. Editorial staffs were highly skilled at appropriating stock footage to create new situations, particularly at Universal. *The Great Alaskan Mystery* (Taylor and Collins, 1944), for instance, fashions events by repurposing feature film material from the Universal library. At Republic, *Daredevils* and *Nyoka* exhibit the serial unit's refinement of the fight sequence into a precisely choreographed, rhythmically edited form. Similarly, cliffhangers from both films receive uncommon attention and elaboration, evidence that formula could encourage and yield artistic refinement. In focusing creative energy on scenes of action and process, serials craft engaging experiences that invite muscular empathy and generate templates for play.

Finally, chapter 7 opens up continuities between the sound-serial formula and its closest cinematic descendant, the contemporary action film. With their emphasis on physical problem solving, fights, and chases, reliance on melodramatic plotting, and employment of basic suspense structures, action films and serials share substantial ground. The James Bond franchise, itself a central model for the contemporary action genre, adapted key elements of the serial formula for an adult audience. Feature films, however, obey a different set of narrative constraints. They demand closure, unity, and overall comprehensibility, which shift the way situations are incorporated and combined. An extended analysis of Steven Spielberg's blockbuster homage to serials, *Raiders of the Lost Ark* (1981), tests and specifies the sound serial's lingering influence. As an industry exemplar, *Raiders*, like *Star Wars* (Lucas, 1977) before it, helped bring serial-inspired action and story to prominence. Rather than copy the older formula, *Raiders* negotiates a place for it within the parameters of a three-act structure. Spielberg and Lawrence Kasdan, the screenwriter, adapt situations and serial rhythms to a recognizable beginning, middle, and end. *Raiders* evokes the chapterplay by employing an action prologue, giving heroes and villains a prize to pursue, citing cliffhangers without developing them, grouping fights and chases together, and cycling through a pattern of hostage taking and liberation. At the same time, character psychology, the romantic subplot, and unifying motifs temper and contain the serial inheritance.

This blending of serial-style action melodrama and contemporary standards of unity and character depth constitutes a general quality of action features, which bears comparison with serials. The chapter concludes with a brief discussion of *The Bourne Ultimatum* (Greengrass, 2007), and other films of the trilogy, in light of the serial formula. At first glance, the conflicted, psychologically complex Jason Bourne (Matt Damon) would seem directly opposed to the serial world. Yet the films' physical problem spaces, episodic situations, fantasy of mastery, and continuing narrative hark back to serial pleasures. Our understanding of the sound serial provides a useful perspective on the structures and appeals of contemporary action, though the relationship between the forms is a matter less of direct influence than of shared aims. The comparison also reveals unbridgeable gaps, fissures between forms, which speak to the sound serial's historical and formal specificity.

The book concludes by speculating about the sound serial's place in film and media history. With regard to popular cinema, the serial broadens our understanding of studio-era classicism and points forward to the attractions of contemporary blockbusters. But the form is also important to the history of moving-image seriality, that is, to other media that construct an ongoing, episodic experience. Television, to a degree, annexed the serial audience and appropriated some of its tactics. The new medium offered regular return to continuing, visual worlds, but its preference for stand-alone episodes largely dislodged the cliffhanger from the serial experience. In developing the ludic potentials of action melodrama, serials also appear to prefigure the playable narratives of videogames and computer games. Games require more formalized rule sets and can get by with even sketchier stories than serials, but they create worlds defined by contests and puzzles, which fans are encouraged to occupy and explore. This book aims to help us identify the sound serial's indirect and multifaceted legacy. But we need not appeal to its influence to make a case for the sound serial; in looking closely at its conventions, aesthetics, and brand of viewer engagement, we can recognize the artistry in a neglected formula.

2

Storytelling on a Schedule

• • • • • • • • • • • • • • • • • • • •

Narrative Form in
the Sound Serial

Sound serials meander frantically and rush nowhere. They are very long films, some lasting over four hours, time enough to get comfortable in the diegesis. However, the whole is divided into strictly defined chapters, each running on an unforgiving schedule. The sound serial's peculiar mix of narrative compression and willful inefficiency, of intense repetition and seemingly endless extension, and of breakneck action without forward progress both assures viewers a confident familiarity with the world and focuses them intently on the feverish present. The formula blends crisis and stability: we are caught up in life-or-death situations that we know will be repeated week after week.

This curious balance of tension and stasis results, in part, from the two scales of serial storytelling: the episode and the series. We might expect that each episode should present a chapter in an ongoing arc, contributing to the large-scale story's forward progress, but the relationship between part and whole is not so intuitive. Some chapters, particularly the first and last installments, bind tightly to the arc; they open up enigmas, refine goals, and generate closure. Most others, though packed with incident, do relatively little to resolve the grand narrative. Instead they engage viewers in navigating from problems to solutions, which are neither entirely independent of nor in service to the whole.

Using *Zorro's Fighting Legion* (Witney and English, 1939) as a touchstone, this chapter explores the distinctive structure of sound-serial narrative. Following the practice of serial writers, we focus on the organization of events within chapters and the implications of formula storytelling for depicting characters and a fictional world. After parsing the five-part format of a standard episode, we will turn to the opening chapter of a serial, which was given special attention by producers, filmmakers, and exhibitors. At its very start, a chapterplay resembles a studio-era feature, but it swiftly departs from that model as it narrows to a stunningly limited, knowable, and cyclical world. Finally, a detailed comparison of serial and feature narrative highlights their differences, particularly with regard to romance, progress, and closure. The narrative formulas discussed here lay the foundation for the remainder of this book; they make possible and set the limits for serial pleasures and artistry.

That chapterplays are not unified, progressive stories that build a totality brick by brick can be clearly gauged by the amount of "wheel-turning" in any given series. *The Golden God*, the first episode of *Zorro's Fighting Legion*, for example, establishes that the mysterious Don del Oro (Bud Geary), who appears to the Yaqui Indians as a sort of Aztec robot, is actually a member of a local council of antifederalist businessmen who seek to control the flow of gold from the San Mendolito Mine and to prevent shipments from reaching Mexico City. Zorro (Reed Hadley) arrives to organize his legionnaires, unmask Don del Oro, and free the gold for Benito Juarez's (Carleton Young) new republic. In the twelfth and final chapter, *Unmasked*, Zorro finds answers to his questions and reaches his objectives. He reveals and defeats Don del Oro, and President Juarez makes Zorro's confidant Ramon (William Corson) the new governor of San Mendolito. Opening and closing chapters approach the goal-driven unity of a feature film.

Episodes 2–11, however, take a circuitous and digressive route to the climax. Don del Oro and the council play an extended game of cat and mouse with Zorro, neither side gaining ground. The main body of the story consists of seven groups of related events, most of which span two chapters:

Chapters 1–2: Zorro protects a gold shipment from attack, but this leads Don del Oro's men to blow up the legion's hideout.

Chapters 3–4: Zorro and the legion discover a secret room in the mine and trace a gun dropped by one of Don del Oro's henchmen, but neither clue leads any closer to the villain's unmasking.

Chapters 4–6: The bad guys hijack Juarez's weapons shipment in order to arm the Yaquis, but Zorro recaptures the guns and delivers them to Juarez.

Chapters 6–7: Don del Oro turns his attention to Ramon and manages to capture him, his sister Volita (Sheila Darcy), and Zorro. They all swiftly escape.

Chapters 7–9: Zorro contrives to trap a known henchman, Manuel (John Merton), who confesses, "Don del Oro is . . . ," before being impaled by a golden arrow shot by a Yaqui assassin.

Chapters 10–11: Zorro and Ramon pursue the assassin and discover that Don del Oro uses a water wagon with a secret compartment to transport arms. This lead, however, becomes a dead end.

Chapter 11: Finally, Zorro rescues and befriends Kala (Paul Marion), a Yaqui prince, who promises to help reveal that Don del Oro is a false god. Their plan fails, and the alliance with Kala comes to naught.

Each set of events traces failed efforts by either Zorro or Don del Oro to gain the upper hand. Zorro's actions are especially frustrating. The clues he discovers never produce results. Chapters 7–9 offer an unbroken span of progress for Zorro, but his plan to extract information from Manuel is cut short by a whistling arrow. Any viewer seeking the narrative pleasure of a well-crafted mystery or even a suspenseful adventure yarn would be disappointed.

Even the thread of action initiated in chapter 11, which seems destined to flush out the villain, brings Zorro no closer to his goal. It is only in the final chapter, when Don del Oro kills his two remaining co-conspirators and is about to (again) rally a Yaqui insurrection, that Zorro confronts and unmasks him, revealing Pablo (C. Montague Shaw), San Mendolito's chief justice. Precious few of the previous 205 minutes of running time seem essential to reaching this moment, and viewers' first reaction to the villain's unmasking might be "Pablo who?" *Zorro's Fighting Legion*, one of the most highly regarded of all serials, spins a directionless, uninspiring tale. The serial's lure lies elsewhere.

The Five-Part Format

Serials match diffuse and aimless large-scale storytelling to episodes that pack incident into a tightly defined formula. Chapters tend to alternate action and exposition in a five-part structure: A-b-C-d-E.

A, C, and E are action sequences spaced at the start, middle, and end of a typical fifteen-to-twenty-minute episode. The remaining two parts, b and d, tend to be dialogue sequences in which heroes and villains lay their plans. The exquisitely silly second episode of *Flash Gordon* (Stephani and Taylor, 1936), entitled *The Tunnel of Terror*, throws the five-part format into sharp relief. *Flash Gordon* is a rare serial that follows the plot of its source material with fair consistency, and so offers an atypical large-scale story. Individual chapters, however, tend to follow norms. *Tunnel of Terror* runs twenty minutes and fifty seconds including credits, with recognizable action beats at 2:38, 10:00, and 17:50 (A, C, and E).

In part A, Ming the Merciless (Charles Middleton) quickly resolves the previous week's cliffhanger by triggering a safety net to stop Flash (Buster Crabbe) and Princess Aura's (Priscilla Lawson) plunge through a trapdoor toward giant "dragons of death" (three iguanas shot in close-up). Ming shows mercy only for his daughter. Exposition (b) takes over when Flash and Aura sneak out a secret door and wander the caverns of Mongo. Expositional sequences, tasked with orienting viewers to the larger plot and linking action scenes, can be slow, talky affairs. The directors, Ray Taylor and Frederick Stephani, keep things moving through six minutes of exposition by crosscutting between the heroic earthlings Flash, Dr. Zarkov (Frank Shannon), and Dale Arden (Jean Rogers). Hiding from guards in the cavern, Flash and Aura pause for a quick exchange:

> FLASH: I wonder what happened to Dale and Dr. Zarkov.
> AURA: No doubt my father is holding them prisoners. . . . (*Stroking Flash's muscular arm*) You *like* the Earth woman.

This economical dialogue raises our concern for the other protagonists and for Flash's Boy Scout innocence. A flurry of quick scenes catches up with two other lines of action that have developed since the last episode. Elsewhere in the palace, Zarkov declares his new laboratory "a scientist's paradise" (it is stocked with Kenneth Strickfaden's electrical devices left over from *Bride of Frankenstein* [James Whale, 1935]) and asks Ming, "But what has become of my friends from the Earth?" In answer, a single-shot scene shows Dale restrained by her ladies-in-waiting, who try to force her into a wedding gown under the smirking gaze of Ming's high priest (Lon Poff). Dale throws the dress at the priest and announces, "I won't do anything until you tell me what's happened to Flash Gordon." Back in the lab, Ming states his intention to conquer the universe with Zarkov's aid. Meanwhile Aura locks Flash inside one of Ming's rocket ships to hide him from the guards, though he protests, "I've got to find out what happened to Dale." She pauses alone outside the closed door to proclaim, "You will never see Dale Arden again." In less than three minutes, all the principals have forthrightly articulated their aims in scenes that locate them in concrete situations.

Flash Gordon presents stretches of plot with unusual dynamism courtesy of Universal's optical department. Each bit of exposition bumps the previous off-screen, with transitions variously designed in the shape of a bolt of lighting, a diamond, a burst of bubbles, a rising circle, and a cross. The complexity of these transitions was a luxury beyond the reach of other serial studios in 1936, though they are now regarded as a cliché of the form. They set *Flash* apart from competitors while also highlighting the importance of crosscut exposition to the serial's structure. Things seem to be moving quickly even as the narration restates the same basic information: Flash wonders where Zarkov and

Dale are, Zarkov asks after Flash and Dale, Dale and Flash each demand to know what happened to the other, and Aura swears to keep them apart. The watchwords for part b are speed and repetition.

This expository stretch concludes by initiating a causal chain that will culminate in the cliffhanger. Back in Zarkov's laboratory, the high priest reports to Ming that Dale refuses to prepare for her nuptials. Ming orders the priest to use "the dehumanizer" on Dale to make her compliant for the duration of the ceremony. Then, at 8.5 minutes (out of 20), the episode explodes into part C, the middle action.[1] A fleet of gyroships piloted by Lionmen attacks the palace as Ming watches on his spaceograph. Flash, conveniently locked in an attack ship, quickly figures out the controls and blasts into a dogfight, much to Ming's delight. This battle royale of sparklers, kitchen funnels, and fishing line climaxes in a spectacular midair collision and crash. The action continues on a smaller scale as Prince Thun of the Lionmen (James Pierce) and Flash climb from the debris of their spacecraft and fight hand to hand. Flash ably disarms Thun, and within moments the two are sworn allies. Thun explains: "You spared my life. I will help you free the prisoners of whom you speak." At the twelve-minute mark, Thun and Flash shake hands, closing the midepisode action sequence and initiating the next phase of exposition. The gyroship attack is an event from Alex Raymond's comic, in which it interrupts Ming's attempt to dehumanize Dale. Raymond used the device to spectacularly resolve Dale's tense situation. Here, the incident is merely an extravagant means for introducing Thun; it comes out of nowhere and delivers relatively little. From a feature-centric perspective, this action sequence is arbitrary and all too quickly resolved. Without prior mention or anticipatory crosscutting, the Lionmen drop from the skies to dispense the requisite spectacle at the appointed time; they get things airborne in an otherwise landlocked episode.

The second expositional sequence, or the fourth part (d) of the five-part structure, prepares the way for the cliffhanger. *Tunnel of Terror* uses the time for characters to specify and embark on plans that they had set out in part b. Ming and the high priest subject Dale to the dehumanizer (an orb of neon tubes attached to a film projector and mounted on a pedestal) and consult the Oracle of Teyo to determine if the god is favorable to the marriage. Meanwhile, Thun and Flash overpower a guard and force him to lead them to Zarkov's lab, where they learn of the impending ceremony. The guard sends Flash and Thun toward the ceremony through a tunnel "guarded by large beasts," while Zarkov and the high priest repair to the secret wedding chamber (an Egyptian tomb set recycled from *The Mummy* [Karl Freund, 1932]). It is a brief sequence of investigation and explanation, of characters moving from place to place and performing simple tasks. *Flash Gordon* connects the dots of plot with efficient clarity.

The cliffhanger comprises the final part of the structure (part E). As chapter 3 will discuss, it is by far the most painstakingly crafted portion of any episode. In *Tunnel of Terror*, a clever suspense device unites the two lines of action before they physically converge. A guard in the chamber informs Zarkov that "on the thirteenth stroke of the sacred gong, the wedding ceremony will be completed." The gong is audible in the tunnel outside the chamber, where a horrible lobster-clawed beast crushes Flash on the eleventh stroke. All appears lost as a wipe to black in the shape of monstrous teeth brings on the title card: "See 'Captured by Sharkmen,' Chapter Three of 'Flash Gordon' serial to be shown at this theatre next week."

The five-part chapter format is action oriented but elastic. Cliffhangers ensure that each episode opens and closes with a physical trap or challenge for the hero, and almost always a chase or a fight occurs in the middle. Viewers are never far from an exciting incident. In *Tunnel of Terror* the format dictates the timing of events in an obvious manner. Neither melodramatic convention nor classical motivation covers the middle action; the Lionmen obey the episode's externally determined schedule. In some cases, causal connections between the parts give an episode a more unified appearance. *Descending Doom*, chapter 3 of *Zorro's Fighting Legion*, presents a more tightly integrated example of the five-part format:

A The first 3 minutes consist of credits, a text recap, and the resolution of the previous episode's cliffhanger, in which Zorro rescues Ramon from the exploding legion hideout by swinging from his whip through a stained-glass window.

b During the next 3.5 minutes Zorro dispatches Juan (Bud Buster) to follow Don del Oro's men and carries the injured Ramon to safety. Juan infiltrates the San Mendolito Mine and discovers a secret room. The next morning, Zorro and Ramon receive a note from Juan describing the secret room, and they ride to help. Zorro, disguised as his foppish alter ego, Don Diego, reaches the mine just as Don del Oro's men discover Juan.

c The next 1.5 minutes dive through a stretch of action in which Zorro helps Juan escape, races down mine shafts, and fights and subdues a henchman.

d Between minutes 8 and 13, four quick scenes set up the cliffhanger. The henchman is killed by an assassin's arrow before he can reveal the villain's identity. Don del Oro, in his robot costume, orders the Yaquis to destroy the mine. Zorro orders Ramon to gather the legion as he departs for the mine. Finally, the legion assembles as Don del Oro's men prepare to blow the shaft.

E The episode enters its fifth part at about 13.5 minutes, as Zorro sneaks into the mine, fights two henchmen, and is knocked out at the bottom of an elevator shaft next to a burning dynamite fuse with the elevator car plummeting toward him (see figure 2).

Descending Doom is more plot-heavy than *Tunnel of Terror*, but this binds action and exposition together. The middle action (C) is set up immediately after the cliffhanger resolution when Zorro orders Juan to spy on the henchmen. The passage from night to morning provides a slight pause at the start of part b and softens the formula by matching the shift into exposition to change within the story world. Zorro's rescue of Juan resolves a hostage situation, in time-honored melodramatic fashion, which further naturalizes the episode's schedule keeping. Part d must cover ground very quickly because, unlike in *Tunnel of Terror*, the cliffhanger has not been signaled earlier. The episode is a model of efficiency. Heroes and villains make plans, which put them on a collision course at the San Mendolito Mine. Zorro's investigation must intersect with the henchmen's attempt to destroy the mine right on schedule, and even this happenstance is motivated. Both parties need to act before the next morning's official mine investigation takes place. *Flash Gordon* and *Zorro's Fighting Legion* present two approaches to the same structure. *Tunnel of Terror* piles spectacle on at regular intervals, while *Descending Doom* camouflages formula with a logical flow from action to exposition.

FIGURE 2 Promotional still from *Zorro's Fighting Legion* (1939). Author's collection.

The five-part structure served more as a departure point than a straitjacket; its flexibility made it resilient. As our discussion of *Perils of Nyoka* and *Daredevils of the Red Circle* will show, fifteen-to-twenty-minute chapters might feather action sequences into continuous stretches of screen time, or integrate units of exposition and eventful action. As running times dropped in the late 1940s, parts might be compressed or truncated, but the format remained in force. Republic's 1944 release *Zorro's Black Whip* (Bennet and Grissell) demonstrates the five-part structure's durability. Having overspent on that year's previous two serials, Republic producers trimmed the budget for *Zorro's Black Whip*, eliminating optical titles, using an economy chapter built out of previously seen footage (chapter 8), lengthening the amount of footage used in recaps of previous episodes, and compacting the already dense format. Jack Mathis reports that the serial cost Republic $134,899, less than the previous twenty-one efforts or any that followed.[2] As part of the effort to economize, the studio cut episodes down to around fourteen minutes apiece.[3]

The screenwriting team, headed by Basil Dickey, developed two options for meeting the new time constraints. They either condensed parts of the structure or strategically eliminated the third or fourth part. Episode 7, *Wolf Pack*, for example, abbreviates the middle action and second expositional sequence (parts C and d). In the first three minutes, the Black Whip (Linda Sterling) survives a bombing attempt. Four minutes of exposition follow, in which the bad guys plan to attack a convoy of settlers and plant a false story to divert the citizens' patrol. This fairly standard stretch leads into a very slight half-minute gun battle at the eight-minute mark. The fight slides into an equally scant two-minute expositional scene as federal agent Vic Gordon (George J. Lewis) alerts the Black Whip and both ride to the settlers' rescue. At ten minutes and thirty seconds, the villains spring their trap, and ensuing chases and fights fill out the remaining four minutes of the episode, ending when the Black Whip is tossed over a cliff. By squeezing in a micro middle action and keeping the subsequent exposition brief, the chapter covers all five parts and retains room for an extended action-cliffhanger.

If five parts proved too cumbersome, the writers would truncate the structure, usually removing the middle action or the second expositional sequence. Episode 4, *Detour to Death*, keeps parts A and b, but then runs the middle action (C) and cliffhanger (E) together as a horse chase turns into a perilous runaway wagon situation. The serial's final episode amplifies the tactic with unusual force. The revelation scene, in which the heroes unmask the villain, is a good candidate for the episode's middle action (C). Instead, it is depicted through an insert of the *Crescent City Herald* front page: "Hammond Exposed as Outlaw Leader: Escapes on Eve of Elections, Aroused Citizens Flock to Polls." From here, the chapter moves economically through exposition until about 7.5 minutes, just past the midpoint, when Hammond's gang opens fire in Crescent City. Action runs continuously until the two-minute denouement that closes the serial. In a sense, all five parts remain in the story, but the plot reduces a major event, the villain's unmasking and his escape, to newspaper exposition. In marking out a middle action but not showing it, the writers obey the five-part template without losing time.

Beginning in 1945, chapter running times fell to just over thirteen minutes, where they would remain until the very end.[4] As our discussion of the one-reel melodramas that preceded the development of the feature film will show, a standardized length of twelve to fifteen minutes can nicely support unified dramatic arcs. Remarkably, jamming chapters down to one-reel proportions did little to encourage this kind of situational coherence. Episode 5 of Republic's late entry *Radar Men from the Moon* (Brannon, 1952) illustrates the rote observance of the five-part format that typifies efforts from the end of the serial's reign. The villain stages a payroll robbery to finance his secret ray gun in the middle action. This failed crime provides an inconsequential action beat, as it did in the nearly identically structured chapter 3 of *The Crimson Ghost* (Brannon and Witney, 1946) six years earlier. But here the action is a particularly dodgy affair. The heist itself is elided, and instead we are treated to a stock-footage car chase (likely from a *Dick Tracy* serial), featuring anachronistic 1930s vehicles. The five-part format, which had always admitted a good deal of padding, especially through travel sequences, withstood contracted running times quite well.[5]

No matter the chapter length, the five-part format accounts for the sound serial's peculiar narrative rhythm. Serials appear fast-paced, moving from incident to incident at breakneck speed. Unlike in a feature film, turning points follow quickly upon one another as characters race from space to space and challenge to challenge. In only ten minutes of screen time, and perhaps an hour of story time, Flash escapes the lizard pit, evades guards, fights a fleet of gyroships, befriends Thun of the Lionmen, and battles a lobster beast on his way to rescue Dale. Serial screenwriters were obliged to keep things moving, and they achieved narrative compression by dispensing with character development, complex motivations, and fleshed-out relationships. Ming succinctly states his desire to conquer the universe, and Aura her desire to conquer Flash. We know that Dale and Flash care for one another because each keeps asking where the other is. Where a feature film might linger, the serial zips ahead. But for all its linear drive, the serial chapter is highly redundant and cyclical. Characters have simple goals and plans to achieve them, and these are subject to near-constant articulation. A benefit of the midpoint action scene is that it opens room for another regrouping of heroes and villains to once again state their goals and make plans. Each episode cycles through the predictable fixed course from action to exposition and planning to action at least once. Stories are repetitive rather than complex.

Compression and repetition work together in the sound serial to forge a cinematic world at once clear, direct, and single-minded but also frantic, compulsive, and focused to the point of obsession. To a certain extent, the long running time and interrupted viewing of a fifteen-chapter serial combine to make redundancy unavoidable. Each episode must quickly reacquaint returning viewers with characters and their traits, while new viewers need to be brought up to speed. A practical concern for clarity between episodes, however, does not explain the exhaustive repetition within each chapter. Consider Ming's wedding plans. The title card that recaps action at the start of *Tunnel of Terror* informs us that Ming, "determined to win the beautiful Dale for his bride, condemns Flash to fight huge ape-like man killers in the arena." The impending marriage is reinforced visually about five minutes later when Dale throws her wedding gown at the High Priest. Two minutes after that, the High Priest reports to Ming that Dale refuses to become his bride, and the evil emperor orders up the dehumanizer. After the midchapter gyroship battle, and about five minutes since its last mention, the High Priest assures Dale that soon she will forget Flash Gordon forever. Two minutes later, Ming uses the dehumanizer and asks his priest to summon the oracle to "determine if the God Teyo is favorable to the marriage." A minute beyond that, Zarkov alerts Flash: "I believe that Ming is going to force Dale to become his wife." Immediately, a guard reveals to Flash that the image on the spaceograph "is the Oracle deciding the marriage."

Repetition is important to all Hollywood storytelling. In feature films, David Bordwell explains, "optimally a significant motif or informational bit should be shown or mentioned at three or four distinct moments.... The Hollywood slogan is to state every fact three times, once for the smart viewer, once for the average viewer, and once for slow Joe in the back row."[6] Where features could be elegantly redundant, restating a motif through varied means, serials are relentless. Mentioning Ming's wedding seven times in fifteen minutes transgresses the feature-film norm of generally inconspicuous narration, which, Bordwell notes, prevents extensive repetition.[7] *Tunnel of Terror* may treat its collective matinee audience as "slow Joe in the back row," but reiteration also contributes to the sound serial in a more positive way. Unlike narration in features, serial narration tends not to recede to the background. The declarative, presentational address of an episode's opening recap and closing cliffhanger makes way for directive and emphatic storytelling throughout each chapter. An episode's narrative compression creates a kind of situational intensity; all roads lead to the next crisis. In this narrational environment, repetition pressurizes the problem space; each mention amplifies the deadline's menace. Moreover, repetition and the five-part-format help make the act of storytelling visible. Even as a chapter builds tension, viewers can recognize the game at hand and appropriate it to play outside the theater.

Serial chapters break norms in another way as well. The five-part format militates against the kind of dramatic unity that typifies studio-era features. By placing an action sequence near the midpoint, serial writers split the dramatic slope in two. If graphed, the ideal feature would resemble a continuously rising incline followed by a quick descent to normalcy. The serial would look more like a mountain range. A, C, and E are all peaks, while b and d represent the valleys. This formula directly mirrors melodramatic situational dramaturgy that, as discussed in chapter 1, Jacobs and Brewster identify in both late nineteenth-century stage spectacles and feature films made in the 1910s. In this model, writers construct plays by combining ready-made "states of affair" into thrilling scenarios. One result was the double and multiple climax plot, graphed by Alfred Hennequin in his 1897 manual *The Art of Playwriting* as a rising and falling line. Plots with multiple peaks built from discrete situations "ultimately break up the rising line of the plot, the emotional and logical continuity of the linear chain of cause and effect," according to Brewster and Jacobs. The results were popular but also frequently criticized for introducing "powerful situations in arbitrary or mechanical ways simply to create 'effects,' a term which was used to refer variously to moments of emotional intensity, of suspense, and of spectacular display."[8]

The one-reel films that preceded the development of the feature could generally develop a single effect across their running time, while later studio-era features aim to unify effects along a continuously progressive path toward climax and closure. The very format of the sound-serial episode, by contrast, almost demands mechanical and arbitrary effects every six minutes or so. Events after the cliffhanger resolution might set up the middle action as in *Zorro's Fighting Legion*, or the midpoint climax might simply drop from the skies of Mongo as in *Flash Gordon*. In either case, the characters must then regroup and climb the dramatic mountainside to the next cliffhanger. The attack of the Lionmen, the pursuit of Don del Oro's henchmen through a mine shaft, and countless chases, crashes, fights, and rescues set the serial apart from both its one-reel and feature-film relatives and connect it to an older, if no more venerable, popular tradition.

Melodramatic situational plotting helped serial screenwriters create eventful narratives, while the five-part format tended to limit complexity. The result is a form that keeps things moving but prevents the deepening or development of characters, their motivations, or our alignment with them. A tightly packed schedule of fights, chases, and races to the rescue demands quick and sure identification of heroes and villains. Moreover, the serial practice of shooting action sequences first with stunt teams or constructing them out of stock footage generally prevents much character individuation during the heat of battle. Any exploration of character traits, psychology, and motives is thus relegated to short expository bursts, where it vies for time with concrete explanations of plans and procedures. The same limits on exposition kept situations themselves from becoming too intricate. Unlike a grand theatrical melodrama that could layer and interconnect baroque plot machinations, the sound serial required situations to swiftly crystalize and dissolve. The convention of summarizing previous events at the start of each chapter illustrates this pressure. For instance, in episode 1 of Columbia's 1952 aviator serial *Blackhawk* (Bennet and Sears), squadron member Stan (Rick Vallin) is lured away by his former countrymen who appeal to him to join their cause. When they fail, they abduct him and send his twin brother Boris (also Vallin) to infiltrate the Blackhawk base. The voice-over recap at the start of chapter 2 must boil the situation down: "Realizing that an enemy in Blackhawk uniform is at large in their headquarters, the Blackhawks try to reach there before the man can sabotage their airbase." Innovative twists like the invader's identity and his relationship to Stan are inessential details when the plot must be compressed into a definition of good guys and bad guys. In the main, the serial episode is disposed to rearticulating central conflicts and goals and maneuvering characters into vivid situations that can be resolved without a major impact on the overarching story. The stories told might not be nuanced or multifaceted, but from episode to episode they are comprehensible, even when a viewer has missed one or all of the previous installments. In putting situational dramaturgy on a timetable, serials managed the steady proliferation of discrete crises while keeping them simple and predictable enough for the playground.

Setting the Game: First Chapters

The bulk of a serial's episodes might have more or less interchangeable formats, but beginnings had their own special requirements. The first chapter was vital to the serial's market identity. Distributors and theater owners coordinated ballyhoo with the start of the serial, and trade papers like the *Exhibitor* based reviews on the initial chapter. Universal's manual *How to Make Money with Serials* makes the point: "If the first installment of a serial intrigues them, the purchasers are sure to become constant. . . . The first chapter of a Universal serial should insure capacity audiences for each of the succeeding episodes. But exploitation and advertising are required to arouse their interest at the start— and to keep them reminded of your play dates on the serial." Preproduction and production also conferred special status. The first-episode treatment served as the guide for writing subsequent chapters, and its final script was generally better polished because it spent more time in revision.[9] Finally, more resources were allocated to the opening. Until the mid-1940s first chapters ran about thirty minutes, which allowed for more extensive exposition and an unequaled scale of spectacle. A serial's opening was expected to lay the foundation of viewership for the entire run.

In launching the large-scale story and initiating the familiar local pattern of exposition and action, opening episodes mix ambition with routine. The narratologist Steven Connor distinguishes between "the world" and "a world": "A world is strongly determined but weakly determining. By contrast, 'the world' is weakly determined but strongly determining." Sound-serial fictions firmly belong to the former category. They are supremely knowable and readily legible to the extent that, in Connor's terms, "we can see round them."[10] Serials create closed and limited worlds, no more detailed than the action requires. But if body chapters present essentially closed systems that make reference to a well-mapped circuit of repeated spaces and situations, opening episodes cut a broader swath of time and space.

The Golden God, the first installment of *Zorro's Fighting Legion*, exemplifies the form. In its first few moments the chapter has epic swagger. After the title, Witney and English rocket through a fifty-second montage depicting the Mexican Revolution. Text informs us, over a shot of marching drummers, "In 1819 the Mexican people revolted against centuries of tyranny." Superimposed images of cannon fire, gun battles, and mounted assaults follow, with the words "Declaration of Independence" and "September 16, 1810" rising above the chaos. The Mexican flag is raised, and a map of the republic appears beneath another title card: "By 1824, the old Spanish provinces had formed themselves into the United States of Mexico." The camera tilts and zooms into an area of the map labeled "Province of San Mendolito." The sequence emulates a feature-length period film's historical sweep, using library footage and title cards to inflate the proceedings well beyond their B-grade means.

This opening volley of imagery projects a grand and impressive fiction around the events to follow. It is as close as a serial can come to "the world," with its massive, uncontainable forces of history, tyranny, and revolution. The effect is similar to the stock-footage montage of global disaster that depicts Mongo's approach to the Earth at the start of *Flash Gordon*, the earthquake and tsunami that apparently devastates New York City in the first episode of *Dick Tracy vs. Crime Inc.* (Witney and English, 1941), or the destruction of the planet Krypton in chapter 1 of *Superman* (Bennet and Carr, 1948). Many films begin by situating their stories in relation to a larger background, but the sound serial's invocation of scope and scale stands out because of both the form's representational inadequacies and the opening's contrast to the resolutely narrow fictions that follow. Producers undoubtedly hoped to give their chapterplays an aura of importance that might distinguish them from the competition and, perhaps, convince viewers that the new serial would be substantially different from the one that had just ended.

To borrow from Huizinga, the serial introductions also "hedge round" the playground, marking off "a world" from "the world." The action of *Zorro's Fighting Legion* circulates among landscapes filmed in Chatsworth, California, at the Iverson Movie Ranch, various generic Western interiors, and the San Mendolito Mine constructed on Republic's standing cave set, a circumscribed and familiar arena. The loud and expansive beginnings of many serials impart grandeur to the routine, giving it a new frame of reference. They also highlight the rift between the imagined world and the one practicably representable, lending the whole enterprise the appearance of make-believe. In either case, these fleeting references to an encompassing context reinforce the sound serial's playlike aspect; characters occupy a closed course, but they behave as though it is "the world." Viewers can replicate the dynamic in their own ludic space, projecting epic circumstances around a playground game of tag.

Producers could occasionally extend the expansive approach across the entirety of an opening chapter as a means of product differentiation. *Flash Gordon* invests a good stretch of its first chapter charting the rocket trip to Mongo, *Adventures of Captain Marvel* (Witney and English, 1941) begins on an archaeological expedition in Siam, *The Lone Ranger* (Witney and English, 1938) opens by depicting its villain's rise and the massacre that forges its hero, and *Superman* does not reach the *Daily Planet* until episode 2. As high-profile adaptations of well-known properties, most of these serials draw on previously developed origin stories to briefly vary the formula. With the notable exception of Universal's flagship *Flash Gordon*, which continues to unveil new regions of Mongo across its run, each serial merely delays the arrival of its regular milieu, settling into the standard kinds of repetition by the second episode. References to vast fictional worlds amount to window dressing on a form that favors predictable familiarity. Serials tend to innovate by burrowing within narrow parameters rather than building outward.

Zorro's Fighting Legion, a serial of typically moderate ambitions, swiftly reverts to business as usual. Opening chapters must quickly narrow the world, and the process by which routine takes hold illustrates the formula's kinship to gameplay. The first scene briefly extends the historical montage's aura of worldly importance. In the Mendolito province council's boardroom, Governor Felipe (Leander De Cordova) introduces Benito Juarez, who beseeches the councilmen to deliver gold to Mexico City because "in your hands alone rests the fate of our newborn democracy." Juarez had appeared earlier that year in Warner Bros.' eponymous biopic (William Dieterle, 1939) starring Paul Muni and Bette Davis, and Carleton Young's stately line readings mimic prestige-film pretension. Like the grand revolutionary battle scenes, Juarez's appearance suggests the sheen of historical gravitas. Despite the pomp of his introduction, he is strictly a minor character, returning only briefly in the second and final episodes.

The serial formula's narrative economy quickly takes command. In short order the episode establishes the bad guys and their plan. As Juarez holds forth on the nation's future, a simple panning shot isolates each of the "brain heavies" in shifty-eyed close-up: "Our republic has internal enemies [close-up]. Selfish [close-up], unscrupulous [close-up], callous men [close-up]." Don Francisco (Guy D'Ennery) marks himself in opposition to the villains when he warns Juarez that Don Del Oro, a three-century-old idol, has been rousing the Yaqui tribe. Francisco confides that he has "organized a group of patriots to combat" threats to the gold train. Our suspicions about the remaining council members are confirmed one minute later as they raise their glasses to Gonzales's (Edmund Cobb) toast: "Francisco and Juarez, how can they interfere with our plans? To Don del Oro's success!" Within five minutes, the episode has closed in on the serial's central Manichaeism and stated the terms of contest. Mexican national history fades, and the squabble over gold shipments from the province's mine sets the narrative agenda.

Abstract oppositions become concrete in the fifth scene when a hidden hand fires a golden arrow signaling the Yaquis' attack on a pack train carrying gold. This first battle sequence is an undistinguished melee without any major characters, but it physicalizes the serial's conflict and initiates the regular alternation of exposition and action. Having met the expectation of gunfire and horseplay, the chapter returns to the council chambers for one minute of exposition in which Francisco protests the decision to halt the gold trains: "Don del Oro or no Don del Oro, our republic's need for gold must be supplied." Action immediately strikes again (at about the eight-minute mark) when the council has Francisco murdered in a rigged duel at a café, and Zorro appears on the scene to drive off the gang of thugs. Francisco's final act is to gun down an assailant who is about to shoot Zorro, prompting our hero to clarify their relationship with a simple "You saved my life, Uncle." Ramon, Francisco's young confidant, cements character identity through repetition. He asks Zorro, "You are Diego Vega?" Francisco offers a bit of deathbed exposition, repeats the relationship, and raises the enigma: "As my nephew you will meet with opposition. Ramon will explain everything. Watch the counselors. Don del Oro is . . . is. . . ." In eleven minutes the episode has focused down from the Mexican Revolution to deliver two fights, announce the villains and heroes, lay out the stakes, and mention Don del Oro in six of its seven scenes. The game is set.

The remaining principal characters are immediately brought into play. Two quick scenes establish the knife-and-gun heavies as they respond to Don del Oro's signal: a tuneless chord strummed by a strolling guitar player named Pedro (Eddie Cherkose). The tenth scene reveals the Golden God himself, seated on a throne behind sliding stone doors deep in the sacred Yaqui volcanic cave. Don del Oro, impressively voiced by Billy Bletcher, who had previously lent his stentorian intonation to the Lone Ranger, has the tribe throw Sebastian (Ernest Sarracino), an erstwhile heavy, into the volcanic pit as "a sacrifice to Yaqui victory." The murder serves the villain in two ways. It impresses the natives with his cruel power and scares the henchmen who attend him behind the doors. At the chapter's midpoint, Don del Oro declares his evil intent: "You saw what happened to Sebastian. Remember the lesson. No man can stop me from using the Yaquis to keep gold out of Mexico City. Then, when I have forced the Republic into bankruptcy, I'll strike, found an empire, become its emperor!" Here, in this boxy suit of armor and surrounded by worshipping natives, is the enemy of democracy: his ruthlessness equaled only by his penchant for ceremony and fueled by a crystal-clear objective.

The Golden God speedily sets the serial's narrative machine in motion. The world, its situations, and characters are whittled down to the capacities of a form that must feature a chase or fight every six minutes. The film's love interest, Volita (Sheila Darcy), the last of the main characters to be introduced, emblematizes this narrowing process. Volita's primary purpose is to be at once impressed by Zorro and disenchanted with his alter ego, Diego, a relationship that entered cinema in Douglas Fairbanks's *Mark of Zorro* (Fred Niblo, 1920), which made romance its centerpiece. Her terse appraisal of Diego in the episode's eleventh scene perfectly condenses her attitude: "Saints protect us. A fop!" Where *Mark of Zorro* derives comedy and tension from the heroine's simultaneous disdain for and attraction to the hero, *Zorro's Fighting Legion* never sparks the love affair.

The structural role of love interest to a dual-identity hero had been previously filled by Joyce Andrews (Helen Christian) in *Zorro Rides Again* (Witney and English, 1937), Republic's first Zorro serial, a contemporary update of the story, and would be more famously occupied by Lois Lane (Noel Neill) in *Superman* (Bennet and Carr, 1948) and Vicki Vale (Jane Adams) in *Batman and Robin* (Bennet, 1949). In none of these cases does the relationship move beyond an initial statement of interest and disappointment. The romantic stalemate stems in part from assumptions about the sound serial's young audience, but it also speaks to a more general quality of first episodes. Major players are swiftly introduced and clearly defined, but their motives, traits, and psychologies will remain more or less static for the rest of the run. First chapters resemble feature films in efficiently delineating a specific fictional world. But where a classical feature's first act establishes a point of departure for characters who might undergo journeys of self-discovery, serials give us figures sketched with as much detail as they will ever receive. While feature films might present characters living in a world, serials array playing pieces that fit onto the formula's game board.

Zorro versus Robin Hood: Serials and Features

Opening chapters introduce a set of procedures, attractions, and conflicts to be replayed from episode to episode, and they initiate the overarching story that binds the pieces together. In terms of plotting, the first episode strongly resembles a feature film's opening act, but the two forms diverge after their initial twenty or thirty minutes. As noted, the five-part format ensures that subsequent chapters keep the action moving without necessarily pushing the large-scale story forward. Long-range plots develop over the course of a serial, but with little of the economy or organicism that we associate with contemporaneous feature films. We can grasp the serial's peculiar narrative design, and better understand its distinctive properties, by comparing it to a studio-era feature-length counterpart.

Warner Bros.' prestige Technicolor production *Adventures of Robin Hood* (Michael Curtiz, 1938) shares a good deal with both of Republic's serial hits of 1939, *The Lone Ranger* and *Zorro's Fighting Legion*. All three are tales of vigilante heroes battling oppressive usurpers. Each is a clear variation on the historical adventure genre, which Brian Taves defines as "the valiant fight for freedom and a just form of government set in exotic locales and the historical past."[11] Indeed, both *Robin Hood* and *Zorro's Fighting Legion* share a common lineage in the Douglas Fairbanks cycle of the 1920s, which cemented conventions of the genre in such films as *Mark of Zorro* (1920), *Robin Hood* (Allan Dwan, 1922), and *The Black Pirate* (Albert Parker, 1926). One need look no further than the identically structured montage sequences in which the hero invites followers to meet him "at the gallows oak" in *Adventures of Robin Hood* and to "head for the old stockade" in *The Lone Ranger*, or the device of the unseen archer whose arrow nails Prince John's (Claude Rains) proclamation to the conference table and the soon-to-be-sacrificed henchman Sebastian's Ace of Spades to the gambling table, to see the influence of Curtiz's spectacle on Witney and English at Republic. All three films are episodic adventures, but only *Robin Hood* is unified around character psychology and a careful causal chain.

As scripted by Norman Reilly Raine and Seton Miller, *Adventures of Robin Hood* follows a three-act structure, the first act of which roughly corresponds to *The Golden God*. Prince John and Sir Guy of Gisbourne (Basil Rathbone) lay out their plans to consolidate power by taxing and dominating the Normans while King Richard (Ian Hunter) is away on the crusades. As if in answer to a montage of oppression, Robin Hood (Errol Flynn) rides to the rescue of Much the Miller's Son (Herbert Mundin) and holds Sir Guy at arrow's point. Broad historical background and political conflict is thus specified around a few characters with personal stakes. In the fifth scene Robin crashes Prince

John's celebration, catches Maid Marian's (Olivia de Havilland) eye, and declares war on the villain. The act climaxes in an elaborate action set piece with Robin fighting off a horde of men-at-arms and escaping the castle. As in the serial, major characters are introduced, plans revealed, and good and evil vividly arrayed, in the first thirty minutes. *Robin Hood's* middle act and climax, however, are different creatures.

Sound-serial narratives are unbalanced. After a seemingly endless cycle of entrapment and escape that ends in impasse, serials swiftly rush to closure at the appointed hour. In fact, the last two chapters present the only discernible turning point common to the form. William Cline proposes a general scheme that he suggests "was the pattern of most serials and the framework upon which could be built stories that might otherwise wander aimlessly or lose all interest."[12] Cline tends to force a progressive structure onto a formula that was satisfied with simple repetition. He suggests that chapters 2–7 or 8 (in a twelve-chapter serial) gradually reveal details of the villain's plan and that in episodes 8 and 9 things go from bad to worse as the villain appears on the verge of achieving his or her nefarious aims. Both observations overemphasize the narrative arc. Villains tend to announce their plans immediately, and it is often impossible to judge their progress because steps are constantly added from chapter to chapter. With every episode culminating in crisis, serials cannot easily escalate tension as Cline suggests.

However, Cline's discussion of a serial's final chapters rings true. He proposes a turning point in chapters 10 and 11 in which "the hero's dogged persistence would begin to pay off" and the villain turns "his attention directly to the task of eliminating the hated hero and setting in motion a final desperate effort to culminate his grand design." Finally, in chapters 11 and 12, which Cline deems "the most meaningful and exciting," heroes and villains collide in battle, ending in the victory of justice.[13] While the hero's progress is not necessarily a feature of the tenth chapter, the final two episodes restate and resolve the serial's central conflict. In terms of melodramatic plotting, the serial's initial deadlock is crystallized and broken, as often by an unforeseen event as by any successful extended effort by the hero.

As the outline of *Zorro's Fighting Legion* indicates, the heroes' investigations repeatedly culminate in dead ends until late in the serial. Zorro's grand scheme to entrap Commandant Manuel and force his confession, which extends from the seventh chapter to the ninth, comes to naught, as does his pursuit of a would-be assassin and discovery of Don del Oro's secret water wagon in the ninth and tenth episodes. The serial's true turning point coincides with the sudden appearance of a new character, Kala, the "hereditary leader" of the Yaqui tribe. Absent from the first nine chapters and barely individuated in chapter 10, Kala is central to bringing down Don del Oro. In the middle action of chapter 11, *Face to Face*, the fighting legion rescues Kala from execution, and he swears a blood oath of brotherhood with Zorro. Kala then serves two important functions. First, he brings Zorro to Don del Oro's cave. Second, he lobbies the Yaqui tribe against Don del Oro and the native hench-man Tarmac (Joe Molina). In episode 12, *Unmasked*, Kala delays the armed insurrection until Zorro can reveal Chief Justice Pablo beneath the helmet. He then restores order: "Return to your homes and live in peace with your white friends. . . . Remember only that if it were not for our brother Zorro, death and bloodshed would have found us." By inventing Kala in the third-to-last episode, *Zorro's Fighting Legion*'s screenwriters provide a convenient solution to the serial's master conflict. His advent reflects melodrama's "wide latitude" for resolving situations through recourse to "external or arbitrary incidents," identified by Brewster and Jacobs.[14] Storytelling in serials is an ad hoc affair; elements are introduced as needed to help the plot hit its marks in twelve or fifteen episodes.

Adventures of Robin Hood stands in stark contrast to this method of plot-ting. The film weaves characters' personal desires and growth with overarch-ing goals, which raises and deepens the stakes in a way wholly absent from the serial. Romance is the key to character development, as Robin tempers his independence with attachment to Marian and she softens to his political agenda. Though hardly complex, Robin has room to grow. He is flawed by pride and arrogance, traits that lead him straight into Sir Guy's trap despite the warnings of his men. After his capture, romance and action intertwine when Marian arranges his escape. Yet Marian declines Robin's request that she join him in Sherwood, explaining that she might better help the cause from within Prince John's castle walls. The lovers are separated by their fealty to the greater good, and they forestall happiness to defeat the villain. Romance is imbricated in the fight for justice.

The timely return of King Richard at the midpoint of *Robin Hood*'s second act cracks the romantic and political deadlock. Like Kala's, his appearance is something of a melodramatic coincidence, but the feature has prepared the way with references to Richard's absence from the start. Unlike in the serial, his arrival is tightly integrated into the causal chain, touching off events that lead directly to Marian's imprisonment and Prince John's overthrow. The Bishop of the Black Canons (Montegue Love) spots King Richard and reports it to Prince John and Sir Guy. Upon overhearing this, Marian attempts to alert Robin of Richard's return, but Sir Guy discovers her and casts her into the dungeon. As the film nears its climax, the final situation crystallizes. In a nicely efficient touch, the Bishop also provides the means for her rescue, since Robin and Richard exploit him to infiltrate Prince John's coronation. In the climactic battle, Robin smites Sir Guy and frees Maid Marian. King Richard's first act is to unite the lovers by giving the hero Marian's hand in marriage, to which Robin responds, "May I obey all your commands with equal pleasure!"

Beyond the parallels between first act and first episode, the sound serial has little of *Robin Hood*'s structural refinement. Absent an actual character arc, no matter how externalized, the sound serial has trouble defining a "second act." Even the makeup of the hero's team tends to remain static, unlike Robin's, which gains members through the middle of the film. Serial heroes are not granted the leeway for flaw and change that Robin Hood enjoys. They may have personal stakes in the fight, most often vengeance as in *The Lone Ranger*, but these are introduced at the start rather than revealed or built during the adventures. Plots tend to add parts and repeat situations rather than develop or grow. *Robin Hood*, with its economical weave of causal threads, shows the difference. The Bishop of the Black Canons links Richard's return to Marian's imprisonment and provides the means for Robin's climactic attack. By contrast, Zorro pursues a series of dead ends before happening on Kala, who bears no connection to any major character. Climaxes don't appear to grow from long chains of events in the serial, they just happen.

Once again, the romantic subplot best illustrates the gulf between serial and feature storytelling. A relationship like Robin and Marian's is impossible when characters must stay aligned with one side of the conflict or the other. Some Mascot productions from the early 1930s attempt to integrate romance and action, as when Tom Wayne (John Wayne) must convince Elaine Corday (Ruth Hall) that he didn't murder her brother in *The Three Musketeers* (1933). Setting the record straight, however, proves to be a simple matter, after which Elaine joins Tom as part of his team. Such complexities are streamlined out of the formula by middecade as familial relationships replace romantic ones. Volita's capture and rescue in chapters 6 and 7 of *Zorro's Fighting Legion*, for example, have little effect on the causal chain. She is caught up in the villain's plans because she is Ramon's sister, not Zorro's lover. Romance usually involves depicting character change within the tale, whereas familial ties can be instantly established at the story's start. This is one reason that the daughters of abducted (or soon-to-be abducted) scientists, professors, and government officials populate the serial world. The static relationships of "intrepid daughter" characters fit easily into the serial's fixed parameters; she might also vaguely occupy the place of love interest as long as no character change is entailed. Robin's final line of dialogue sums up the adventure's interlacing of character desire, action, and meaning. Only by returning Richard to the throne can Robin follow his command; the romantic couple had been kept apart because they needed to fight Prince John, but the couple was also forged by that battle. Robin wittily remarks that his pleasures, serving his king and getting the girl, are indistinguishable. All of this is foreign to the sound serial. The pleasure of serial narrative rests less in moving forward toward a goal than in keeping things in motion, extending the possible engagements in a series of suspenseful situations. The form is designed to maintain interest in the moment and to hold open playable scenarios between chapters: a continuing projectable world rather than a journey to closure.

Conclusion

Comparing sound serials to major-studio feature films risks defining them by what they lack. *Zorro's Fighting Legion* is not a thematically unified or emotionally rich work. Characters are thin, events predictable, and the drama doesn't build so much as repeat itself. But viewing serials as inadequate versions of Hollywood features misses the point. They aim to involve viewers with regular bouts of rapidly unfolding action in heightened but familiar worlds and to leave them with vivid, inhabitable scenarios. Formulaic narrative structure enabled time-and-budget-strapped producers to hit these marks more often than not.

A cinema of immediacy, serials prioritize legible parts over complex wholes. The five-part format ensures a steady flow of pursuit, entrapment, and conflict but puts limits on exposition. Likewise, chapters that climax in dire crises prevent larger-scale modulations of tension. Sound serials may tell lengthy tales, but they invite intensive focus on the critical moment; film and spectator live in the present. Narrative is geared toward placing well-defined figures in equally well defined situations. In this sense, the best analog to the serial story is neither the epic adventure nor the feature film but the game. Each chapter restages a variant on the same contest along a rigid timeline. Major characters divide cleanly into opposing teams, while those in the middle, the third factions like the Yaquis in *Zorro's Fighting Legion*, must eventually choose sides. Both heroes and villains are defined by functions and affordances, as the practice of categorizing henchmen by weapon suggests. Zorro, with his whip and sword, faces wave after wave of knife-and-gun heavies. While character depth and development serve organic fictions well, they would cloud the serial's field of play. Like so many pawns and knights in a game of chess, heroes, sidekicks, villains, and henchmen must be known quantities. As the next chapter illustrates, the serial world has the quality of a narrative architecture in which figures maneuver through obstacles, engage in contests, and solve physical puzzles.

Of course, unlike in a game, in a serial the outcome is always the same. But if the heroes win at the appointed hour, they spend most of their time on the point of defeat. Our interest is less in following their journeys to victory than in watching them struggle with the present dilemma. That dilemmas are constructed from familiar, recycled parts, and obey an externally imposed timeline, further aligns serials with games. Chapter breaks that freeze dilemmas for a week open the game to the viewer. Serial figures can serve as appropriable roles, and well-drawn situations supply exportable parameters for play. Once the opening chapter sets things in motion, repetition rules the serial narrative, giving the impression that it might cycle endlessly through rounds of capture and release. Huizinga points out, "In nearly all higher forms of play the elements of repetition and alternation . . . are like the warp and woof of a fabric."[15] In reaching arbitrary closure in the final two episodes, serials seem to stop because of convention rather than to conclude on their own. It is the nature of play to continue until it is broken off.

Narrative structure is quite possibly the least interesting aspect of the sound serial. The five-part format and the twelve-to-fifteen-chapter limit resemble rules for play. In themselves, they are necessary but empty guidelines. I will argue that these patterns give shape to our experience of the serial world and that they can generate innovation and enable virtuosity. But for the spectator, they merely provide a familiar framework to support other pleasures. Responding to criticism that serial narrative is uninterestingly formulaic, Ruth Mayer observes, "The fact that the narrative layout is familiar allows the narrative's recipients to focus on other things—the special effects and mediatized interventions, the formal particularities and iterations, the action rather than the agents."[16] The next chapter turns to these "other things," the components and attractions of the serial world.

3

The Serial World

• •

During the early exposition of *Phantom Empire*'s opening episode, Betsy visits Frankie's secret laboratory hidden in a barn loft and discovers his new gadget, a radio signal "direction finder." The plot point is simple, but procedure is everything. To access the lab, Betsy spins a wagon wheel that lowers a rope ladder from the barn ceiling. She climbs onto a rung and spins the wheel in the opposite direction, which whisks her through a trapdoor to the upper level. Once there, she presses a secret button that illuminates a light and sounds a buzzer on Frankie's desk. In response, he pushes another button and a portion of the wall slides upward, allowing Betsy to enter. Frankie demonstrates his new device, built from a stolen "cyclometer tube," which floats in a jar of water and spins to point toward the origin of any radio signal he tunes in. First, the finder turns toward San Francisco when Frankie finds a music station. Then bizarre signals interrupt the broadcast and the direction finder points straight down, our first indication of Muranian activity below Radio Ranch. Frankie and Betsy hurry to another trapdoor, slide down a pole, and rush off to alert Gene Autry. The entire scene runs just under three minutes, an ample slice of the first chapter's half-hour running time.

Compare this step-by-step detail with the following episode's handling of a conventionally tragic event. In *Secret Weapons*, Frankie and Betsy take part in a staged shootout between radio-drama villains and the Thunder Riders Club, part of Gene Autry's daily Radio Ranch broadcast. During the pretend battle, a real bullet strikes the siblings' father. Still in character, Betsy and Frankie rush to his side, congratulate him on the realism of his fall, and, while pretending to bandage him, discover that he has died. Frankie cradles his father's head and stifles a tear. The children's encounter with death and grief runs just thirty seconds.

This contrast typifies sound-serial priorities. Physical and mechanical procedures dwarf emotional expression and character psychology; the serial presents an operational world. As noted in the last chapter, despite their sprawling stories, serials tend toward repetition, which helps them create bounded, lucid diegeses: "a world" as opposed to "the world." The effect is a visually intelligible space within which situations can be played out. Though characters may find themselves lost within labyrinths, spectators usually have a clear vantage on the action, and after one or two episodes can probably anticipate most outcomes. Serials throw emphasis behind "how" things happen, rather than "what" happens, and this presumes a high degree of clarity regarding causes and likely effects. The serial world is thus a bizarre mix of outlandish adventure and almost tactile familiarity.

In part, the world's closed quality stems from the way most serials regularly return to familiar locations. For example, the council chamber and Don del Oro's Yaqui cave appear in every episode of *Zorro's Fighting Legion*, commonly between the action sequences. Repeating sets made for efficient production by allowing directors to shoot many scenes in a short period and to schedule actors associated with each set for fewer days' work. For the viewer, the repetition signals a familiar rhythm of return, cycling back to known spaces between fights and chases. Columbia's *Blackhawk* lays bare the device when the cell of red spies abandons its lair week after week, only to take up occupation in the identical set. The heroes, who regularly raid the enemy stations just as they are being evacuated, reason that the duplicate interiors are meant to confuse prisoners. These interiors also clarify, to the point of boredom, exactly the sort of action that is about to take place. The dominant means for building a serial world involve replication and recapitulation rather than expansion or development. This relative stasis, however, often coincides with, and sometimes enables, the display of mechanisms, devices, and causal systems at work.

Mechanics and Operations

The sound serial's gadgets, gimmicks, traps, and in a sense the form itself evince "the operational aesthetic," a term suggested by Neil Harris and specified with regard to cinema by Tom Gunning and Charles Musser. Harris, analyzing the life and work of P. T. Barnum, observes that the showman's success in the nineteenth century derived from an "approach to reality and to pleasure" that directed attention to the "structures and operations" of activities and objects. The curiosities, machines, and performers that Barnum presented to his public "appealed because they exposed their own processes of action." Harris points to the popularity of how-to manuals, scientific description, science fiction, and mystery stories as evidence of the era's passion for procedural detail, which he deems culturally pervasive enough to merit the status of an "aesthetic."[1]

Gunning and Musser link early cinema to this late nineteenth-century desire, in part because audiences were fascinated with demonstrations of the moving-image apparatus. Film subjects, too, engaged the aesthetic. Musser, for example, identifies the operational aesthetic in crime films like Edwin S. Porter's *The Great Train Robbery* (1903), which details step by step the titular heist's procedure. Gunning associates it with silent comedy, beginning in simple gag films like the Lumieres' *L'Arroseur arrosé* (1894) and reaching unparalleled grace in films like Buster Keaton's *Our Hospitality* (Keaton and Blystone, 1923).[2]

Gunning's analysis of the cinematic gag is particularly relevant to the sound serial. Gag films revolve around three elements: the mischievous trickster, the victim, and, between them, the mechanism. As Gunning notes, "A detour is taken through an inanimate object, or arrangement of objects. As a mediatory visual element which takes some time to operate, the device possesses its own fascination." The gag film's apparatus renders the distance between setup and punch line as a physical chain of cause and effect, an observable process. Gunning compares the gag device to the cartoonist Rube Goldberg's absurd but functionally clear mechanical diagrams of complicated gadgets that accomplish simple tasks. Like a Goldberg machine that takes thirteen steps to crack a nut, cinematic gags "mine the fascination that spectators of the industrial age had with the way things work" by stringing together vivid nonproductive and "nonpsychological" actions. For Gunning, the gag device was a "showstopper," both because it uncoiled with inordinate complexity and because it provided an autonomous and direct pleasure unsubordinated to a larger dramatic aim.[3]

The operational aesthetic's immediacy, its ability to capture and hold attention without much dramatic support, suited the serial's episodic narrative and broken continuity. Ilka Brasch points out that silent serials exploited the operational tradition by showcasing technological marvels. *Exploits of Elaine* (Gasnier, Seitz, and Wharton, 1915), for example, focused chapters "around at least one remarkable mechanism to be demonstrated and used by the villains or detective," while Pathé promoted the authenticity of each week's scientific contraption. Like Gunning, Brasch connects the appeal of the aesthetic to modernity and "its constant supply of new mechanisms."[4] At one remove from the turn-of-the-century mechanical revolution, sound serials maintained this tradition as a formulaic element. Cliffhanger deathtraps, considered in the next chapter, present the form's most obvious debt to Goldbergian design, but chapters regularly dwell on observable technologies and processes. Betsy's visit to Frankie's lab exemplifies the serial's procedural embellishment of routine tasks: wagon wheel, rope ladder, trapdoor, hidden buzzer, and sliding wall must all cooperate to accomplish the simple task of entering a room. The process, which might generally establish Frankie's engineering prowess and secrecy, is also a pleasurable end in itself, an intricate mechanism constructed from common materials of the children's rural environment.

The same appetite for visualizing machines fuels *Flash Gordon*'s protracted demonstrations of future technology. Chapter 3, *Captured by Sharkmen*, for example, fills out its middle section with a presentation of the "aqua-cycle." The sequence details six stages in launching the submarine, cutting between detailed miniatures, insert shots of the sharkman manipulating controls, and Flash's reactions. It is a virtual aquacycle training manual: pulling a lever and turning a knob opens the floodgate in the submersible's dry dock, filling the chamber with water; another lever opens a sliding double door to the ocean; turning a knob activates the submarine's twin propellers; twisting a dial turns the craft to face the door; turning another knob restarts the rotors, to accelerate out of the dock; finally, by adjusting a crank and dial,

FIGURE 3 Twelve shots, reading across in three rows, depicting the operation of an aquacycle in *Flash Gordon* (1936).

the sharkman controls its speed and dives toward the ocean's bottom (see figure 3). Having attentively followed these procedures, Flash confides to Dale: "You know, I'm going to learn to operate one of these things. It might come in handy." He never has the opportunity, however, as this is the aquacycle's only appearance. The display of procedure serves no greater purpose.

While Gunning, Brasch, and Harris connect the operational aesthetic to the rise of modernity, something more specific seems to be at work in the sound-serial era. As stand-alone units of visual entertainment, the obsessive mechanical demonstrations offer serial screenwriters a ready way to pad out stretches between action situations. Like comic gags, procedures and operations entertain viewers without necessarily requiring knowledge of a larger plot or story

context. These sequences are also malleable, easily extended or compressed by adding steps or devoting more or less time to any particular component. Though serial plots appear to rush forward, their investment in repetition and their general lack of unifying structures like character psychology encourage a loose organization open to modular elaboration. Moreover, the fact that serial machines consist of highly visual causal chains makes them ideal for viewers likely to get antsy during scenes of dialogue. For these reasons, the resources of early, preclassical cinema found continued relevance in the sound serial.

The operational aesthetic also resonates with the serial's ludic qualities. As Harris and Gunning point out, America's obsession with novel machines was supported by an avid community of amateur tinkerers who devoured diagrams, manuals, and publications like *Popular Mechanics*, which began publication in 1902.[5] Industrialization had spurred a new pastime, an active counterpart to viewing and reading about mechanisms, which thrived because "technology was still primarily a matter of the hand and the tool, and within the reach of most folks."[6] The early twentieth century brought technological monkeying to the playroom. Mass-produced construction toys, some of them still sold today, appeared in quick succession. Frank Hornby first marketed his Meccano sets in 1902 under the name "Mechanics Made Easy"; Erector Sets followed in 1913, introduced as "The Erector/Structural Steel and Electro-Mechanical Builder"; Tinkertoys reached stores in 1916 and Lincoln Logs in 1918. Maaike Lauwaert suggests that sets with identical, interlocking pieces were "designed to be about design on the level of both play practices and play subject." Unlike free-form building blocks, "second-generation construction toys" foregrounded the arrangement of interacting parts into functioning mechanisms, which, once assembled, were then broken down and repurposed. Toys replicated the concern with design and mechanical problem solving that Harris identified; the tasks of building and engineering were pleasurable in and of themselves.[7]

Expensive construction sets were largely the province of middle-class homes, but bricolage was a common part of American childhood. Simon Bronner defines children's material folk culture as the practice of appropriating and "manipulating resources and structures to shape things." As an illustration, he cites children of the 1930s who built clubhouses from scraps of lumber, corrugated tin, refrigerator cartons, and "left-over cement drippings" from construction sites.[8] Tinkering with industrial materials had become a part of children's culture by the 1930s, and sound serials appealed to, represented, and modeled the impulse.

More fundamentally, like play, serial mechanisms elevate process over the goal. Play scholars have often noted that the pleasure of procedure characterizes children's games. Huizinga signals this quality when he proposes that "play is superfluous . . . never a task" but also that "it creates order, *is* order."[9] In their seminal study of street play Iona and Peter Opie observe that in games of tag and chase "little significance is attached to who wins or loses" and that "each stage, the choosing of leaders, the picking-up of sides, the determining of which side shall start, is almost a game in itself."[10] Jean Piaget considers early play to consist of the application of known schemas "without any external aim." Pleasure obtains from rehearsing something already mastered, assimilating "the real to the activity itself without effort or limitation."[11] The operational aesthetic, with its emphasis on causal legibility of systematically organized materials, serves as a ready vehicle for play's brand of rational inconsequence. The machines of the serial world exult in a playlike superfluous order; they celebrate activity rather than result. In depicting visually transparent, unambiguous causes and effects, the operational aesthetic mirrors the reassuring nature of play as Huizinga describes it: "Into an imperfect world and into the confusion of life it brings a temporary, a limited, perfection."[12] The sound serial's arsenal of contraptions and devices convey a world in which parts mesh neatly together.

The serial's operational aesthetic intersects with the gamelike structure of the contest in the figure of the "weenie," a physical object over which villains and heroes struggle. Pearl White, the queen of silent serials, reportedly originated the term in the teens, and it was part of sound-serial filmmakers' common vernacular.[13] Equivalent to Hitchcock's more famous MacGuffin, the weenie is a contrivance to motivate action and lend some unity to a serial's macronarrative. Often the prized object takes the form of a machine that is tested, built, or repaired across the length of the run: a progressively revealed apparatus in need of tinkering. Typically, these machines change hands, serving both as weapons and as targets of pursuit. In their design and operation, they bring to mind objects of play.

The popularity of ray guns and power beams exemplifies this convention. Their appearance in the serial world increased during the 1940s in the wake of atomic research and declining production budgets. Cash-strapped producers could depict a power beam with little expense beyond a sound effect and stock footage of an exploding plane or collapsing building. The radium energy machine prized by the Wasp (Edward Earle) in *Mandrake, the Magician* (Deming and Nelson, 1939), the paratron ray coveted by enemy agents in *The Great Alaskan Mystery* (Collins and Taylor, 1944), and the Wizard's (Leonard Penn) remote-control ray in *Batman and Robin* (Bennet, 1949) well illustrate the trend. The energy they emit is intangible, but each is a satisfyingly mechanical contraption, subjected to detailed demonstration. The radium machine, which looks something like a deco piece of radio equipment with a steel tube on top of it, features toggle switches, neon lights, and a small pedestal that allows the operator to aim it in the general direction of the target. When switched on, it emits the whir of a small electrical motor that quickly climbs in pitch as various lights glow on its casing. Professor Houston (Forbes Murray) demonstrates it to Mandrake (Warren Hull) and his friends, carefully cloaking himself in protective gear and aiming the device at an old filing cabinet, which duly explodes. Likewise, Dr. Miller's (Ralph Morgan) demonstration of his paratron in *The Great Alaskan Mystery* has the air of a magic act. The scientist aims a device that looks and sounds like a canister vacuum cleaner placed on a pedestal toward his assistant, who holds a large concave mirror connected to a beaker that collects particles teleported through the air. The Wizard's remote-control machine in *Batman and Robin* is a more imposing room-sized installation, consisting of four cabinets replete with switches, gauges, and dials, and a smaller desktop unit, similar to an oscilloscope, through which the operator views his target. The full-sized version seems beyond the means of the common tinkerer, but in chapter 1, Mr. Williams (Emmett Vogan), the head of an electronic research lab, demonstrates a small working model of the machine for Batman (Robert Lowery) and Robin (Johnny Duncan) in his office; he controls an electric train and a toy truck on a tabletop by fiddling with radio knobs across the room, literalizing the parallel between gadget and toy. These demonstrations connect props and physical procedures to their potential effects. We are told that the radium energy machine "could paralyze all communications, wreck buildings, cities," that the paratron holds "the secret of atomic energy," and that with the remote-control machine "one man could control the industry of an entire city" (see figure 4).

Yet there is a marked disparity between the enormity of power that these machines wield and the intuitive simplicity of their operation. Users merely point and shoot, or tune a few radio dials. The apparatus itself, seemingly

FIGURE 4 Power beam machines. Top row: the radium energy machine from *Mandrake, the Magician* (1939); the paratron ray from *The Great Alaskan Mystery* (1944); and the remote-control ray from *Batman and Robin* (1949). Bottom row: A small working model of the remote-control ray demonstrated with toys.

cobbled together from familiar forms, echoes the arbitrariness of play. Brian Sutton-Smith identifies the "schematic" quality of toys, which allows them to "be subsumed to the player's own causes, to be 'assimilated' to the player's own fantasies," as when a child uses a toy car as a boat or baseball bat as a gun. According to Smith, new and complex toys must become familiar before serving as vehicles for play; the peculiar must be made schematic enough for repurposing.[14] With no direct visible connection between the device and its effect, any technical-looking object with switches or buttons might serve as a ray gun or beam generator. The props' resemblance to radio equipment or a vacuum cleaner has the added benefit of making their fantasy power projectable onto objects available in the viewer's world. These science fiction gadgets are not far removed from the shields and spears that the viewer quoted in chapter 1 recalled fashioning out of wash-boiler tops and sticks for his play. They are imitable and interchangeable with other schematic representations. Moreover, these machines are likely to change functions as the serial story requires it, which emphasizes their arbitrariness. The paratron, for instance, begins as a device for teleporting matter, but Professor Houston discovers it to be even more powerful as a ray gun. Similarly, the Wizard finds that using the remote-control machine and the anti-remote-control machine together renders their target invisible. Situational dramaturgy discourages coherence, and because weenies stick around for the length of the serial, they are prone to inconsistency. Such convenient flexibility seems isomorphic with imaginative play; like toys, ray guns can be repurposed as the situation demands.[15]

As illogical as they are, weenies often appear to structure the overall plot. They occupy the shared ground between story and game, which Janet Murray identifies with the puzzle and the contest.[16] Building and powering these devices can be an extended process of problem solving; meanwhile, opposing teams vie for their possession. Each of the three wonder machines noted above, for instance, requires additional raw materials, the acquisition of which generates cliffhangers. The remote-control machine runs on diamonds, which motivates the villains to become jewel thieves. The radium energy machine and paratron ray require characters to search for and battle over the rare minerals of platenite and energized quartz, respectively. Each step in assembling the machine can launch another crisis or pose another conundrum.

Though it is not an invention, the golden scorpion idol in *Adventures of Captain Marvel* reveals how serial weenies can intertwine game structure, the operational aesthetic, and imaginative play. When members of Professor Malcolm's (Robert Strange) archaeological expedition discover the scorpion relic, they demonstrate its improbable combination of powers: rearranging lenses held in the statue's pincers produces a ray that either explodes objects by smashing their atoms or turns any metal into gold. Upon concluding that the combined temptations to avarice and belligerence are too great, the scientists divide the five lenses among themselves. After one of the team disguises himself in a black hood and robe and steals the figurine, the heroes must race to solve the mystery of his identity and to prevent his collecting all the lenses. The terms of victory and loss are defined with the clarity of a board game: acquiring the lenses means winning the contest. In this sense, the weenie grants the plot an itinerary and identifies narrative progress with constructing the machine. It extends operational logic across the plot as a whole and holds out the promise of another demonstration. But like the serial gadget itself, the appearance of order masks loose contrivance. In contrast to the tight system of a rule-bound game, the serial world is indefinite and open to ad hoc variation. Lenses, diamonds, and minerals can be obtained and lost as often as twelve to fifteen chapters will permit, and machines can change their function if that facilitates a new situation. Weenies create structures that resemble games, but they remain toys, whose principal purpose is to prolong play.

The operational aesthetic governs the serial world, constituting its chief source of invention and novelty. It approaches the status of a formal dominant, which Kristin Thompson defines as a work's organizing principle that "determines which devices and functions will come forward as important defamiliarizing traits and which will be less important."[17] In serials, the dominant encourages artists to seek opportunities to foreground process and procedure. Filmmakers often treat expositional sequences, for instance, as dull necessities. The stolid, actionless weekly council meetings in *Dick Tracy vs. Crime Inc.* and *Zorro's Fighting Legion*, scripted in stilted dialogue and shot with minimal coverage, typify the serial's stylistic zero point. From all accounts, audiences were unimpressed. After visiting a showing of *Don Winslow of the Navy*, the sociologist J. P. Mayer reported that during scenes of lengthy dialogue "restlessness and boredom were expressed freely by moving about and chattering," and Mary Parnaby and Maurice Woodhouse, who attended the entire run of *Jungle Queen*, observed that "there are scenes of mere talk and sentiment which bore the children, but they are not numerous, nor, as a rule, do they last long."[18] Faced with this audience, filmmakers could not enliven exposition by refining actor performance, developing emotional stakes, or increasing story complexity. Instead, they innovated by introducing and layering operational elements. Meetings of El Shaitan's (Robert Frazer) cult in *The Three Musketeers* and of the Si Fan organization in *The Drums of Fu Manchu* (Witney and English, 1940) feature ritualistic trappings and mysterious appearances by the master villain, while the Wasp in *Mandrake, the Magician* and the Mask (Hans Schumm) in *Spy Smasher* (Witney, 1942) materialize to their henchmen over giant television screens. In the highly repetitive serial idiom, depictions of procedure, both technological and ritual, are the most likely means of artistic embellishment.

Don del Oro's cave offers a good example. The first chapter of *Zorro's Fighting Legion* introduces the villain's lair from behind two great stone doors that slide apart to reveal Yaqui warriors arranged around a pit emitting steam and light. The reverse shot reveals the object of the Yaquis' worship, Don del Oro, clad in presumably gold armor and a chiseled mask, rising from a throne adorned with human skulls and flanked by shirtless guards with spears and headdresses. On his order, the warriors force a victim into the volcanic pit, demonstrating the lethal trap that will be turned on the villain in the final episode. A cut to the side of the throne reveals the mechanical workings of the sliding door and a smaller chamber where the false god confers with his white henchmen. Week after week, visits to Don del Oro's cave showcase the sliding door, throne, and volcanic pit. Ceremonial procedure and operation convert a space of routine exposition into rich narrative architecture.

Procedure's formal dominance shapes the serial's routine stretches and transitional sequences as well. The serial world keeps characters in transit, which lends the impression of forward momentum even when the narrative progress is nil. For the dramaturge, scenes of travel are flexible units that pad out episodes and impart some of the urgency of a chase by equating elapsed time with space covered. The mode of transportation, be it car, horse, elephant, airplane, submarine, or rocket, can supply operational novelty, especially for juvenile viewers restricted to travel by foot or bike. Once again, operationalism meshes with practical concerns: travel scenes are easily written and make good use of limited production resources. They can be built from reusable footage (as in the horse riding in *Zorro's Fighting Legion* or any Western serial), staged before rear-projection screens (as in the endless auto pursuits in the Dick Tracy serials), and create the impression of a large space by repeating contiguous shots of a single set (as in the caverns of Ming's palace). They can also be expanded or trimmed to suit a chapter's length. Even when they bide their time, serials present moving parts.

Finally, the operational inclination informs smaller-scale repetitions and motifs that serve as trademarks or signatures. The electric buzz of *Flash Gordon*'s space ships and the flash-pot explosions that accompany Captain Marvel's transformation highlight processes ripe for projection onto the playground. To return to our running example, Zorro's special sword that wraps around his waist like a belt gives him a unique, imitable action to perform in each episode. Similarly, his whip, delivered cinematically via close-ups and sound effects, telegraphs his presence when he enters a fight. The whoosh of the whip and swish of the belt-sword are concrete sonic emblems. The same might be said of the golden arrow shot by a mysterious hand as warning to victims of Don del Oro, a descendent of the "whistling arrow" fired by the mystery hero of *The Painted Stallion* (James, Taylor, and Witney, 1937). Each golden arrow is accompanied by the sound of the bow's release (*doinnng*) and the arrow's landing (*thwack*). Repetition trains the fan in the serial's action grammar, helping episodes move more economically and engendering embodied response. The sharp rhythm of *doinnng* and *thwack* renders procedure tactile, a sensory nugget of sound and image identified with the serial world.

Characters and Serial Psychology

Given their emphasis on action and physical process in tightly paced chapters, serials can devote few resources to character development or psychology. As noted in chapter 2, characters have little if any "internal" life in the sense of a struggle with, or discovery of, the self. This lack of characterization, rather than posing a critical liability, reinforces the sound serial's play value. In studying fictional figures that cross various media, Shane Denson and Ruth Mayer draw a distinction between "series characters," which exist in a "closed fictional universe" and "show a certain extent of depth," and "serial figures," which are "flat, familiar, and iconic." Serial figures tend to be visually striking but empty, and this gives them a "capacity for reinscription, inversion, appropriation." Iconic figures like Tarzan, Fu Manchu, or Dracula, according to Mayer, are malleable, traveling between media as "vehicles to express very personal agendas and individual programs of self-fashioning."[19] This quality pertains to the characters within sound serials as well; visually potent but one-dimensional, they are plainly defined facades, ripe for adoption. Like toys, serial characters tend to be schematic and appropriable to the playground.

Born from the sound serial's synthesis of melodrama and play, characters are vivid, quickly readable, and static. The serial's Manichaean world polarizes inhabitants into virtuous and villainous camps, and visibly marked alliances with one side or the other stand in for psychology. Of character complexity, Peter Brooks notes: "There is no 'psychology' in melodrama in this sense; the characters have no interior depth, there is no psychological conflict. It is delusive to seek an interior conflict, the 'psychology of melodrama,' because melodrama exteriorizes conflict and psychic structure, producing what we might call the 'melodrama of psychology.'"[20] Like the workings of an operational mechanism, serial psychology must be visible and clear. Characters, villains especially, are prone to self-nomination, the forthright announcement of their moral identities. Brooks draws a distinction between melodrama and tragedy that might apply equally well to serials and feature films.[21] If soliloquies in tragedy "exteriorized a mind divided against itself," in melodrama they become "pure self-expression, the venting of what one is and how it feels to be that way, the saying of self through its moral and emotional integers."[22] Generally, heroes and villains simply and candidly state their plans and affiliations, sometimes directly to the viewer as in Aura's aside to the camera saying that Flash "will never see

Dale Arden again" after she locks him in a spaceship. Villains define themselves through announcements of greed and a general appetite for power,
heroes by their opposition to the villains. The Wizard's introductory declaration in *Batman and Robin* is representative. Clad in a black cape and
face mask, he congratulates his heavies on their use of the remote-control
ray: "Your reward will be a share of the great power this machine will give
me. . . . With this in operation, I'll be able to control everything that moves,
including man himself."

Melodrama serves serial efficiency well, but in a pared-down fashion. Generally, serials lack the expressive amplification that Brooks notes in stage melodrama; they don't multiply "moral and emotional integers" through elaborate
language. Often, the saying of self is not even a matter of dialogue but of action
and appearance. The Wasp, for instance, materializes before his henchmen on
a wall-sized television screen, seated at a control panel in his secret chamber,
enwrapped in a satin cape, and sporting a foil face mask and a fedora. It is a
customarily bizarre image that condenses high technology, mysticism, and
hard-nosed gangsterism into visual shorthand for malevolence. Melodramatic
extravagance is achieved not by "venting what one is and how it feels to be that
way" but through emphatically vivid depiction.

These conventions spare serials from much exposition about why characters
act as they do. As Brooks observes, "Motivation is in fact often summary and
benefits from the briefest of explanations. And in almost every case it appears
somewhat inadequate to the quantity of villainy unleashed. The villain is simply the conveyor of evil . . . because evil in the world of melodrama does not
need justification." Such instant legibility supports situational immediacy;
past events need not bear on the crisis of the moment. When plots feature
character revelation, as in mystery-villain serials, the unmasking is perfunc-
tory. Brooks describes melodramatic revelation scenes as "breaking through
disguises and enigmas to establish true identities," but sound serials reduce
this convention to its rudiments.[23] The true evildoer is often an unexcep-
tional background figure of whom we know little; the mask has more depth.
For instance, the Wasp's dramatic revelation in the final episode of *Mandrake,
the Magician* as Dr. Andre Bennett, an undistinguished member of Professor
Houston's cadre, supplies his wholly unforeseeable motive: "I was barred from
the practice of medicine. It was then that I resolved to have more power than
any other doctor, than any living man."[24] Questions of professional reputation
have never been broached in *Mandrake*, and his scant explanation has little
bearing on events. However, masked figures, largely defined by costume, offer
readily inhabitable masquerades. Before the villain is individuated, he remains
a vehicle for personal agendas, a guise to take up in play. In keeping identities
secret until the last minute, serials forestall narrowing the role; they benefit
more from the mystery than revelation.

Figural characterizations can be ported to almost any ludic scenario involving moral opposition, allowing flexible repurposing for games of "cops and robbers" or "cowboys and Indians." Moreover, formulaic consistency means that situations from one serial are open to reenactment with characters from another. In terms of action, Captain Marvel and Superman are more or less identical, as are Buck Rogers and Flash Gordon, the Lone Ranger and Zorro, Dick Tracy and Holt of the Secret Service, and Captain Midnight and Captain Bob Dayton, hero of *Sky Raiders*. Likewise, villains, especially the masked variety, seem interchangeable. Only minor differences distinguish the Wizard from the Scorpion, the Lightning, or the Wasp; one might just as well slip into another's fiction. *The Phantom Empire* models this portability of character and situation within its world. Gene Autry offers his fictional radio audience Thunder Riders costume patterns and sketches scenarios for them to emulate. As noted in the opening of this book, his band performs a scene of invaders attacking a homestead. The operational detail of the victim replacing his front door's locking bar with his own arm as the villains attempt to batter it open presents a tactile procedure, and the amateurish acting of Autry's band stands in for its playground reenactment. Meanwhile, the Thunder Riders Club, on-screen juveniles dressed in futuristic capes and helmets imitating the guards of the lost scientific city of Murania, speed to the homesteaders' rescue. Science fiction iconography and the instantly recognizable Western situation are basically compatible in the serial world; they are equally available components of play. The kids' gang in the film schematizes and imitates the "real" Thunder Riders, and they directly urge viewers to follow their lead. Characterization, whether defined by cape and helmet or cowboy boots and hat, amounts to a pose that players take up in this serial-within-a-serial.

We can appreciate the schematic simplicity of serial heroes by comparing them to their feature-film counterparts. In his study of the historical adventure film, Brian Taves convincingly demonstrates that the protagonists of films like *Robin Hood* (1922 and 1938), *Captain Blood* (1935), and *Beau Geste* (Herbert Brenon, 1926, and William Wellman, 1939) live by "the code of adventure," which requires valor, selflessness, the "voluntary willingness to face danger," and overcoming the fear of death. The code commits heroes to "the valiant fight for freedom and a just form of government," which Taves views as essential to the historical adventure's depth and meaning. In comparison, serial heroes follow an ideologically naïve protocol. Certainly they are valorous, and serials based on historical adventure characters like *Zorro*, or those that project freedom fighters into the future like *Flash Gordon's Trip to Mars* (Beebe and Hill, 1938) and *Buck Rogers* (Beebe and Goodkind, 1939) place their heroes in opposition to antidemocratic usurpers. But in all cases, the fight remains more important than the cause. Serial heroes lack the historical adventurer's "thematic commitment" to an "integrated social and spiritual ideal." They also lack character change. Through ordeals, Taves explains, the feature film adventurer "experiences self-discovery . . . to achieve a new, nearly spiritual, threshold."[25] In contrast, the serial hero who faces death every ten to twenty minutes bounces back unshaken and unchanged. If a coherent ideal unifies serial heroes, it is faith that immediate physical action can surmount obstacles and save the day. Serial heroes thrive in a world of moral clarity and physicality; they are defined by their abilities to carry out weekly actions against the villain. Psychological stasis allows the game to continue, and the situations to accumulate, indefinitely.

Serial villains may be no more complex than the heroes, but they are considerably more important. The strong and immediate establishment of malevolence is essential to creating the serial world. Indeed, the very existence of villainy defines the possibility of heroism. If the serial formula resembles a game's external rules, placing constraints on and enabling play, then the villain functions like a game master within the fiction. By laying traps, villains transform the world into a space of physical challenge, focusing the serial's operational aesthetic into a contest for survival. In his genre study of movie thrillers, Martin Rubin compares their conspiratorial worlds to labyrinths. Labyrinths may appear unknowable and fraught with peril but are intentionally organized so that "it should be possible to reach the exit by deduction, by figuring out the design rather than just by aimless trial and error." For Rubin, the pleasure of thrillers lies in the way they transmute the ordinary into adventure, creating labyrinths from the stuff of modern life. Akin to Jenkins's narrative architecture, the labyrinth is, in part, "a spatial equivalent to the emotion of suspense."[26] Serial villains are designers.

Though few serials achieve a thriller's conspiratorial complexity, each week villains convert the environment into a suspenseful space. The convention is literalized in *Mandrake, the Magician* and *Batman and Robin*, in which criminals wire entire buildings for destruction and track the heroes' progress through corridors on mazelike electric displays that represent people as proto-Pac-Men, blinking lights along a twisting path. But under the pressure of a deadline or in the presence of a malicious force, even mundane tasks are charged with tension. The sound serial's instant labyrinths have the practical benefit of implying adventure on a budget. When enemy agents plant a pressure-sensitive bomb under a basement step in chapter 10 of *The Great Alaskan Mystery*, for example, the heroes' routine trips up and down the stairs become a matter of life and death. Cliffhangers routinely leave viewers with unresolved labyrinths. The villain's transformation of the world remains in effect; situations are held open for those who wish to continue the game.

Melodrama without Time for Tears

The contrast with which we began this chapter, between Betsy's passage to Frankie's lab and the scene of their father's death, points toward the adaptation of melodramatic convention to the terms of play. The serial world embraces morally polarized characters speeding from situation to situation, but it more or less rejects the hyperbolic emotion that Neale and others identify with melodrama. If melodrama, as Linda Williams proposes, depends on the "dialectic of pathos and action," then sound serials are clearly unbalanced. Suffering, the violation of innocence, and the recognition of loss are, for Williams, inextricably linked with the thrill of action through which heroes struggle to regain and defend virtue.[27] Sound serials, and cliffhangers in particular, rehearse the threat of physical suffering defeated by daring action, but they divorce the thrill from pathetic emotion.

As noted in chapter 1, the form's situational vocabulary is notably narrower than that of nineteenth-century melodramatists like George Polti. Serials favor playable scenarios of abduction and deliverance over emotional deadlocks involving adultery, mistaken jealousy, and the like. The premise that loss is reversible, that, as Williams puts it, "'in the nick of time' defies 'too late,'" undergirds the serial world.[28] Tears are not entirely banished; in fact, they appear more frequently in early 1930s serials, especially those produced by Mascot. Even so, the recognition of powerlessness is best suited to early chapters where it can spur heroic exploits and where our attachment to characters has been brief. For example, *The Hurricane Express* (Schaeffer and McGowan, 1932) and *The Three Musketeers* (1933), both starring John Wayne, use the murder of loved ones to get the plot off the ground. *The Hurricane Express*, particularly, milks the situation. Aviator Larry Baker (Wayne) fails to prevent a train collision that kills his father (J. Farrell MacDonald), an engineer. Witnessing the cataclysm, Larry pulls his father's body from the wreckage, learns of foul play, and tearfully declares: "My father was murdered, and I'll bring that murderer to justice if it takes the rest of my life." The loss is unusually cruel because it follows swiftly on an opening scene of good-natured bonding in which Larry and his father rib one another about the speed and safety of trains versus airplanes. Narrative compression exaggerates the emotional disparity between the two sequences, leaving viewers in the lurch. Mascot's *The Vanishing Legion* (Beebe and Reaves Eason, 1931) is even more surprisingly weepy. When young Jimmie Williams (Frankie Darro) sees Rex the Wonder Horse trample his father (just after a scene of father-son bonding), he cradles the limp body, sobbing, "You killed my Daddy. . . . Daddy, Daddy, speak to me!" Concussed but not dead, Jimmie's father (Edward Hearn) is almost immediately kidnapped by the bad guys, who are framing him for murder.

Emotionally raw, and out of keeping with the tone of their respective serials, these pathetic scenes powerfully demonstrate the hero's virtue by violating his innocence. In these rare cases, primal scenes of violence forge heroes and emotionally implicate viewers; they are effective curtain raisers. Once the serials get under way, the five-part format eliminates most opportunities for pathos. When loss occurs even slightly later in the Mascot serials, as with the second-episode murders of Frankie and Betsy's father, or of Tom Wayne's copilot in *The Three Musketeers*, the moment passes quickly so that the adventure may continue.

As the decade progressed, scenes of pathetic loss became somewhat less frequent. A mixed viewership always frequented serials, but judging by the *Exhibitor* reviews, from the late 1930s onward their address to juveniles became ever more pronounced. Where the paper could praise *Custer's Last Stand* (Clifton, 1935) for being "excellent in love interest, action, and historical authenticity," by the 1940s *White Eagle* (Horne, 1941) aimed at the "matinee trade," received top rankings because it could "have the kids sitting on edge and that's what serials are for." *Spy Smasher* epitomizes the sound serial's dominant priorities after the mid-1930s. At the start of chapter 4, *Stratosphere Invaders*, Captain Pierre Durand (Franco Corsaro), Spy Smasher's (Kane Richmond) French counterpart, condemns himself to a watery grave in a flooded submarine chamber so that he can jettison the hero to safety through a torpedo tube. The film puts all its eggs in the basket of valiant sacrifice, using Durand's death to resolve the cliffhanger and combining it with a heavy dose of operational gimmickry, including an underwater respirator, a gauge marking the rising flood waters, and the torpedo tube itself. In return, Durand receives a meager two lines of dialogue as recognition and remembrance. In the next scene, Spy Smasher shows his colleague a French flag that Durand pinned to him and proclaims, "Someday I'll fasten that on top of the Eiffel Tower in free Paris, in honor of Pierre Durand. I found this official dispatch in the submarine log. I have every reason to believe it's important." The serial elaborates Durand's death for the sake of action, and then brushes him aside to make room for the next clue in the case.

In reducing melodrama to action elements, serials capitalize on situational plotting in the name of adventurous but reassuring fantasy. Remarkably, filmmakers still occasionally explored loss, albeit in a limited way. The death of a character, especially a parent, was a powerful way to create moral opposition and grip the audience, but it could also derail action and overwhelm young viewers. The tactics for introducing and regulating pathos reveal a careful negotiation between raising the stakes and maintaining momentum. For instance, 1940's *King of the Royal Mounted* (Witney and English), a serial pegged for young "Saturday afternoon customers" by the *Exhibitor*, kills off two parental characters. In the first episode, the villains murder Thomas Merritt (Stanley Andrews), scientist, mine owner, and father to love interest Linda Merritt (Lita Conway) and young Corporal Tom Merritt Jr. (Robert Kellard). The chapter buries the elder Merritt's death in an action sequence that quickly leads to investigation. His role has hardly been established, and his death is a swiftly disposed-of plot catalyst. The implications of the second killing, unusually placed in the cliffhanger between chapters 3 and 4, are not so easily dismissed.[29] This time, the victim is a regular character, Inspector King (Herbert Rawlinson), father to the serial's hero, Sergeant Dave King (Allan Lane). Inspector King electrocutes himself when he short-circuits a buzz saw before it can kill his son. The screenwriters give the father's sacrifice pride of place as a take-out; his final action interrupts the infernal machine, a suitably operational death. But in the aftermath, the episode deals with its effect on the hero. Dave King rushes to his father, cradles the body, and utters a single word, "Dad," as he shifts his gaze to the horizon. The chapter then cuts to a military funeral rendered in two shots and accompanied by weeping strings. The funeral ends with a medium shot of Dave standing at attention, which dissolves to a graphically matched photograph of his father that adorns the hero's desk. A pan from the photograph to Dave reading aloud the order giving him command of the post completes the transition of power. At every point, the filmmakers channel irreversible loss of the father into the son's consolidation of the hero's role. Expositional dialogue cements the link between both fathers' deaths and the heroes' overarching goals. Dave King explains to Tom Merritt Jr: "Tom, Garson killed your father, and he was responsible for the death of mine. Together you and I are going to get to the bottom of this compound X business, capture Garson and the men he's connected with." Turning the death into an opportunity for regular repetition of the goals gets the plot back on track within two minutes. When the sound serial admits melodrama's "too late," it does so to motivate concrete action.

Formula abets bounded experimentation, and like the five-part structure or the cliffhanger situation, the sound serial's approach to pathos was a norm from which filmmakers could selectively depart. Innovation generally amounts to varying conventions without challenging fundamentals; serial producers might eliminate exposition within an episode, or accelerate the cycle of hostage taking and liberation, but they are unlikely to eliminate a cliffhanger or kill off the hero. The sound-serial world, which emphasizes physical solutions to concrete problems, constrains filmmakers from differentiating their product by elaborating emotional stakes or acknowledging mortality. Republic's hit *The Lone Ranger* tests this principle, and in doing so maps the serial world's capacity for pathos. The studio's main innovation in adapting the radio drama was to reverse the standard mystery of identity so that it was the hero rather than the villain who remained unknown until the end. The Lone Ranger's origin story, in which his entire company is gunned down in an ambush (invented for the serial), is already uncommonly dark. After a bizarrely expressionist sequence in which Tonto (Chief Thundercloud) searches through the bodies and finds the surviving hero, he confirms the finality of the violence: "Other Rangers, all dead." Our hero immediately converts loss to action. Gripping his metal star, he vows: "The only one, the Lone Ranger. I'll never rest until those deaths are avenged!" This somber introduction presages the serial's exceptional morbidness. The writing team, lead by Barry Shipman, extends the mystery of identity by introducing five potential heroes in the first episode and then killing them off one by one until the last man standing must be the true Lone Ranger.

William Witney, one of the serial's directors, regarded the plot device as "a stroke of genius" because "this was the first time in a serial where you didn't have to cheat the audience to show how the lead miraculously escaped being killed. We could actually knock him off."[30] The format grimly commits the serial to depicting the mortality of heroes, with Rangers dying in episodes 5, 12, and 15. Cliffhangers, though, remain survivable until the end. Only one Ranger perishes in an episode's climax, an event in the next-to-last chapter when Dick Forrest (Lane Chandler) sacrifices himself by bringing a cave ceiling down to protect a group of innocents. By withholding this Pyrrhic victory until the final cliffhanger, the writers avoid undercutting the serial code by which climactic catastrophes are reversed. Viewers who took the situation up during the intervening week could assume the hero's escape, and at the end of this episode they could move on to a fresh chapterplay. Additionally, the shooting of another disguised Ranger quickly follows Dick's demise and diverts attention away from the loss and onto the enigma of the remaining hero's identity. When the Lone Ranger interrupts his comrades' funeral in the film's final moments, the excitement of revelation overwhelms pathos and logic. Despite having buried the four other Rangers, no one seems to have figured out who the real hero is. Love interest Joan Blanchard (Lynn Roberts) eagerly asks the Lone Ranger to unmask himself and verifies his identity for the viewers: "Allen King!" (Lee Powell). This ultimate naming of the hero answers the founding enigma and primes viewers for further exploits; the Lone Ranger's final line of dialogue is directed at the camera: "Till we meet again!" Death and loss are mere bumps along the trail of adventure.

One of the four Rangers' murders, however, pushes at the sound serial's confines. Jim Clark's (George Letz) death is handled with staggered emphasis. Shot during the middle action of chapter 5, Clark survives long enough to be rescued from gunpoint by the real Lone Ranger. His liberation comes as a double relief since it also confirms that he is not the actual masked hero, and his predicament is quickly displaced when the Lone Ranger's struggle with a henchman over a lava pit develops into the episode's cliffhanger. Having momentarily shifted viewer concern to make way for action, Shipman and his screenwriting team dwell on Clark's death and its repercussions in the exposition sequences of chapter 6. The remaining Rangers gather for a brief funeral in part b, and the Lone Ranger calls for action: "We promise that the ideals you fought for and died for will continue to be our ideals until the power of Marcus Jefferies is forever broken. I pledge that your death shall not go unavenged." The narration typically, if cynically, turns the funeral into an economical means for exposition.

Surprisingly, mourning lingers nearly a minute longer during an elegiac scene of Tonto in silhouette singing toward the sunset, an iconic moment lifted from Jacques Tourneur and Clarence Brown's racial melodrama *Last of the Mohicans* (1920). The pause in the action treats Native American ritual as an exotic attraction, yet it also generates an unmistakable and anomalously somber atmosphere. Later, the second exposition sequence (d) unexpectedly squeezes another drop of sorrow from Jim Clark's death when the Lone Ranger visits his slain comrade's parents and finds Mama Clark (Jane Keckley) feverish and confined to bed. She mistakes the Lone Ranger for her son and then tearfully corrects herself: "No, I forgot, Jim can't come back." Together, the scenes underscore the irreversibility of death almost beyond necessity since the five Rangers are scarcely individuated even through the serial's end. Chapter 5 exemplifies the standard serial procedure of sweeping past loss to deliver the regular flow of thrills. Chapter 6, though, reminds us how tightly measured the form's handling of time and emotion usually are. To be sure, the investment in pathos is a by-product of *The Lone Ranger*'s plot gimmick, and it is wedged into brief sections of the standard five-part format, between energetic action sequences. But even in this circumscribed and qualified form, Jim Clark's passing troubles the serial world's forward momentum. It marks consequence rather than process and points to the past instead of the ever-frantic present. This rare surfacing of despair points to the sound serial's melodramatic origins and reveals how tenuous the balance between pathos and action may be. Just beneath the thrill of rescue lurks the threat of loss.

Conclusion

Schematic, tactile, familiar, and bizarre, sound serials tender predictable worlds shot through with operational novelties and vivid situations. Like construction toys, they arrange modular parts, easily grasped, broken down, and repurposed. The formulas that permitted rapid and efficient production of long narratives made the serial world portable and projectable. Repeating sets, footage, plot elements, and character types from chapter to chapter and film to film, for instance, created a common reservoir of templates available to both filmmakers and fans. Melodrama supplied a sturdy moral framework and a steady stream of exciting happenstance at the cost of causal and dramatic unity. But if the films lack comprehensible overarching plots, they find coherence in a familiar cyclic world. Describing the movie audience in 1939, Margaret Thorp identified serials' appeal with their familiarity: "You can have your weekly artistic experience, if you are a serial fan, without the labor of adjusting yourself each time to a wholly new environment. The devotee of *The Lone Ranger* watches his tenth adventure with the same comfortable ease with which the experienced musician hears a new conductor's reading of Beethoven's 'Seventh Symphony.'"[31] Condescension aside, Thorp's comparison points to the way repetition engenders fluency. Serials regularly return to the known and knowable, freeing viewers to focus on ritual, technology, and physical process rather than plot twists or dramatic development. Immediately identifiable characters serve as vessels for action, unburdened by psychologies that might limit their potential for appropriation. Splitting the difference between game board and playground, the serial world structures action and gives roles meaning, while inviting imaginative exploration of narrative architectures.

Few films exemplify the interaction of melodrama, play, and appropriation better than *Dick Tracy vs. Crime Inc.* (Witney and English, 1941). In the last of Republic's four Dick Tracy serials, producers raided the previous three for stunts and cliffhangers. As a result, the film's world is unusually expansive, introducing new locations throughout, but a standard-issue masked villain plot anchors it all. The Ghost (Ralph Morgan), a disguised member of the crime-fighting "Council of Eight" that meets with Tracy each week, wages a campaign of industrial sabotage and murder to eliminate the other counselors, who are responsible for his criminal brother's execution. Weekly confrontations between G-men and henchmen revisit set pieces from earlier serials, including a race between a military tank and a speeding train, Tracy's daring transfers between a speedboat and an airplane, aerial bombardment, and collisions of cars and planes, boats and ships. Since each member of the council captains a different industry, the Ghost has a convenient variety of weekly targets, and this helps thread together disparate situations. Nonetheless, *Dick Tracy vs. Crime Inc.* seems even more arbitrary than most other serials. Tracy's discovery of a tank outside a train station, for instance, has no motivation beyond the producer's desire to repeat an archived cliffhanger. The practice throws the sound serial's priorities into stark relief. Operational spectacle dominates the story, vivid parts dwarf the whole, and the entire enterprise has the capricious opportunism of play.

The Ghost provides the serial with a specific kind of operational novelty. Throughout, he appears wearing a skintight black rubber mask that eliminates facial expression and prevents individuation. As though this emptying out of character weren't enough, the Ghost performs most of his crimes while invisible, rendered so by a power beam controlled by his henchmen. He may be undermotivated and barely defined, but the Ghost's device is satisfyingly complex. In the backseat of a sedan, henchmen operate a control box, with radio dials and a spinning illuminated disk that sends an invisibility beam to anyone wearing the special amulet. Each week, the Ghost dissolves from view via an optical effect, but only after the easily copied procedures of donning the amulet and tuning the control dials. The filmmakers grant further concreteness to the otherwise imperceptible beam by giving it a sound: a high-pitched drone, which accompanies the invisible man. Described by characters as "a peculiar whirring sound," it foregrounds the machine's operation and clarifies action by alerting viewers to the Ghost's whereabouts. Finally, we are told that tubes in the device burn out after about ten minutes of operation, which imposes a deadline on the Ghost and heightens our awareness of the contraption's inner workings. The machine imposes a logic of affordance and constraint on the villain; it sets rules of play. More fundamentally, ritual, sound, and technical detail make the invisibility process palpable and imitable.

The prominence of operation and procedure in the serial world helped the films model and enable play, and it could inspire novel repurposing by the filmmakers. In depicting the technology of the climactic episode, Witney, English, and the Republic production staff reach an avant-garde level of experimentation. Tracy rigs his own contraption to counter the Ghost's power. Having analyzed a recording of the whirring sound, Tracy's team isolates the beam's wavelengths and produces an "ultraviolet" light bulb that interrupts its effects. The filmmakers signal the bulb's operation by switching to a negative image, which affects the entire frame, rendering the Ghost's black rubber mask in glowing white and all bright areas in deep black (see figure 5). The effect harkens back to the origins of the operational aesthetic in cinema, particularly

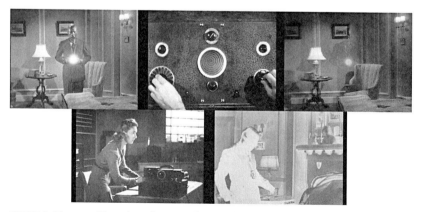

FIGURE 5 Top row: Three shots depicting the invisibility ray in *Dick Tracy vs. Crime Inc.* (1941). Bottom row: The device that reverses the invisibility ray, represented with a negative image.

to trick films like Frederick S. Armitage's *Ghost Train* (AMB, 1901), which consists of the negative image of a passing locomotive. In foregrounding the photographic process, the technique makes the operation of Tracy's trap coterminous with that of film itself. To be sure, the Republic unit did not set out to produce a modernist work, but shifting between positive and negative inescapably calls attention to form. It marks the cinematic means of storytelling and makes process briefly observable. The moment is a nice metaphor for the affinity between serials and play, both of which create worlds from available materials and elevate the pleasures of procedure above fictional unity or coherence.

The sound serial's narrative structures and worlds create the conditions for playful interaction. Yet the form's situational plotting, operational aesthetic, and figural characters do not in themselves account for its distinctive appeal. Only by sundering the viewer's connection to the ongoing world at the height of a situation does the serial fulfill its ludic promise. During the weeklong break between chapters, narration abdicates its authority over the moment and leaves spectators to dwell upon and within the scenario. This regular rupture activates the world's familiar routines and novel devices as playable frameworks. In the next chapter we turn to the nexus of serial engagement, the cliffhanger.

4

Cliffhanging

• • • • • • • • • • • • • • • • • • •

Cliffhangers are the sound serial's central and most distinctive feature. They are test departments for generating suspense and offer insight into the nature of cinematic storytelling. But cliffhangers also merge suspense with the seemingly antithetical appeals of spectacular catastrophe and puzzle solving. Each week, viewers could witness the hero's demise and yet be assured of his or her survival; each week they could anxiously anticipate imminent disaster and ponder the narrative deceptions that would reverse it. Serials inherit and repurpose the basic techniques of one-reel melodrama and break situations in two, which complicates our engagement with them. Cliffhangers could simultaneously absorb viewers into tautly drawn situations and promote awareness of narration, a dynamic consonant with make-believe. This chapter explores cliffhangers by first considering the rudiments of the race to the rescue as it was refined in early narrative cinema, and then looking at how serials reconceive the formula around the contradictory mandates to deliver a climax and continue the story. We will bring forward issues of anomalous suspense and levels of film narration in order to pin down the peculiarities of serial storytelling. Finally, we review the lexicon of perils and chart cliffhanging's major variables, which lay the groundwork for artistic achievement within the bounds of formula.

According to Ben Singer, cliffhangers "with the protagonists precariously near some sort of graphic death" had become standard in silent serials by late 1914 or early 1915. This convention had a clear profit motive, encouraging, as Singer notes, "a steady volume of return customers, tantalized and eager for the fix of narrative closure withheld in the previous installment."[1] Cliffhangers were particularly valuable at a time when serials and early features vied for dominance. In the sound era, when national advertising campaigns of the majors were geared toward first-run houses, cliffhangers helped neighborhood and unaffiliated theaters compete for attention. Ideally they could regularize attendance by building a Saturday routine for schoolchildren, who had an institutionalized gap in their schedules, and by spurring some adult trade. From commercial imperative sprang a unique blend of experiences unavailable in other popular cinema: spectacular cataclysm, engaging suspense, and the parameters of an inescapable dilemma left unresolved for an entire week.

Mascot's 1933 *The Three Musketeers* provides an excellent model of cliffhanging mechanics. An in-title-only "updating" of the Alexandre Dumas story, the serial follows American aviator Tom Wayne (John Wayne) in his struggle to put down an Arab rebellion and clear his name of a false murder charge with the help of three French Foreign Legionnaires who call themselves the "Musketeers." The serial's cliffhangers are generally undistinguished, with Wayne dodging bullets, surviving falls from his horse, or besting his attackers in hand-to-hand fights. The conclusion of chapter 6, *Death's Marathon*, however, presents a nicely embellished version of a melodramatic staple. Colonel Duval (Gordon De Main), the corrupt officer who is in league with the serial's masked villain, has sentenced Wayne to death before a firing squad. Elaine Corday (Ruth Hall), Wayne's girlfriend and the sister of the man he is accused of murdering, has obtained a reprieve from the commanding general in another part of the country. After she is forced to make an emergency landing in her sabotaged airplane, Elaine undertakes a long march through the desert to deliver the reprieve. The episode crosscuts between Elaine's ever more desperate struggle through the desert sands and the orderly routine of Wayne's execution. The lines of action are thusly arrayed:

> Elaine sets out from her damaged plane.
> Cut to: Legionnaires march to Wayne's cell, retrieve him, and march away.
> Cut to: Elaine comes over a hill, weary, out of breath.
> Cut to: Legionnaires march Wayne through the barracks.
> Cut to: Elaine charges ahead with renewed determination.
> Cut to: Legionnaires march Wayne to the firing range, as the evil Colonel Duval observes.
> Cut to: Elaine stumbles past the camera, barely upright.
> Cut to: The Legionnaires raise their rifles and take aim.
> Cut to: Elaine arrives at the barracks, shouting and waving the reprieve.

The situation is hardly novel, but the contrast between the somber ritual and the heroine's frantic race has kinetic force. Moreover, the firing squad's lockstep progress through the barracks as their commander barks orders lends the proceedings the sense of operational inevitability. There is no way of knowing how long the executioners will take, but their formal procedure stands in for a literal ticking clock. Each return to Wayne's line of action signals the impending deadline, while vague geography strengthens the narrator's hand. How far apart are Elaine and Wayne? How far must the Legionnaires march? The filmmakers may compress or expand space as they see fit to draw out the tension. The firing-squad ritual crescendos with a very precise and lethal action; soldiers raise and cock their rifles as the commander prepares the order to fire. It would be an opportune moment for interruption, leaving the spectator a week to sweat out the situation.

Death's Marathon, though, carries the proceedings past the moment when the lines of action converge. The episode's final five images are (see figure 6):

> The Commander shouts the order "Ready!" as Legionnaires raise their rifles.
> Cut to: Elaine waves the reprieve shouts for them to stop, as the Commander orders, "Aim!"
> Cut to: In a reverse shot, Elaine races toward the firing squad, crying, "I have a reprieve!"
> Cut to: From a long shot of Wayne, the camera pans swiftly left to reveal the firing squad. The Commander barks, "Fire!" Elaine screams. The rifles erupt.
> Cut to: Title "Next Week *Naked Steel*" over the sounds of screams and gunfire.

Where self-contained features and one-reel films would contrive interruptions and delays that stretch out the moment before the innocents meet a terrible fate, sound serials arrest the action after a lethal event. In this case, the doom is doubled. Not only has Wayne apparently been shot, but also his would-be rescuer has hurled herself between him and the guns. The deadline has passed;

FIGURE 6   Four images from the cliffhanger of chapter 6 of *The Three Musketeers* (1933).

both the hero and heroine are lost; justice is fully defeated. Except that, of course, this is not the end. If the soundtrack gives uncontestable evidence that the rifles have fired and Elaine has been hit, the title card it accompanies reassures viewers that the heroes will return and nearly perish next week. This is the nature of cliffhanger suspense: it leaves the hero not dangling from the edge but plunging beyond it to certain ruin.

Cinematic Suspense and the Cliffhanger's Origin

The form has precedents in popular serialized literature and in melodramatic theater, but its cinematic forebears are the one-reel action melodramas that helped to stabilize the nascent American film industry between 1907 and 1912. These short films packed violence, abduction, and hair's-breadth escape into twelve-to-fifteen-minute stand-alone narratives, which fed the maw of the burgeoning nickelodeon trade.[2] The connection between the one-reel thrillers and the serial format is fairly direct. With the ascendance of feature films, and the failure of the Motion Picture Patents Company, some producers and exhibitors turned to serials as a less risky model of storytelling. The Kalem Company, for instance, transformed its output of one- and two-reel railroad thrillers into the *Hazards of Helen* series in 1914.[3] Serials bridged the distance between the one-reel standard and longer films, sparing wary producers and exhibitors the cold leap to stand-alone features.

Action melodrama was a staple during the nickelodeon boom, during which filmmakers honed the crosscut race-to-the-rescue formula. One-reel films raided the storehouse of theatrical melodrama for sensational situations that revolved around easily visualized moral poles. In this way they developed suspense into a fundamental hook for narrative cinema and gave serials a basic formula. Time and again, innocent women, families, or children were set upon by villainous criminals, transients, or racial others and rescued by heroic suitors, husbands, or father figures. In the sound era, these structures and

mechanisms were integrated into thrillers and adventure films, but the serial played them out with unmatched regularity. Serials are the foremost studio-era carriers of some very old cinematic DNA. We can learn a great deal about the cliffhanger and its eccentricities by first considering its one-reel ancestor.

The race-to-the-rescue climax of D. W. Griffith's Biograph short *The Unseen Enemy* (1912) typifies the tradition and clearly illustrates the game between filmmaker and audience that the sound serial develops. Dorothy and Lillian Gish play adolescent orphans, left alone in their country home with a large sum of money in the family safe while their older brother (Elmer Booth) bicycles to his office. Smelling blood in the water, the girls' "slattern maid" (Grace Henderson) and her criminal accomplice (Harry Carey) lock the girls in a sitting room and attempt to crack the safe in the adjoining parlor. To prevent the girls from escaping while also concealing her identity, the maid holds a gun on them by reaching through a small hole in the wall between the rooms (an unused stovepipe hookup). The girls phone their brother and, after some delay in talking to his assistant, alert him to their predicament. Just as the situation dawns on him, the maid fires her pistol, forcing the older sister (Lillian Gish) to retreat from the telephone and take refuge in the back corner of the room. The maid, now drinking heavily from a whisky bottle, becomes increasingly trigger-happy by the minute. Mad with fear and rage, the brother commandeers a passing auto and races to his sisters' aid. But just as the younger sister (Dorothy Gish) is approaching the gun, the brother's car becomes trapped on a swing-bridge, which is rotating to allow a boat to pass. The younger sister faints as the maid's gun turns to point directly at her head, and her older sister covers her body with her own. This is the "all is lost" moment, and the viewer may well expect *An Unseen Enemy* to join the ranks of those rare one-reel melodramas in which the rescue fails (as in Griffith's *Death's Marathon* of 1913). The rescuer has been delayed, the drunken gunwoman holds both sisters in her sights, and the accomplice is on the verge of breaking into the safe.

A sound serial might well sever the episode at this point, but one-reel films must resolve the situation quickly. Griffith does so, rather ingeniously, by reintroducing a character that has been more or less forgotten: the younger sister's "boyish sweetheart" (Robert Harron). He first appears toward the end of the film's first act, after the brother has departed, to ask the younger sister for a kiss before he leaves for college. She denies him, a point succinctly emphasized by the stinging intertitle "No Kiss." Thus he is still moping about, wandering the grounds and gazing wistfully through the sisters' window. Heartbreak turns to timely intervention when he opens the window and frees the sisters just as the burglars blow the safe with explosives. Meanwhile, the brother clears the bridge and arrives in time to nab the villains. All is well in the final shot when the family and money are reunited, and the younger sister, prodded by her siblings, allows her sweetheart to steal a kiss.

We have detoured through this early film because it can tell us much about the basic suspense techniques that undergird the serial cliffhanger. *Unseen Enemy*'s success lies partly in its visual clarity. Griffith has constructed the sitting room as something of a compositional infernal machine for his innocents. The space is split into three or four zones of action. In the foreground right sits the telephone, the girls' only hope of contacting the outside world. But the gun in the wall, midway down the left edge of the room, prevents them from reaching help. Instead, the girls seek cover in a third zone behind a bureau in the far left corner, out of sight of the maid, and also well way from the phone. Hope and fear are spatially triangulated. The cinematographer, Billy Bitzer, wisely underplays the presence of the window at the rear right (a potential fourth zone of action). It remains just visible on the edge of the frame (entirely cropped out in most video transfers), but the actresses never approach it or call attention to it. The window is well within range of the gun and so, like the phone, is an escape route that has been cut off. Still, by focusing all attention on the three key areas, Griffith keeps viewer attention from wandering and stealthily hides the ultimate means of liberation in plain sight. The maid's cleverness and increasingly drunken desperation give the situation mounting tension. It is only a matter of time until her accomplice cracks the safe, but within this horizon the situation intensifies the stakes, first by having the maid remember the stove hookup and put her plan into action, and then by progressively impairing her judgment. Just before she begins firing, an intertitle warns "The Drink Has Its Effect."

Unseen Enemy is a working model of narrative. Griffith translates the suspenseful trap into physical design; danger seems built into the set. Richard Gerrig describes such arrangements as suspenseful "problem spaces." For Gerrig, a cognitive psychologist, suspense is a participatory structure that cues viewers to seek some piece of withheld knowledge. The "problem space" analogy compares problem solving to searching a space for information that will allow one to achieve a goal. The contours of the trap and the aim of getting away are clear, but the means of liberation, the escape hatch, remains hidden: "To make the reader really feel suspense, the author must sufficiently constrain the space of possible solutions so that the situation appears beyond hope." *Unseen Enemy* develops tension by introducing and then discarding potential solutions to the problem. The viewer, literally scanning the space of the room, will notice the telephone, prominent in the foreground. This seems the way out, but the gun's emergence from the wall (punctuated by the film's only true close-up) eliminates the option. When the younger sister boldly returns to the phone and speaks to her brother, the maid opens fire, assuring the sisters, and the viewer, that she means business. If the telephone is off-limits, at least the sisters can seek shelter behind the bureau at the far corner of the room, out of the maid's sight. Griffith negates this solution, too, when the younger sister sneaks up to the gun, calling the killer's attention to their hiding spot and bringing them within the line of fire. As Gerrig notes, a successful suspense situation "mimics the process of problem solving . . . by specifying and then eliminating potential means for escape."[4] From all appearances, the sisters cannot solve their problem from within the confines of the trap.

The one-reel action melodrama introduced to cinema the value of vivid and legible problem spaces, laying the foundation for sound-serial exploration of narrative architecture. The graphic clarity and simplicity of Griffith's triangulation of the gun, the girls, and the phone, for instance, anticipates the trap in *Three Musketeers*. The direction of Elaine's race to the firing squad will place her squarely between the rifles and their target, and though the camera reframes to remove her from the screen, the spatial dynamics are emphatically clear. One mark of a good cliffhanger is that a cut to black does nothing to diminish the vividness of the deathtrap. Both films design the possibilities of suspense into concrete space.

Of course, most viewers of *Unseen Enemy*, and maybe the victims themselves, pin their hopes on the brother's race against time. As soon as Griffith begins crosscutting between two lines of action, he activates a narrative template made familiar by countless other one-reel melodramas and thus primes viewers for a last-minute deliverance. But the film begins teasing and shutting down solutions on this narrative line as well. First, the brother is not even in the office when the sisters call; second, he owns only a bicycle. The major obstacle, and the one that seemingly eliminates the brother's rescue, is the swing-bridge that traps the rescue car just as the younger sister is approaching the gun. This suddenly restricts the problem space, knocking out our best prospect for a solution.

The boyfriend's reintroduction, then, is the surprise escape hatch, the unanticipated solution to the problem. *An Unseen Enemy* relies on what Gerrig calls "functional fixedness" to block our anticipation of its solution. Crosscutting encourages us to focus entirely on the brother's progress, and to disregard other narrative agents, including a moping comic boyfriend. The eventual solution, as in so many serial cliffhangers, emerges from outside the realm of possibilities that the sequence has delineated. It is beyond the immediate narrative architecture, but still near enough to the viewer's reasonable range of expectations that it doesn't feel like a "cheat." The boy's timely arrival is coincidental, but not on the order of a true deus ex machina. Rather, because he has been planted in the story, and because his arrival is motivated by conventions of character trait and romantic closure, the boyfriend solution allows the viewer to, in Gerrig's terms, "indulge in pleasurable self-recrimination: Why didn't I think of that."[5]

The concepts of narrative architecture and problem space tend to emphasize complications and obstacles that are built up from within the fictional world. But they also refer to the game played between narrator and viewer, of which no character can be aware. Again, the one-reel melodrama sets the terms that serials follow by imposing a pattern of interruption and delay onto the unfolding action. In *Unseen Enemy*, crosscutting directs viewer expectations with impeccable timing. From the moment that the older sister picks up the telephone, Griffith alternates between three lines of action: the sisters in the parlor, the villains in the front room, and the brother and his assistant in his office and then on the road as they race home. Action shifts between locales at a blistering pace, alternating a full thirty-seven times (most often between the sisters and their brother) in about five minutes. The thirty-eighth shift introduces a fourth line of action, the lonely boyfriend revisiting the place of his denied kiss. Once the means of escape has been revealed, the lines of action quickly converge. In only four more alternations the boy arrives at the sisters' window, and four after that, the brother's car is on the scene. In tracing the evolution of this technique, which began around 1908 in Pathé films, Tom Gunning notes that Griffith pushes crosscutting to the center of his storytelling system and "makes the progression of time palpable through its interruption, imposing a rhythm on the unfolding events."[6] Editing intervenes in the flow of events, expands and compresses time, and orchestrates viewer expectations.

Griffith's most powerful technique involves cutting on the "fatal gesture," Gunning's term for action that occurs just before all is lost.[7] In *An Unseen Enemy*, the fatal gestures escalate, each seeming to more surely signal the violation of innocence. After the gun is briefly withdrawn from the hole, the older sister makes her way back to the phone, and Griffith alternates between the two ends of the conversation. This pattern is broken with the title "The Drink Has Its Effect" and a shot of the front parlor, where the maid puts down her bottle and picks up her gun. A proximate deadline is thus imposed on the action; how long, the viewer asks, before the maid opens fire? Griffith cuts back and forth between the ends of the telephone conversation once more, delaying by a tiny bit the maid's action of pushing the gun through the wall. When the gun reemerges in the background, the sister drops the phone, prompting a lingering shot of the brother's panicked reaction. Griffith withholds the outcome of the first fatal gesture, the gun's reappearance. In the next round, the gesture becomes more final. As the older sister attempts to sneak back to her corner, the gun fires and smoke jets across the frame. Cut to the brother, gaping in horror as he overhears the shot and assumes the worst. Interruption maximizes suspense by blocking our access to the solution. When we return to the girls' room, they are both safely huddled in the far corner, and the drunken maid fires again. Apparently, she is a poor shot (see figure 7).

Meir Sternberg's discussion of suspense helps us characterize this give-and-take between storyteller and viewer. In Sternberg's model, the

FIGURE 7 Four shots that demonstrate Griffith's cutting on the fatal gesture in *An Unseen Enemy* (1912).

storyteller raises our interest in some future uncertainty and then delays closure, drawing out our anticipation. The reader's task is to form hypotheses that might fill in the missing exposition, guided by the story's limits on what counts as a "warrantable expectation." Sternberg prefers classical storytelling that hides the narrator's hand to melodrama's embrace of virtually any means for sustaining engagement. He regards a well-wrought detective story, for instance, as bound by "the limitations of fair-play convention," which requires that all the information for solving the problem be available within the diegesis, but cleverly obfuscated to "prevent the mystery from leaking out."[8] By these standards, the one-reel thriller and the serial both fail. But crosscutting can marry the narrator's manipulations to the pulse of our engagement, burying the intervention within the cascade of hypotheses running through the viewer's mind. Cutting on the fatal gesture amounts to finding the visual moment at which fear outstrips hope and then arresting the tragic outcome. From within the flow of action, the boyfriend's return hardly seems warrantable, but in the heat of the moment we accept, even embrace, the felicitous turn. This is a game well played, and it is essentially melodramatic.

Serial cliffhangers give pride of place to fatal gestures and their timely interruptions, but unlike one-reel films they cannot finesse improbable contrivance with film form. External retardation, Sternberg's bête noire, is built into the formula and emphasized by the narrator's voice that breaks out of the story to implore viewers to "return next week" at each episode's end. *An Unseen Enemy* might mask melodramatic artifice by rushing the story forward, but the pause between serial chapters invariably underscores it. Here, the cliffhanger radically departs from its predecessor, and in doing so reorients the viewer's relationship to suspense. Fans are left until the next installment to search the problem space for a solution, however improbable, all the while knowing that the crisis will pass.

Curiosity, Suspense, and Knowing Better

The majority of serial chapters conclude not with the bomb still ticking but with the explosion, fatal shot, unsurvivable plane or car or train crash, collapsing building, trampling by stampede, etc.—a point driven home by the voice-over narrator in Columbia serials like *Mandrake, the Magician* (1939), who regularly describes the hero as "hurtling to a *certain death*." Images might just barely curtail our access, but off-screen sound can guarantee the springing of the infernal trap. Self-contained narrative films (one-reel or feature) involve viewers in the tense play of hope and fear, while the sound serial, week after week, ends at the moment that the latter prevails. The episode constructs a problem space for the viewer in which visual and aural evidence contradicts the foregone (and invariable) conclusion that the heroes are safe.[9] The keen viewer has a week to mull the resolution to this contradiction. Cliffhangers convert heat-of-the-moment problems into puzzles to solve, terrains to explore.

This convention requires a different understanding of suspense. For Sternberg, the viewer's knowledge of a situation's outcome downshifts suspense to a weaker emotion: curiosity. It creates a "more purely retardatory . . . suspense" in which the spectator hypothesizes "how" over what: "All the reader does is eagerly or resignedly await the inevitable end as it draws nearer and nearer with each twist of the action that retards it."[10] In the cliffhanger, the viewer has an absolute assurance that the peril will be reversed so that it can be averted in the next episode. The salient knowledge regulated by cliffhanger narration is not the fate of the hero so much as the means of his or her liberation. Certainly the forced rupture of narrative progression just after an apparent cataclysm amplifies the importance of "how" hypotheses. But this account minimizes the lingering sense that our heroes are in danger and that the future of their mission is uncertain. Just because we know Tom Wayne cannot die doesn't mean that we don't fear his death.

Gerrig terms situations in which viewers experience tension despite knowing the outcome of events "anomalous suspense." For Gerrig, suspense is a powerfully resilient emotion able to withstand inhospitable conditions like the viewer having seen a film more than once, or knowing full well that things will turn out right. The sound serial is something of a powerhouse of anomalous suspense. Our general knowledge of genre conventions is bolstered by formulaic episodes that essentially reteach the rules of the game. Not only is Wayne the hero of the story, we have witnessed his survival in chapters 1–5. How much uncertainty can really endure by the time he finds himself face-to-face with a firing squad? As a cognitivist, Gerrig casts narrative in terms of information processing, and this leads him to an intriguing hypothesis. Cognition, Gerrig reasons, is hardwired with an *expectation of uniqueness*: "Our natural stance—as we are immersed in the ongoing stream of life—is always to act as if we cannot know what is going to happen next." This expectation may have the evolutionary advantage of keeping us alert to change, helping us expect the unexpected. Suspenseful fictions, according to Gerrig, tap into this innate predisposition, which encourages us to entertain the prospect of uncertainty: "Because life is made up of unique experiences—we undergo repeated types but not repeated tokens—readers do not ordinarily have reason to search memory for *literal* repetitions of events."[11] Though we can almost invariably predict the cliffhanger's outcome, and though the question of "how" weighs more than "what," there is something about the way our minds work that keeps us interested in the fate of our hero.

Not all suspense is created equal. As Gerrig admits, in response to criticism from the analytical philosopher Noel Carroll, the viewer must be adequately drawn into a fictional situation for the expectation of uniqueness to do its work.[12] Carroll offers a clean and precise explanation of how fictions can reliably draw viewers in: a formula that bears directly on the cliffhanger. Suspense occurs when a character the viewer aligns with is caught in a situation with two clearly defined opposed outcomes, a desirable "moral" outcome and an undesirable "evil" one. For Carroll, the "evil" outcome must be as likely as, or more likely than, the "moral" solution. Suspense necessarily requires uncertainty, as Carroll explains: "As the frenzied horses thunder toward the precipice, pulling a wagonload of children toward death, we feel suspense: Will they be saved or not? As long as that question is vital, and the outcome is uncertain, we are in a state of suspense. Once the outcome is fixed, however, the state is no longer suspense. If the wagon hurtles over the edge, we feel sorrow and anguish; if the children are saved, we feel relief and joy." Several features of Carroll's formula are particularly suited to melodramatic cliffhangers. First, the viewer must have a strong rooting interest in the fate of the fictional character, and a swift means for achieving this is to rely on simple moral binaries and conventional types. The wagonload of children, like most serial heroes and heroines, constitutes a pretty unambiguous site of virtue; they are worthy of our concern. Second, situations that progressively tip the balance of probability toward the evil outcome are excellent vehicles for suspense. Every moment that the horses thunder toward the precipice further endangers the children: "Time is running out on the good and therefore evil is becoming more likely." Finally, the success of a suspense situation rests largely on riveting the viewer to the story and keeping the probable outcomes "vividly before the audience."[13] Melodramas, with their visually spectacular dilemmas, traps, and pitfalls, fit the bill.

Character alignment, moral polarity, increasing danger, and vividness help anchor the viewer to the story world, driving attention to the problem space as it is constituted within the diegesis. For Carroll, this solves the apparent paradox of suspense "recidivism," his term for anomalous suspense in which viewers still feel engaged with films they have already seen. Following a fiction entails not an actual belief in the events depicted but a willingness to entertain the thought (or nonassertive propositions) of those events. In other words, just because we know that Wayne and Elaine must live, and even if we know how they survive, we can still experience suspense as long as we entertain the thought of the situation before us. The formulaic repetition of serial episodes, if not entire serials themselves, makes every viewer a virtual recidivist. Properly motivated, however, the viewers dwell within the fiction. As Carroll explains it, we rate the "internal probability" of an outcome because, for instance, "from a viewpoint external to the fiction there is no probability that King Kong will be killed because King Kong does not exist."[14] If Gerrig is right that we are cognitively predisposed to expect uniqueness (a disposition sorely tested by the sound serial), Carroll's account helps explain how fiction might exploit that.

Serial fans may be a community of recidivists, but chapters must nonetheless give some reason to entertain suspenseful thought. The longevity of the serial suggests that week after week filmmakers tended to succeed in crafting compelling situations. The conclusion of *Death's Marathon* is something of a virtuoso cliffhanger because Elaine, the means of rescue to which our attention is conducted by crosscutting, suddenly becomes a victim of the very machine that she is trying to halt. As in *An Unseen Enemy*, the race-to-the-rescue format encourages functional fixedness, which masks the ultimate solution for the time being. Not only does the reprieve arrive too late, the messenger is killed; the one solution we have fixed on is consumed by the space of the problem. This twist, which is vivid and high-stakes, helps buy our continued imaginative engagement.

One way to capture the cliffhanger's mixture of curiosity and suspense is provided by Edward Branigan's discussion of narrative comprehension in film. Branigan conceives of narration as involving "levels," or various frames of reference that delimit the way spectators process information. One frame of reference remains within the diegesis, allowing viewers to make sense of causes and effects more or less alongside the characters, with access to the world as it exists for them. At this level the hero's fate hangs in the balance, and the balance is shifting quickly toward defeat. Nondiegetic material, like a propulsive orchestral score, is registered, of course, but it tends to support hypotheses formed within the bounds of the story world. It is within this frame of reference that viewers can experience "anomalous suspense"; that is, we entertain the thought of uncertainty although, on another level, we know the outcome.

A key feature of Branigan's model is that different frames of reference, or "levels of narration," operate simultaneously, which means different routines for making sense of the story coexist. While we are engaged in weighing the possibilities of the hero's survival at one level, at another we identify the game being played and anticipate (even appreciate) the cliffhanger's contrivances.[15] As the countdown to the episode's end begins, we sense a storyteller deploying old tricks to wind us up; when the cliffhanger comes into focus, so does our faith in its resolution. In reference to the race-to-the-rescue scenario, Linda Williams observes, "Paradoxically, it is as if the more the temporal prolongation of suspense builds, the more sure we can be that the investment of time will have a successful outcome."[16] In a serial, there is no surer sign of the hero's survival than the emphasis on his steadily approaching doom. The very formal structures that generate suspense can actually negate it. This dynamic pertains to many formula fictions, from horror films to romantic comedies, in which audiences engage in stories with full awareness of conventions. Serials, though, present an extreme. The compressed running time of each episode, and the sheer repetition of structures from week to week and from title to title, make formulas ridiculously conspicuous. Branigan's theory helps explain why they are nonetheless engaging.[17]

And yet, no matter how engrossed in the story world we have become, the weeklong break ejects us from the scene, grants us an unusual awareness of the narration, and invites deliberative thought. As both Carroll and Gerrig have noted, the hypotheses made while consuming a fiction tend to remain tacit and unacknowledged unless viewers are wrenched from the story and made to focus attention elsewhere.[18] On one hand, this feature is a windfall for the narrator, whose goal it is to prolong the experience; it builds in a delay in exposition. On the other, the narrator necessarily loses command of the viewer's attentional pulse; spectators have the breathing room to test hypotheses, question probabilities, and think beyond the internal range of knowledge. Action melodramas thrive on happenstance, and the serial breaks narration and releases viewers to contemplate various possibilities. What little information we have about serials' young viewers suggests that they took this seriously. In his Payne Fund volume, Blumer noted with concern the tendency of children to reflect on cliffhangers and discuss "how the escape will occur."[19] Parnaby and Woodhouse similarly observed that the matinee audience spotted "slight alterations in the timing" of events that enabled escape: "It is interesting to note that the children detected this crude artifice, and occasionally expressed disappointment and annoyance that such unfair technique had been employed."[20]

Serial makers seem to have been aware of this, as evidenced by the convention of posing explicit questions over the end credits. *The Three Musketeers* is bare-bones in this regard, simply offering the title and number of the next episode, but later serials elaborate the convention. Columbia's *Brenda Starr, Reporter* (Fox, 1945) concludes each episode by replaying highlights of the cliffhanger just witnessed with a voice-over that lays out all the questions. For instance, chapter 2, *The Blazing Trap*, ends with Brenda (Joan Woodbury) apparently crushed beneath a collapsing staircase in a warehouse. The narration, by the ubiquitous voice actor Knox Manning, intones: "How can Brenda survive this terrific crash? How can Chuck help her with two murderous gunmen closing in on her? And what will happen, even if she comes out of the wreckage alive? Don't fail to see *Taken for a Ride*, the third thrill-packed chapter of *Brenda Starr, Reporter* at this theater next week." Narration seeks to cement the questions that viewers ask at the point of interruption. The big question, of Brenda's survival, is purely redundant and serves only to underline the cliffhanger convention and repeat a bit of spectacular footage. The second question, though, aims at casting doubt on the most likely solution, the intervention of Chuck (Syd Saylor), Brenda's partner, who is outside the warehouse. The third question implicitly acknowledges what the viewer well knows and directs attention beyond the current situation: She will live, but what will happen next? Only time and the price of a ticket can settle these matters. The internal recap is one last, slightly desperate attempt to constrain and guide the viewer's navigation of the problem space.

Cliffhangers are the very opposite of Sternberg's ideal of fair play in which we have all important information at hand to solve a mystery. Following any narrative involves a continual recasting of knowledge according to new frames of reference for previous events, but no popular form is as consistently radical as the sound serial.[21] In doubling back over action to present an unseen event or simply changing those events, serials regularly and overtly mislead the viewer. For example, the staircase that collapses at the end of *Brenda Starr*'s episode 2 actually protects her from rubble at the start of episode 3. More egregiously, Happy Cardigan (Harry Carey), visibly pummeled beneath the hooves of stampeding wild horses in the second chapter of Mascot's *The Vanishing Legion*, finds last-minute protection beneath an automobile at the start of the next chapter.

Serial screenwriters wield discontinuity as a common tool, demanding that viewers make accommodations, accept contradictory depictions, and revise previous understandings. Chapter 9 of Republic's *Flash Gordon*–inspired *Undersea Kingdom* (Eason and Kane, 1936) offers a famous example. The episode concludes with the hero, Crash Corrigan, strapped to the hood of a battle tank being slammed into a gate, complete with a plume of debris and horrified expressions from onlookers. Chapter 10 reveals, though, that at the last minute the gate was opened, and the tank passes unobstructed through the barrier in a restaged version of the event devoid of crashing sounds or debris.

Having been fed a contradiction, we must revise and reject previous knowledge in order to make sense of the story. Our disappointment is bought off, in part, by a swift change in topic. At one level we must let the aberration pass in order to keep up with the story; it helps that no one in the fiction notices anything strange about witnessing a collision that never happened. At another, simultaneous level of narration, we see that we have once again been deceived, but we also know that it probably doesn't matter in the long run; we must grant the narration this leeway if we wish to engage in other serial pleasures.

The resolution of our *Three Musketeers* cliffhanger is better developed, and it plays a game with the knowledgeable viewer. Chapter 7 opens with a written recap of the situation, illustrated by drawings of the stars. The action restarts with a story event that had previously been elided. A title informs us: "A last-minute appeal to Colonel Duval is also being made by Major Booth, of the American Embassy in Paris." Booth (Robert Frazer), who wants Wayne extradited for trial in Paris, has been circling the margins for several episodes, and it appears that he will be our "escape hatch." Cliffhangers direct viewers to notice the act of storytelling by openly withholding and revealing important exposition. Without subtlety or cleverness, the narration simply announces previously unseen major events. Booth's interpolation requires the plot to return to an earlier point and repeat events, a conventional procedure that is nonetheless conspicuous.

Serial fans could expect such convenient and undisguised interpolations as a matter of course. In fact, "cheating" refers only to cliffhanger solutions that obviously alter the repeated footage, not to the more common practice of opening up a scene to previously unseen action. The limits of fair play were roomy. In this episode of *Three Musketeers*, however, the interpolation is just a tease and Booth's last-minute appeal comes to naught. Duval, bent on eliminating Wayne, refuses the request, and our only hopes are once again pinned to Elaine's desperate journey across the burning sands. The scene adds little, but it illustrates that even meretricious storytelling can engage viewers in a sophisticated way. By dangling a false solution, the narration momentarily throws serial fans off the trail and acknowledges the savvy of its audience.

Once Duval dismisses Booth, the film returns to the events from the previous episode, shot for shot. Guards retrieve Wayne from his cell, Elaine rushes over a hill, and Duval watches as the firing squad lines up its shot. In all, one minute and fourteen seconds of footage are replayed, bringing the viewer right up to moment of execution. The shot of Elaine racing into the middle of the firing range is followed by the leftward pan from Wayne against the wall to the rifle barrels, and, once again, they blast while Elaine's scream issues from off-screen. Like a magician tapping the inside of a box to assure the audience it is empty, the narration recounts its steps, showing that our heroine is at gunpoint, and that no protection intervenes between Wayne and the soldiers. Then the film cuts, not to another line of action, or even an angle that reveals the trick, but to Elaine's stunned reaction. The scream, which bridges the cut, does not match the image, for instead of recoiling in terror Elaine looks merely confused. A quick pan to the sergeant reveals him widening his eyes in incomprehension. Next, the riflemen glance quizzically at one another and inspect their guns. Finally, the camera whip-pans to the right and lands on John Wayne's wonderfully inadequate reaction as he checks for injuries. In one of the sound serial's great moments of accidental modernism, the performers, the characters, and the audience all seem to experience the same shocked incredulity. "How have we managed to escape certain doom, again?" (See figure 8.)

The answer is delayed a moment longer as Duval questions the sergeant and each soldier swears that he aimed at the prisoner. Then, upon inspecting one of the rifles, Duval declares: "Why, this clip is full of blanks!" A quick two-shot of the Musketeers settles the matter. Schmidt (Francis X. Bushman Jr.) asks "What did you do with them bullets?" and Renard (Raymond Hatton) responds, "Dropped 'em down the well." Elaine presents her reprieve, Duval grudgingly orders Wayne returned to his cell, and at almost exactly one-third of the way through the episode, the cliffhanger is resolved. The Three Musketeers have once again materialized on the scene to solve our hero's dilemma.

To the screenwriters' credit, their solution had been planted in the previous episode when the three were detailed to the firing squad despite Clancy's (Jack Mulhall) violent objection. When reminded of the penalty for refusing to obey, Renard holds his friend back and assures him, "That won't do our friend Wayne any good." The saviors are thus positioned to intervene, though their success depends on the serendipity of Elaine's arrival with the reprieve. Both events seem equally unlikely, but as in *An Unseen Enemy*, the race to the rescue locks the viewer into a closed scenario in which the players are functionally fixed. Crosscutting seems to assure us that Elaine will be the rescuer; our attention is diverted from the good guys already on the premises. If the suspense situation works, it is because we have temporarily forgotten Wayne's accomplices and focused instead on Elaine's seemingly failed mission. The interpolation of Booth's futile attempt to dissuade Duval may further throw us off the track since it displaces the point in the chronology at which the heroes are drafted into the firing squad. Where episode 6 showed us Elaine's crash landing and the Musketeers' assignment, episode 7 shows Booth talking to Duval.

By serial standards this is an elegant cliffhanger. The end of *Death's Marathon* cheats, but only slightly, on the soundtrack. Elaine's scream of terror, which provides an effective curtain for the episode, does not match her

FIGURE 8 The hero escapes unharmed at the start of chapter 7 of *The Three Musketeers* (1933).

expression of surprise in *Naked Steel*. In fact, the audio and visual tracks contradict one another, with the scream bridging a cut to Elaine resolutely not screaming. Of course, plausibility is never the form's strong suit, and like most suspense situations, this one crumbles at the faintest intellectual pressure. If we are to remain in the film's community, we must simply accept the happy coincidence of Elaine's arrival, the Musketeers' new assignment, their ability to reload every gun on the squad, and the discontinuous scream. If the incongruence should flag the narration's misdirection for the viewer, it is swiftly trumped by a change of topic. The hero, safe for the moment, is marched back to his cell, and the episode switches its focus to El Maghreb (George Magrill), Tom Wayne's would-be assassin, who races away from the failed execution on his horse. The remainder of the episode concerns El Maghreb's desperate plan to kill El Shaitan (Robert Frazer) before the masked leader punishes him for failing to eliminate Wayne. The hero himself does not directly reappear in the episode, a truly unusual tactic for a sound serial.[22] Having cheated fate once more, Wayne disappears from the proceedings, and the narration plays a shell game by distracting spectators with a side plot.

Because solutions can so rarely live up to expectations fostered by cliffhanger hyperbole, the screenwriters dispense with them quickly and divert the viewer with another situation. Thus, in chapter 3 of *The Vanishing Legion* the wild stampede disappears off-screen (to become someone else's problem, we assume) and Happy Cardigan finds himself face-to-face with suspected evildoer Caroline Hall (Edwina Booth), abruptly switching the story to a new narrative track:

CAROLINE: Are you badly hurt?

CARDIGAN: (*Quickly recovering*) Well, it looks like I owe you my life, Miss Hall. It would be easier to thank you if I didn't know that it was you that planned the attack against me.

CAROLINE: *I* planned the attack against you?

CARDIGAN: Jimmie heard and told me that you phoned in a disguised voice and threatened me if I fail to leave the district.

Their exchange is interrupted by the abduction of young Jimmie Williams (Frankie Darro) by the Voice's (Boris Karloff) mysterious gang, obliterating any lingering concern for Cardigan's near-fatal trampling. Characters promptly bounce back from trauma, never learning from, and barely registering, their experience. Even when the solution is reasonably well motivated, and not a cheat to be swept under the narrative rug, chapters rarely sacrifice more than five minutes to it, and far less to its repercussions. Having brought viewers back to the theater, the cliffhanger is summarily dropped, and a new game begins.

Engaging with the Cliffhanger

Cliffhangers entail a curious inflection of Hollywood's standard viewing procedures. They manage knowledge in a predictable way, broadcasting the direction of events with utmost clarity. But unlike its feature-film counterpart, the serial episode disposes spectators to anticipate interruption and delay rather than closure and resolution. From the moment that the perilous situation begins to take shape, we rest assured that goals will remain blocked and the story's progress halted. Episodes are paced with such regularity that spectators can easily detect the start of a cliffhanger in the last quarter of a chapter's running time. Chapter 6 of *The Three Musketeers* sets the gears in motion at about thirteen minutes into the sixteen-minute episode, when a nefarious henchman cuts the rudder cable on Elaine's airplane. Like a shot of a whirling buzz saw or a ticking bomb, this detail of sabotage is enough to activate cliffhanger-viewing strategies. It primes viewers to anticipate both interruption and the spectacle of catastrophe. We can indulge in disasters that would end a continuous narrative, because we know the cataclysm will eventually be neutralized.

Our engagement depends on our recognition that cliffhangers are somehow independent of the larger story. Their intensity is out of proportion with their impact on the causal chain. One moment our hero faces certain death before the firing squad; the next moment all is more or less forgotten. This autonomy becomes especially clear in so-called economy episodes, which recycle material from earlier chapters through flashback. For example, in chapter 13 of *The Lone Ranger* the cowboy heroes return to their cave and recount previous adventures around a fire. The thirteen-minute episode spends six minutes in flashback. Without warning, the heroes' prisoner escapes, climbs to a rock ledge, and holds them all at gunpoint. Dick Forest (Lane Chandler), one of the potential Lone Rangers, sneaks up behind the heavy, but they both tumble from the precipice and take the "fatal plunge" of the episode's title. The cliffhanger is pro forma, and its timing is entirely determined by the length of the episode. The prisoner, who is generally forgotten after his capture, could escape at any point but waits until the final two minutes to generate a crisis. Economy episodes bare the device because the cliffhanger is so divorced from forward narrative momentum or specifically stated goals. Crisis arises at the regularly appointed time.[23] But all cliffhangers are modules plugged in at regular intervals, and they are short-term structures, generally irrelevant to any larger story arc.

The story world and the storyteller seem to operate on different principles. The former is strongly linear, driven by unforgiving deadlines and impending crises; the latter is undisciplined and prone to gaps, revision, and contradiction. Instead of attributing narrative developments to a goal-oriented protagonist within the fiction, serial stories arbitrarily construct themselves in order to extend the running time and keep the melodramatic locomotive chugging along. The cliffhanger cleaves apart levels of narration that feature films bind together. The suspense we feel over the hero's peril within the world diverges from our curiosity about how the storyteller will arrange his escape, how the game will be played. The deliberate care with which Wayne's firing-squad dilemma is laid out in both chapters, and the false hope of Booth's intervention, challenge viewers to detect manipulations, while still emphasizing the situation's danger. Two levels operate simultaneously and in opposition to one another.

Cliffhangers set up a distinctive relationship between spectator and film. They break action, sunder our connection at the very moment that it should be strongest, and exhort us to consciously contemplate an unsolved predicament. In contrast to a classical Hollywood feature that seals the lines of action and closes the story world, the serial invites the leap to make-believe. It extends participation with the story world by keeping the situation open, the possibilities alive. Carroll, Gerrig, and Sternberg all contrast suspense as an emotion, earned and structured by the narrator, to a game of pretend initiated by the spectator. The latter, as Carroll notes, involves a good deal of conscious activity like role-playing, while suspense demands only "imaginative engagement" with thoughts to which we react emotionally.[24] In releasing the storyteller's grip, the end of an episode leaves viewers with a vividly drawn scenario, essentially a set of parameters, roles, and stakes to feed make-believe during the intervening week. Overt narration also sensitizes viewers to the ways of delay and revision, modeling the manipulation of the scenario. Even as they absorb us into the game at hand, cliffhangers make us aware of how it is played. Continuing the movie becomes a matter of pretend.

Inspired by the narratological literature on the nature of suspense, our discussion has focused on cognitive aspects of cliffhangers. We must not, however, lose track of their kinetic and sensual appeals. Cliffhangers provide spatially delimited physical challenges, drawn with such schematic clarity that the puzzle can become inhabitable. As noted in the first chapter, film phenomenology casts spectatorship as an embodied activity, and this can reveal continuities between matinee and playground. Cliffhangers tend to be intensely corporeal in fixating on the body's liberation from a tactile threat. They inspire us to entertain tangible, concrete, and literal thoughts. All of the strategies for generating suspense noted above encourage the felt assimilation of problem spaces defined by physical containment. In posing conceptual dilemmas between desirable and likely outcomes, they also prime us for muscular empathy. Lisa Purse argues that contemporary action films involve viewers in a sensorial fantasy of physical mastery and escape, accessed with each visit to the cinema.[25] The sound serial concentrates that fantasy into modular and portable scenarios that we can carry with us and access at will. Cliffhangers crown a package of appeals that include imitable procedures, character types, and ritual action, all of which promote imaginative and physical engagement. Beyond waiting a week to buy a ticket, viewers are set to continue an active and conscious encounter with the story, to take up the mantle of both narrator and participant. The cliffhanger opens the window for play.

A Repertoire of Perils

The aims of this book are analytical rather than taxonomic, but the cliffhanger's modularity and repetition urge an accounting of basic forms and variations. Cliffhanger perils require only the appearance of certain doom, usually a spectacular physical calamity, but it is far from an open form. True to their roots in situational dramaturgy, sound serials build from a relatively small group of elements. Ron Backer's fan-oriented book *Gripping Chapters* documents serial's narrow lexicon. By far the most common perils are what Backer dubs the "cliffover," in which the hero alone, on a horse, in a truck, or in some other conveyance, plunges from a deadly height. Close competitors are crashing airplanes and entrapment in exploding or collapsing buildings. Backer classifies the remaining contrivances thusly: trains (which either crash or rush toward a track-bound hero); bridges (which tend to collapse); boats (often heading toward a waterfall); elevators (crashing or threatening to crush a hero trapped in the shaft); conveyor belts (into furnaces, buzz saws, stone crushers, and the like); machines and other devices (industrial machinery, death rays, and killing machines); gun traps (in which a gun's trigger is attached to a door, a clock, or a steering wheel); rushing waters and mine tunnels (with either rivers of water or flame overtaking the hero); rope bridges and city high wires (which invariably break with the hero partway across); pits and pendulums (bottomless pits and slowly advancing knives, swords, spiked balls); jungle spike traps and other sharp objects (including guillotines); closing walls and sliding floors (which crush heroes or drop them into pits); wild animals (including stampeding horses, attacking lions, hungry alligators); and avalanches (usually boulders).[26]

Backer's list covers the great majority of cliffhangers, itemizing a fairly economical set of gags that allowed producers to churn out product by recycling situations, and even footage, between series. Perils are situational in Jacobs and Brewster's sense; they are preexisting, visually sensational story modules. Thus the same truck could crash into a power station and explode in Republic's *Daughter of Don Q* (Bennet and Brannon, 1946), *G-Men Never Forget* (Brannon and Canutt, 1947), and *Radar Patrol vs. Spy King* (Brannon, 1949); and the same building could implode in Universal's *Junior G-Men* (Beebe and Rawlins, 1940), *Gang Busters* (Smith and Taylor, 1942), and *The Master Key* (Collins and Taylor, 1945).[27] Even relatively specific situations, like the firing squad in *The Three Musketeers*, were bound to resurface sooner or later. When the hero of Columbia's *Holt of the Secret Service* (Horne, 1941) finds himself before a firing squad in chapter 12, viewers might anticipate the revelation that his partner had loaded the guns with blanks in chapter 13. Undisguised reuse and appropriation are the rule.

Serial producers were under little pressure to hide the seams because their formula prioritized vividness over dramatic unity. At their most bald, cliffhangers are as random as the passing bear that harasses the heroine in chapter 7 of *Sign of the Wolf* (Webb and Sheldon, 1931) but is easily shooed away at the start of chapter 8 and never seen again. Stitching the pieces together through narrative integration and internal consistency is less a standard goal than a source of variation and, sometimes, evidence of artistic virtuosity. The more tightly bound a situation is to a particular sequence of events, the less flexible it becomes. For example, the threatened revelation of the protagonist's identity might seem classically motivated within an episode. However, it could only be deployed in serials with masked heroes and did not generally entail their apparent demise. In chapter 9 of *The Lone Ranger*, for instance, the henchman has determined that one of his four prisoners is the real Ranger because he is missing a spur lost earlier in a fight. The episode ends with the evil Kester (John Merton) exclaiming, "So *you* are the Lone Ranger." The stakes are tightly connected to the serial's premise, and the solution involves cleverness rather than physical daring. The start of chapter 11 reveals that all four suspects have removed a spur, rendering Kester's investigation inconclusive. As situations go, threatened unmasking is more specific (if less vivid) than a passing bear, but it is nonetheless a preconstituted option from the serial lexicon. The same peril occurs in chapter 4 of *The Masked Marvel* (Bennet, 1943), chapter 5 of *Zorro's Black Whip* (Bennet and Grissel, 1944), and chapter 9 of *Adventures of Frank and Jesse James* (Brannon and Canutt, 1948), among others. Rather than view these cliffhangers as organic outgrowths of action, we should recognize them as more specialized modules, which require purposely crafted narrative contexts. Employing them involves a trade-off in surprise and spectacle, making them relatively rare.

The more common method of attenuating a cliffhanger's autonomy involves working within the situation to achieve internal consistency between crisis and resolution. This parameter has become a favorite critical measure for modern commentators like Backer, Jim Harmon, and Donald Glut and is frequently discussed in the online community.[28] As noted earlier, outright cheats and restaged action are ordinary, but solutions that remain within the original problem space have the distinction of a well-played game and better reward the return customer's sustained attention. In fact, both cheated and elegant resolutions coexist in the same serial, and they range not simply from honest to false but between more and less nuanced deceptions.

Two cliffhangers from Republic's *The Tiger Woman* (Bennett and Grisell, 1944) illustrate the scale of possibilities. At the end of chapter 4, henchmen chase Tiger Woman (Linda Stirling) toward a waterfall in a speedboat. She exchanges fire with her pursuers and manages to kill one before her own driver is shot. In desperation, Tiger Woman climbs into the driver's seat, but then catches sight of the rapidly approaching precipice and dives down beneath the boat's dashboard. Two shots, a low and a high angle, show a speedboat rocketing over the waterfall and tumbling into the rapids below (see figure 9). The physical intelligibility of the chase (two boats, four combatants, one shot on each boat, and an ever-nearing deadly drop) grants the situation enviable clarity. Allen Saunders (Allan Lane), Tiger Woman's partner and sometime rescuer, follows the action from the vantage of his car rushing along the shore, powerless to intervene. Tiger Woman's problem space is locked tight.

The solution in chapter 5 relies on subtle restaging of action. First, the recap reveals a previously hidden ellipsis. Before making her way to the driver's seat, Tiger Woman blasts her rifle, taking out her remaining pursuer. Next, her dive under the dashboard is revealed to have been not a reaction to the impending crash but an effort to help her driver sit up before she takes the wheel. This is followed by a stunningly lucid long shot that shows Tiger Woman's boat veer away from the falls while the pilotless pursuit boat maintains a direct course

FIGURE 9 The final four shots of chapter 4 of *The Tiger Woman* (1944).

over the edge (see figure 10). The points of revision in the cliffhanger are well hidden, in part, because the scene doesn't actually change any of the repeated actions. Meanwhile, the regular crosscutting between pursuer and pursued in the first version of events masks the change in the second: it is unlikely that a viewer would remember exactly which of the henchmen Tiger Woman had shot. Finally, the substitution of boats is a particularly sophisticated alternative to revealing that the boat did not actually shoot the falls, which would require a much more pronounced modification.

Chapter 9, sensationally titled *Cruise to Cremation*, repeats the basic situation but with far less grace. In this case, Tiger Woman is held captive, unconscious, on a speedboat while Allen Saunders pursues. When Saunders guns down the henchman, Tiger Woman's boat is left without a pilot just as an unexpected (and spectacularly illogical) riverboat crosses its path. Tiger Woman revives just in time to see the riverboat, scream, and duck back down below the seat before an explosive collision obliterates both crafts. The solution in chapter 10 places stress on the point of revision. In this case, instead of screaming and ducking down, Tiger Woman courageously steps to the edge

FIGURE 10 At the start of chapter 5 of *The Tiger Woman* (1944), the heroine steers away from the approaching cliff, allowing an unmanned boat to crash.

of her boat and leaps to Saunders's before he peels off (see figure 11). Compared to chapter 4's cliffhanger, this one draws attention to the restaging by eliminating Tiger Woman's scream and altering her most salient action. Narrative haphazardness is heightened by the appearance of a riverboat in an otherwise isolated jungle outpost and by the casual killing of its passengers and crew. The contrast between the two cliffhangers is telling. Both are technically cheats, but episode 4 displays surprising precision and delicacy. Attention to narrative integration and internal consistency allowed filmmakers to refine their craft. Convention need not be artless.

Conclusion

The cliffhanger is at the center of the sound-serial experience, and it is largely responsible for the form's appeal. Few narrative formulas are so charged with contradiction. Cliffhangers depend on both suspense and foregone conclusions. They present vivid climaxes but forestall closure. They depict the relentlessly linear approach of a deadline but freely reverse and revise events to suit narrative convenience. They focus attention intensively toward a crisis that

FIGURE 11 Top row: at the conclusion of chapter 10 of *The Tiger Woman* (1944), the heroine crashes her craft into a passing riverboat. Bottom row: At the start of chapter 11, she courageously crosses to another boat, which peels away.

will be unceremoniously dropped as a new situation arises. Finally, they eject the viewer from the flow of action at the same time that they encourage continued engagement beyond the theater. These qualities make the cliffhanger a potent testing ground for theories of anomalous suspense, levels of narration, and separately functioning cognitive routines. If hallmarks of classical Hollywood storytelling include ease of comprehension, the binding of discourse to story, and the masking of narrative contrivance with coherent, psychologically motivated cause and effect, then the serial cliffhanger is an apparently radical alternative. The narrator's hand is never deeply hidden, and it can be willfully arbitrary. Cliffhangers rupture the story world with direct address and feed viewers contradictory and discontinuous information. From this perspective, they resemble modernist, fiction-bursting, and anticlosure critiques of normative storytelling.

At most, however, the cliffhanger belongs to the category of vernacular modernism proposed by Miriam Hansen.[29] Its purpose is to entertain popular audiences, but it does so by departing from the classical dramatic curve. Serials compress, break, and repeat action instead of tracing its smooth rise to crisis and fall to resolution. They do not, however, radically challenge coherence or oppose the kinds of pleasure more routinely offered by film narratives. Cliffhangers and the frameworks that support them constitute a parallel track to the studio-era feature. Both forms share structures, emotional appeals, and stylistic tactics, but serials trade in a unique mix of suspense and narrational gaming. They engage distinctive viewing procedures.

Cliffhangers rarely seem to serve any higher order, but they do encapsulate the sound serial's central attraction. Crystallizing wild implausibility and strict conventionality into a single narrative unit, they proffer a basic and constant fantasy: the reassurance of survival and success in the face of staggering improbability. For the hero, the cliffhanger is a malevolent and inescapable space from which he invariably escapes. For the fan, it is a familiar novelty, a life-or-death struggle without real consequence. Each pair of episodes rehearses the scenario of being consumed by unconquerable forces and then beating impossibly stacked odds. Like the sound serial as a whole, cliffhangers promise young viewers the confident mastery of a thoroughly arbitrary world. Popular formula, however, need not entail indifferent filmmaking. The next two chapters consider how serials can achieve formal and narrative refinement within the bounds of viewer expectations.

5

Narrative and the Art of Formula

● ●

We have assessed conventions and potentials of serial plots, worlds, suspense structures, and viewer engagement. This chapter and the next analyze how specific films achieve virtuosity through formula. Using *Daredevils of the Red Circle* (Witney and English, 1939) and *Perils of Nyoka* (Witney, 1942) as case studies, supplemented by additional examples, we first take up issues related to narration and plot, and then (in chapter 6) problems of cinematic form. Close attention to story and style requires detailed description, but the aim is not to synopsize or catalog. Together these chapters seek to deepen our understanding of serial strategies by dwelling within specific works and parsing their creative possibilities, to get under the film's skin and better capture the textures and intricacies of the serial experience.

The speed and economy of sound-serial production encouraged formal proficiency across the industry. Between 1936 and 1946, the so-called golden age, Universal, Columbia, and Republic issued about ten serials each year, with independent producers contributing four in 1936 and one in 1937.[1] *Daredevils* and *Nyoka*, both products of the vaunted Republic unit, demonstrate the finesse that studio achieved in the late 1930s and early 1940s, but we should resist blanket assessments of quality. All three production companies borrowed heavily from one another and innovated with the form. Cliffhanger situations, especially, traveled between studios and in the process were varied and developed. Moreover, the elevation of parts over wholes makes most serials uneven: uninspired efforts can boast imaginative sequences. Steady and stable formulas gave filmmakers the means to meet tight deadlines with passable results, and this chapter argues that they also supported experimentation and refinement. Before turning to our case studies, then, we might note how the sound serial's conventions could inspire passing moments of ingenuity in routine films.

Passing Ingenuity: Storytelling in Batman

Generally dismissed by contemporary commentators, *Batman* (Hillyer, 1943) and *Batman and Robin* (Bennett, 1949) may lack the action and pacing of their Republic counterparts, but in at least two instances they tune formula to explore the possibilities of narrative comprehension. In chapter 14 of *Batman*, Dr. Daka's (J. Carroll Naish) henchmen knock Batman (Lewis Wilson) out cold, lock him in a pine box, and deliver him to the villain's waxworks across town, where he is dumped into an alligator pit. In the final shot, Dr. Daka leans forward into the pit as screams issue from off-screen. The situation's design is hardly innovative; creativity lies in the manner of telling. The setup is extraordinarily painstaking. Before Batman is lured to his apparent demise, Dr. Daka feeds his hungry alligators, explaining, "That was just a little appetizer; the main course will be served when Bruce Wayne gets here." To set their trap, the henchmen transport Linda Page (Shirley Patterson), who has become one of Dr. Daka's zombies, in the pine box. Like stage illusionists demonstrating their apparatus, the henchmen unlock the box, remove Linda, and place her on a chair in the center of the room, and then relock the box, leaning it against a rear wall. Arriving on the scene, Batman assures Robin (Douglas Croft) and Alfred (William Austin) that he will call for help on the "Batman Radio" and rushes to Linda's rescue. Within moments, the henchmen pistol-whip Batman, retrieve the box, and lock him inside.[2]

The serial's poor reputation among serial fans owes something to its often-plodding delineation of simple action. Yet all this time spent moving, opening, loading, and closing the coffin also makes the process concrete and creates an aura of inescapability. In the face of Batman's certain survival, the chapter depicts the process of his entrapment with ridiculously redundant detail and clarity. A similar thoroughness of operation informs the next few scenes that show the unloading of the box at the waxworks and its lowering into the pit by two of Daka's radio-controlled zombies. Methodical specificity may pad the chapter, but it also addresses spectator suspicions. When the narrator spends so much time saying so little, the serial audience watches how the story is told. The sequence draws attention to its aching completeness, inviting scrutiny of procedure while hiding a surprisingly lengthy ellipsis revealed in the next installment.

Chapter 15 begins with Batman's entrapment but then continues through a large narrative expanse that had been neatly covered by a cut to the coffin's delivery to the waxworks. Such hidden ellipses are the most common means of resolving cliffhangers.[3] Frequently, in replaying last week's peril the serial fills in some relatively brief but important action such as a timely leap from a car or horse just before it races over a precipice (as in episode 12 of Republic's 1939 *The Lone Ranger*, in which all three heroes leap from a crashing stagecoach in the nick of time), or the donning of a parachute before an airplane explosion (as in episode 4 of Columbia's 1942 *Captain Midnight* and innumerable aviation serials). *Batman* expands the conventional ellipsis into an entire line of action. A cut to inside the coffin shows the hero using his "Batman Radio," a Morse code device, to contact Robin and Alfred. Robin scales the building, sneaks through a window, and unlocks the coffin, allowing Batman to knock out his guard. The caped crusaders lock the guard in the box and then follow the delivery truck. The box is unloaded from the truck as before, but this time crosscutting reveals Batman and Robin parked across the road and formulating a plan. Once again, the zombies retrieve the box and dump it into the pit, but upon hearing the screams Dr. Daka exclaims, "That's not the Batman, that's Wallace!" Meanwhile, Alfred stages a distraction at the front of the waxworks, allowing the heroes to sneak inside. Moments later Daka once again takes Batman hostage and straps him to "the zombie chair," effectively voiding any forward progress since the previous episode.

Of course, it isn't unusual that the momentarily liberated hero should find himself so swiftly reimperiled. *Batman*'s originality lies in the scale of revision to viewer knowledge. Our initial experience of the events put so much emphasis on the encasement of Batman in the coffin that his escape and substitution comes as a formidable revelation. Where the majority of serial episodes treat cliffhanger ellipses as passing but necessary deceptions, the new material in chapter 15 exaggerates, even celebrates, the serial form's narrational freedom.

Chapters 10 and 11 of Columbia's sequel *Batman and Robin*, produced by the notoriously cheap Sam Katzman, elaborate the technique further (see figure 12). This time, during a punch-up with thugs in an office building, Batman (Robert Lowrey) is thrown through a window and plunges to certain death on the sidewalk below. Robin (Johnny Duncan), parked in a delivery van outside the building, watches helplessly as his mentor plummets. The next installment takes the rare tactic of briefly obscuring the means of the cliffhanger's resolution. At the start of chapter 11, Bruce Wayne (Batman's alter ego) calmly approaches Robin's van, declares that it was Vicki Vale's (Jane Adams) ne'er-do-well brother Jimmy (George Offerman Jr.) who fell from the window, and promises, "I'll explain later." The cliffhanger is resolved in the sense that the hero's survival is quickly assured, but the puzzle remains.

In the following scene, as they drive, Bruce Wayne narrates the cliffhanger's solution as a flashback. He explains that he was defeated by the Wizard's elaborate system of electrified doorknobs. While he was knocked out from the

FIGURE 12 Lobby card for chapter 10 of *Batman and Robin* (1949). Author's collection.

shock, Jimmy Vale seized the opportunity to switch clothes with Batman as he, too, was being pursued by the Wizard's men. This contrivance repurposes the cliffhanger solution from chapter 11 of Republic's *Spy Smasher* (Witney, 1942), in which the hero's twin brother steals his costume and is killed. In *Batman and Robin*, the trick is more surprising and modular because Jimmy Vale is not a regular character and his resemblance to the hero has never been established. Moreover, the recap at the chapter's start maintains the ruse, leaving Batman's flashback to fill in the ellipsis. Viewers must double back over a set of events they have twice witnessed and revise their understanding.

Serial narration regularly withholds events and reverses outcomes, but in this case the deception is repeated and the new material framed as a character's memory. No one would credit *Batman and Robin* with narrative sophistication, but for a serial this is an uncommonly complex manipulation. The requirement of regular cliffhangers prompted Columbia's screenwriters to innovate by elaborating previously elided actions and, in the process, draw us into a game of narrative comprehension.[4] These examples illustrate how even relatively mundane serials might facilitate bravura storytelling. The cliffhanger formula predisposes filmmakers to experiment with the mechanics of narration, and viewers to be aware of it. Convention inspires elaboration.

Craft, Invention, and Republic Studios

Daredevils of the Red Circle and *Perils of Nyoka* stick close to the same formulas as *Batman*, but they more consistently display an assured manipulation of convention. They deserve a close look not because they depart from norms but for their creative adherence to them. Republic's reputation among contemporary critics and commentators has tended to focus attention on its serials, a tradition to which this book consciously adheres.[5] During the high point of serial production, the *Exhibitor* critics favor Republic product slightly ahead of Universal's and well ahead of Columbia's. Republic accounted for 37.5 percent of the serials ranked "excellent" between 1934 and 1947, while Universal brought in 34.4 percent and Columbia 25 percent. The tastes of fans and a single trade paper are hardly proof of aesthetic superiority, but they highlight an area of historical interest. Republic's unit managed to produce polished work with fewer resources than larger firms, and many of its best efforts innovate from within conventional limits. Universal occasionally reached for a broader audience by raising budgets, especially with *Flash Gordon* and *Riders of Death Valley*, and Columbia's unit, particularly under Sam Katzman, exploited high-profile properties in routine efforts. Republic tended to make the most of meager means to please a faithful audience.

If serial history has a Republic bias, it is in part due to the meticulous work of Jack Mathis, who handled the studio's advertising and spent the later part of his career documenting production and plot details in his self-published volumes *The Valley of the Cliffhangers* (1975) and *The Valley of the Cliffhangers Supplement* (1995). In addition, the Republic director William Witney, who entered the studio in his late teens, became a vocal raconteur, appearing at collectors' conventions and detailing his career in the biography *In a Door, into a Fight, out a Door, into a Chase* (1995). Republic films enjoy a surprisingly rich and accessible research base for so marginal an enterprise. These resources make analyzing *Daredevils* and *Nyoka* an appealing task, but these serials are also particularly sharp and well-paced examples of the form. In them, we can see how constraint facilitates skilled refinement.

Daredevils and *Nyoka* nicely represent trends in Republic's output. The former is an urban master-criminal thriller, sharing mise-en-scène, car chases, and gunplay with the studio's Dick Tracy films, *The Masked Marvel* (Bennet, 1943), and significant portions of *The Mysterious Doctor Satan* (Witney and English, 1940), *Captain Marvel*, and *Drums of Fu Manchu*. *Nyoka*, which the *Exhibitor* called "a western in African togs," gallops across the well-trod ground of the Iverson Ranch, a property in the Simi Hills of Chatsworth, California, that the studio rented for outdoor shooting, and the Republic cave set shared by other outdoor serials like *King of the Royal Mounted* and *King of the Texas Rangers* (Witney and English, 1941), Westerns like *Adventures of Red Rider*

(Witney and English, 1940), and the Zorro films, and of course other "jungle" serials including *Jungle Girl* (Witney and English, 1941) and *Secret Service in Darkest Africa* (Bennet, 1943).[6] Urban and outdoor serials comprised the bulk of Republic's "golden age" output, with some productions like *Captain Marvel*, which moved between Siam and the United States, mixing the trends.[7] More central to our study, the serials illustrate two standard ways of structuring plots. *Daredevils* takes the form of a villain-driven labyrinth, extending the story through repeated confrontations with a game-playing, trap-setting mastermind. *Nyoka* follows a spatial itinerary as heroes and villains engage in a particularly elaborate hunt for the prized Tablets of Hippocrates. Each structure emphasizes different potentials of the formula.

Masterminds and Weenies: Large-Scale Plotting in *Daredevils* and *Nyoka*

The spark of malfeasance starts the dramatic engine in *Daredevils*. As Peter Brooks notes: "In the clash of virtue and villainy, it is the latter that constitutes the active force and motor of the plot. . . . Our starting point must be in evil."[8] Escaped criminal Harry Crowel (Charles Middleton), who takes his prison number 39013 as his name, governs the action. 39013 strikes weekly at the industrial holdings of the Granville Corporation, flooding tunnels, burning oil rigs, blowing up gas plants, and perpetrating other acts of sabotage. The master-criminal plot frees the *Daredevils* team of writers, led by Barry Shipman, to combine eclectic situations, limited only by what they can attribute to the Granville empire. Without a weenie or masked villain, however, this premise does little to structure overall action. 39013 vows "to settle the score" with Horace Granville (Miles Mander), who sent him to prison, but offers no specific goal by which we can measure his progress. In fact, as the serial opens 39103 has already gained control of Granville Industries and imprisoned his enemy in a reproduction of his former jail cell. Most serial plots are loose enough for ad hoc extension, but they also give the appearance of advancement toward an end. 39013 possesses seemingly infinite means and manpower with which to carry out his vendetta and, having little else to gain, appears free of any deadline (see figure 13).

In lieu of an endgame, *Daredevils* taps into the sound serial's operational aesthetic to achieve a semblance of unity. Disguised as Granville, 39013 has moved into the family estate, where he holds his hostage in a long-term cliffhanger. Just beyond Granville's cell bars stands a balance scale. On one arm the villain has placed a container of water that drips away at a steady rate; on the other, glass spheres filled with poison gas. 39013 explains his contraption in the opening episode: "If anything happened to me so that I fail to come down here and refill this reservoir, the water would drip entirely away. When the

FIGURE 13 Promotional art for *Daredevils of the Red Circle* (1939). Author's collection.

reservoir became lighter, these lethal gas capsules would break upon the floor. The gas would kill you in a very short time, Mr. Granville. So you see, your life depends on nothing happening to me." The poison-gas device performs like a macro-peril, a single machine to generate suspense across the first eleven episodes (until Granville is freed). Each time 39013 refills the reservoir he restarts the clock on Granville's life. The extended deathtrap emblematizes the sound serial's formula of endlessly blocked progress. The device signals the deadline's relentless approach, even while the clock itself is ritually reset. Time is always running out, but the story can go on forever.

The gas pellets are a distinctly serial method of unifying narrative. Where a feature might weave additional causal threads or develop and vary motifs, *Daredevils* returns to the gimmick. In practice, the threat remains in the background for most of the serial, more a potential thrill than salient suspense. The device appears each week, but usually as an adjunct to exposition as 39013 explains his schemes and taunts Horace Granville. As the serial nears the end of its run, Shipman brings the machine forward in the plot. In episode 10, *The Infernal Machine*, 39013 discovers that Granville has been punching secret messages into newspaper pages with a pin, so he escalates the peril by speeding up the device; now he must return every half hour to prevent the gas release. The move constricts problem space and narrows the window for action. By cutting to detail shots of dripping water, the film reminds us that when our heroes engage the villain they also endanger the victim by preventing 39013 from resetting the scale. *Daredevils* raises the deathtrap, usually a modular crisis, to the status of narrative armature.

Having installed the hostage situation at the plot's center, the serial layers operations and rituals around it. Passage down to the cell begins with the push of a concealed button that opens a wall panel in Granville's office, revealing a flight of stairs leading to a heavy sliding steel door. The cell appears in all but one chapter, and Witney and English stage the complete trip between the office and hidden chamber in five of them. Beyond inconsequential padding, the concrete physical procedure of moving from space to space contributes a kind of progressive rhythm, an appearance of purpose to 39013's wanderings.

More spectacularly, the weekly meetings between villain and victim showcase 39013's powers of disguise. Witney and English accomplish the villain's convincing impersonation of Horace Granville by having Miles Mander play both roles. When 39013 visits the cell, the filmmakers handle conversations between the two through split screen and shot/reverse-shot using foreground stand-ins for Mander, who appears on either side of the iron bars. The novelty of identical characters enlivens expository dialogue and turns performance into something of a special effect. Whether viewers accept that the two characters are identical or understand that a single actor has been duplicated, the staging of these scenes draws attention to cinematic craft.

If the visual manipulation should go unnoticed, 39013's regular transformations from Mander to Middleton throw it into stark relief. Next to the gas-pellet device, Granville's cell features a makeup table, an unlikely piece of procedural equipment. Witney and English stage the transformations in a continuous frame, with the camera facing Mander over his makeup mirror. As he talks, Mander rubs his temples, jaws, and forehead, apparently loosening his mask. Then, in the midst of conversation, he bends down so that the mirror momentarily occludes him and Middleton appears (see figure 14). The effect is seamless, achieved either through stop-frame substitution using a locked-down camera or simply hiding one actor off-frame. Seven episodes feature the transformation with slight variations. Continuity makes the gimmick conspicuous. A cut away to Mander behind bars, or to some other detail in the room, would better blend the trick with the flow of events, hiding it behind the cloak of invisible editing. Instead, the directors place the effect front and center, turning it into a visual trademark.

The staging resembles a Georges Méliès transformation, and it has the presentational character of a magic trick. Like a showman stretching out his act,

FIGURE 14 Three frames from an apparently continuous shot depicting 39103 removing his disguise in *Daredevils of the Red Circle* (1939).

the serial introduces small changes in procedure to keep novelty alive. Chapters 3 and 7, for instance, reverse the process as Middleton changes into Mander, and chapter 7 inserts a side view of Middleton's preparations in front of the mirror before returning to the standard angle. In embellishing the trick and revealing previously unseen facets of the operation, these variations reach toward what Gunning calls the "aesthetics of astonishment." The film becomes a monstrator, "making visible something which could not exist, managing the play of appearance in order to confound expectations of logic and experience."[9] The ritual never fully attains the direct address of early cinema, in part because 39013's makeover sessions have value to the story. They remind viewers of the villain's disguise and clarify his relationship to Granville. Still, the split-screen conversations already accomplish this, and, confined to the estate and surrounded by henchmen who know him, 39013 has little practical reason ever to remove his disguise. Like an early trick film, the makeup table transformations display an illusion and challenge viewers to discover the sleight. The scenario also equates identity with role-play, and changing character with an imitable procedure. Repetition turns the special effect into both a puzzle and a model for play. *Daredevils* is founded in the sound serial's operational bedrock. 39013 possesses few aspirations beyond cruelty, but in place of forward progress, chapters concatenate devices, attractions, and captivating procedures.

Where *Daredevils* lacks trajectory, *Nyoka* follows a map. The screenwriters, led by Ronald Davidson (who also worked on *Daredevils*), organize events and characters around the hunt for the Tablets of Hippocrates, somewhere in North Africa. Structurally, the weenie plot seems far removed from the master-villain option. Instead of centering on freely arranged weekly confrontations, stories revolve around the extended, competitive pursuit of a prized object. Weenies entail more opportunities for overall coherence, with each chapter marking a step toward the larger goal. The serial's emphasis, however, remains on modular situations. *Daredevils* and *Nyoka* occupy two ends of the serial plot's spectrum, each accommodating the form's priorities in different ways.

Weenie plots define characters by their relationship to the prized object. In *Nyoka*'s case, the Tablets of Hippocrates bear a map to untold riches and the cure for cancer, a sensational amalgam of noble and wicked possibilities. The villain, Vultura (Lorna Gray), and her partner Cassib (Charles Middleton) chase the tablets for personal gain. In the opening episode Vultura declares that the treasure will make her "ruler of the desert," thus tying her megalomania to a clear and specific goal. Meanwhile, Dr. Larry Grayson (Clayton Moore) and his partner Professor Campbell (Forbes Murray), aided by their trusty mechanic Red (William Benedict), embark on an expedition to cure disease, intending to use the treasure to fund "a chain of cancer clinics." Desert warrior Nyoka (Kay Aldridge) joins the hunt because, she explains, the Tablets are "the only clue I have for locating my father," Professor Henry Gordon (Robert Strange), who vanished on a similar expedition years before. The weenie motivates characters, signals their moral standing, and aligns psychology with action. Heroes and villains remain static and instantly legible figures, but in *Nyoka* they have long-term ambitions (see figure 15).

By framing action as a quest, this weenie plot moderates the appearance of melodramatic contrivance. Situations can appear as obstacles along a character-initiated path rather than as freestanding modules. *Nyoka* elaborates the Tablets of Hippocrates into a suite of clues that sets the serial's itinerary. The first component is a papyrus, which tells how to seek the tablets. Nyoka translates the papyrus in chapter 3: "Go to the Lair of the Eagles; after penetrating to its far end you will come to the Tunnel of Bubbling Death; passing through this tunnel you will then reach the ancient Valley of the Tuaregs; within the Tuareg caves there is an inscription which points the way to the golden Tablets of Hippocrates." This keeps adventure on a clear linear track. In chapters 1–3 Vultura and Nyoka's team fight over the papyrus. By the end of chapter 3, Nyoka has made it through the Lair of the Eagles and into the Tunnel of Bubbling Death for her cliffhanger. Chapters 4–6 take place in the Valley of the Tuaregs, where Nyoka discovers her father, who, having lost his memory, is now chief of the Tuareg Sun Worshippers. In chapters 7–10, Professor Gordon becomes the weenie when Vultura learns that he may know where the tablets are hidden. He is rescued from Vultura in chapter 10 and recalls that the tablets are in the Tomb of the Moon God. The tomb turns out to be a dead end, but in chapter 12 all are led to the Vault of the Wind God and finally discover the tablets, which mention the last location of the treasure trove, the Shrine of the Evil Bird. Vultura swiftly confiscates the tablets, and in chapter 14 she seeks a translation of the ancient text in the city of Wadi Bartha, where the adventure began. The Shrine of the Evil Bird, it turns out, is the long-forgotten name for Vultura's hideout, where the good guys stage a final showdown and win the treasure.

From the Lair of the Eagles to the Shrine of the Evil Bird, and from the papyrus to the buried treasure, the weenie forms a through-line and lends

FIGURE 15 Promotional art for *Perils of Nyoka* (1942). Author's collection.

the impression of progress toward a defined end. While 39013 keeps his plot turning by simply attacking different parts of the Granville empire, characters in *Nyoka* slowly but surely close in on the Tablets. In the sound serial, however, the appearance of unity must be tempered by the flexibility to arrange situations. Imposing a tight and substantive causal line would make for a rigid overall structure and tax screenwriters with obeying continuities instead of combining vivid perils. For viewers, it might overemphasize the retention of plot details from chapter to chapter at the cost of immediate and accessible thrills. The weenie's through-line, then, amounts to a loose chain of arbitrary links, with each location providing a cliffhanger and each piece of the puzzle contributing another object of endless contest. *Nyoka* gleefully celebrates its ad hoc storytelling during the ultimately pointless trip to the Tomb of the Moon God when Larry inadvertently triggers an unusual contraption:

LARRY: What's that?
NYOKA: Why, it's a sacrificial altar! Why, it's rising out of the floor.
LARRY: Are you thinking the same thing I am?
NYOKA: Yes.
LARRY: It makes me nervous.

Within moments Nyoka is knocked unconscious on that altar as it slowly rises toward a swinging blade and the episode ends. It is easy enough to imagine the screenwriters stretching this itinerary of happenstance ad infinitum or just as plausibly, and at any point, bringing it to a screeching halt. The fact is highlighted by Vultura's convenient unearthing of the shrine in her own backyard at the serial's end. The plot suddenly forges this final link in the chain because it has reached the fifteenth chapter. As a form devoted to regular catastrophe, the sound serial resists unity. Weenies, at their best, provide a pretense of coherence.

Nyoka stands out from the mass of serials, in part, because Republic's writers use the weenie plot and other devices to suggest structural integrity. The papyrus, for instance, helps establish a narrative architecture in Jenkins's sense of laying the adventure out in spatial terms, creating a loose map for us to follow. Each location implies a challenge that must be met for advancement to the next, and viewers can anticipate the upcoming stages. We know, for instance, that the Valley of the Tuaregs is not the final resting place of the Tablets, but that the inscription found there will bring the heroes nearer their goal. Further, Nyoka's recognition of her father in chapter 6, the team's discovery of the tablets in chapter 12, and Vultura's return to Wadi Bartha in the penultimate episode give the story a recognizable shape with points of advancement and closing symmetry. Neither these plot points nor the stations on the map are strictly connected to the intervening actions and perils; rather they mark out points of brief alignment between the makeshift accumulation of situations and the hunt.

Perhaps encouraged by the quest narrative, *Nyoka*'s screenwriters burnish the plot by paralleling heroes and villains and by reincorporating information between chapters. Similarities come forward as the film alternates between the two teams navigating the same map. Nyoka and Vultura are strong leaders of men, women who initiate action and willingly enter the fray. Their fathers each have a claim on the Tablets of Hippocrates: Professor Gordon discovered and then protected them as chief of the Tuaregs, while Vultura's father, we are told, conquered the entire desert including the Shrine of the Evil Bird where the treasure is buried. Larry and Cassib, the secondary hero and villain, flank Nyoka and Vultura. Cassib follows Vultura's plans, but he is more her equal than her henchman and shares equally in the treasure. Larry, the conventional masculine hero, joins forces with Nyoka after she rescues him from Vultura and Cassib. He, too, has equal designs on the Tablets, and the two develop a balanced partnership in which they surmount obstacles together.[10] In the final episode, crosscutting between Larry struggling with Cassib and Nyoka squaring off against Vultura cements the parallel. Symmetry even holds for tertiary characters. Vultura's henchman Maghreb mirrors Larry and Nyoka's sidekick Red. Satan (Emil Van Horn), Vultura's evil gorilla, is balanced by Nyoka's heroic capuchin monkey Jitters (Professor) and trusty dog Fang (Ace).

When characters return to previously charted spaces, they draw on their earlier experiences to solve new problems. In chapter 13 the heroes find themselves trapped in the Tuareg caves. Their elaborate escape plan involves stealing the key to open a sun-window in the mountain, details that feature in the cliffhanger that spans chapters 6 and 7. During the action, Larry evades his pursuers using a trapdoor that had provided the cliffhanger in chapter 4. Likewise, a passing mention in the very first chapter that Nyoka lives among the Bedouins pays off in the serial's climax when she rallies them to attack Cassib's stronghold. These interconnections stand out in a form where characters rarely learn from the most traumatic occurrences, and, like the parallels, they give *Nyoka* an uncommon aura of coherence. The Republic writing staff achieves structural sophistication without sacrificing flexibility.

Doubling and Tripling the Players: Plotting Multiple Characters

Daredevils and *Nyoka* present well-wrought versions of conventional serial plots, reaching toward overarching design while emphasizing immediacy. They both also multiply roles: *Nyoka* doubles the heroes and villains, and *Daredevils* triples its heroes and features two actors as the villain. The strategy extends each serial's situational possibilities simply by increasing the pool of characters to be imperiled, rescued, or challenged. It also poses creative problems of

narrative clarity by forcing filmmakers to make more characters readily identifiable without expanding exposition. *Nyoka* owes its relative complexity to
the convention of pairing female heroes with male counterparts. Serial heroines formed a novel trend in the sound era that also included Republic's *Zorro's
Black Whip* (Bennet and Grissel, 1944), *The Tiger Woman* (Bennet and Grissel, 1944), *Daughter of Don Q* (Bennet and Brannon, 1946), and *Panther Girl
of the Kongo* (Adreon, 1955), as well as Columbia's *Brenda Starr, Reporter* (Fox,
1945), Universal's *Perils of Pauline* (Taylor, 1933), and *Jungle Queen* (Collins
and Taylor, 1945). In *Nyoka's* predecessor *Jungle Girl* (Witney and English,
1941), Republic courted novelty by featuring a woman.[11] Witney recalls: "For
the first time since sound had come into the picture business, we had a serial
built around a girl. In the silent days there were Pearl White and Ruth Roland
serials. Now we were hoping this one would have the success that they had."
In every case, producers cautiously paired their new serial queens with male
heroes because they perceived their viewership as largely male. In casting a
female villain, Republic sought to inject *Nyoka* with further novelty. Witney
reveals his assumptions about the serial audience and about Vultura's appeal
when he comments: "I figured the little kids wouldn't notice, and the big kids
would go home and throw rocks at their sisters. She was just plain sexy."[12] Cassib, like Larry on the heroes' team, offsets an unconventional choice, and this
doubling undoubtedly planted the seeds for the film's extensive parallels. The
symmetry also helps viewers keep track of characters; men and women balance
one another on either side of the equation.

The *Daredevils* screenwriters set themselves a more difficult challenge in
casting three similarly athletic (and similarly dressed) male heroes. Preceded
by *The Lone Ranger Rides Again* (Witney and English, 1939), and followed by
Dick Tracy's G-Men (Witney and English, 1939) and *Zorro's Fighting Legion*,
Daredevils was Republic's only 1939 serial to feature original characters.
Lacking a presold property familiar to viewers, the film swiftly and cleanly
delineates its heroes. Chapter 1, *The Monstrous Plot*, defines the characters
according to their physical skills and introduces them with a spectacular and
efficient origin story. The three Daredevils are carnival performers, each with
a specialty tailored to the exact specifications of a serial world. Gene Town-
ley (Charles Quigley) is a high-diver, Tiny Dawson (Herman Brix) a (not
so tiny) strong man, and Bert Knowles (David Sharpe), an illustrious escape
artist. At the chapter's start, a carnival barker (Earl Hodgins) at Granville
Amusement Center introduces the Daredevils' act, providing exposition and
exhortation along the way. He draws his crowd by promising "the Daredevils
and their triple death-defying, hair-raising, world-famous stunt." The banner
behind him confirms that the Daredevils are the "World's Most Famous Stunt
Trio," imparting an air of renown to Republic's latest creation. Even before
their adventure begins, the trio seems destined for serial action. Their day job

consists of spectacular, if pointless, physical play, organized as though it were a cliffhanger.

The barker explains the mechanics as the Daredevils take their places. Tiny, "by himself and without any assistance," supports an eighty-foot ladder by biting a cable that runs between it and his teeth. Meanwhile, Gene climbs the ladder holding a flare that, when lit, "burns for exactly two minutes." Finally, the barker explains that Bert, "strapped in a standard approved straitjacket and with his feet chained together, will be hoisted, head downward," to the top of the structure. Gene lights the flare, and Bert has two minutes to escape his bonds while Tiny strains to hold the ladder upright. Bert slips from his straitjacket just as he reaches the top, and Gene tosses the still burning flare to the surprisingly shallow water tank below. Gene (doubled by Charles Soderberg, an actual carnival diver who was paid a hundred dollars for two takes) then executes a graceful dive into the tank, and Bert zip-lines down Tiny's cable into a safety net.[13] Drumrolls reverberate as Tiny releases the cable and shakes his head in relief (see figure 16).

The scene is as pure and direct an introduction to serial heroes as any ever filmed. The carnival huckster embodies the serial ethos; his spiel diagrams the impending peril for his audience, selling the preposterous with hyperbole. The members of the trio, meanwhile, are delineated only to the extent that the problem space requires it. They have crafted an infernal machine to be defeated by the combined efforts of a strongman, an escape artist, and a high-diver. As stunt performers, the team's job is to deliver physical thrills, and

FIGURE 16 The Daredevils' stunt show in *Daredevils of the Red Circle* (1939). Top row: the carnival barker (Earle Hodgins) announces the act; Tiny (Herman Brix) supports the eighty-foot ladder with his mouth; Gene (carnival diver Charles Soderberg) climbs to the high dive. Bottom row: Bert (stuntman Jimmy Fawcett) escapes from a straitjacket; Gene performs a high dive; Bert rides a zip line to safety.

they do so without even rudimentary causal logic. The burning time of Gene's flare sets an arbitrary deadline for Bert's escape. That escape may appear daring because he is hoisted high over the water tank, but there is no indication that he would fall should he fail. Likewise, Gene has no compelling reason to dive from the ladder, beyond proving that he can. Tiny struggles to hold the cable throughout, but apparently he is strong enough to support both Gene and Bert as they have a casual conversation on the ladder's platform. The stunt's operational logic is wholly contrived, but also vivid. In essence, the Daredevils' stunt act bares the device, and advertises the serial's wares, absent of any stakes. The heroes have already constructed and rehearsed the labyrinth; they are just waiting for a villain. Later in the episode, 39013 need only make one modification to render the procedure deadly: replace the water with gasoline.

This introduction establishes a repertoire of skills to be integrated into subsequent action scenes. Gene climbs to dangerous heights in episodes 2, 4, 6, 7, and 9 and falls from those heights in episodes 2 (into a pool of burning fuel) and 7 (shocked at the top of a utility pole). The title of episode 9, *Ladder of Peril*, sums up the serial's cut-to-fit dangers. At chapter's end, the villain pushes Gene's stepladder from high atop an industrial gas tank; who but a professional ladder climber could survive such a dirty deed? Bert practices his escape artistry in chapters 4 (slipping knots, removing hinges), 5 (filing bolts off of a locked door), 8 (slipping knots again), and chapter 10 (picking the lock to a cell door). Tiny calls on his brute strength to hold a door closed against four henchmen in chapter 4, break down a heavy cellar door in chapter 5, support a broken bridge strut in chapter 9, lift a heavy steel door in chapter 11, and punch through a solid wall to reveal the villain's secret passage in chapter 12. *Daredevils of the Red Circle* exemplifies the convenient malevolence of the serial world, where problems match the heroes' abilities to solve them.

Having unveiled the new heroes in action, the chapter devotes one additional expository scene to expand character traits. During a break between acts, the trio offers advice to Sammy (Robert Winkler), Gene's twelve-year-old kid brother and unofficial junior member of the Red Circle stunt team. Backstage, the Daredevils are Sammy's de facto parents, each eagerly contributing to the boy's education in adventure. Bert walks on his hands, explaining, "See, it's balance first, and strength afterwards." His demonstration effectively adds acrobatics to Bert's résumé of skills. When Tiny asks Sammy what he wants to do when he grows up, the boy's obliging answer fills in a few more details: "Well, first I want to be as strong as you, Tiny, then I want to be as fast as Bert, and then I want to have a lot of brains, like Gene." Sammy cannily distributes traits among the three heroes and models a juvenile perspective for the serial audience. Tiny's strength, an all-purpose asset, needs no embellishment. Bert's speed, balance, and flexibility, more adaptable traits than his ability to escape straitjackets, will be on display in virtually every fight and chase from here on out. Finally, we learn that Gene, who has the narrowest of all the skill-sets, possesses the brains for leadership and for any ratiocination that might come their way. This scene also establishes a shared trait, the trio's protective compassion for Sammy. In accordance with the form, these serial heroes are now fully fleshed out; they are functionally outfitted for perilous encounters. None of these characters need to be deepened over the remaining three hours and twenty-five minutes; they are known quantities. Together, they function more or less like a Swiss Army knife, each member of the team representing a different utility or blade. Furthermore, they are each recognizable in a fight; character and action are coterminous.

With neither a weenie to seek and protect, nor a recognizable master plan to foil, the plot of *Daredevils* lacks two of the conventional motivations for its heroes. Shipman's screenplay pins the stakes to the death of an innocent; Sammy is viciously murdered in the first third of chapter 1. As inciting actions go, Sammy's killing is unusually commanding because it is so unexpected. A boy among men, the character is set up as an obvious surrogate for the film's intended audience. Witney recalled that he preferred having "a child in the picture because we thought it would give our audience, which was supposed to be all kids, someone to identify with."[14] Though he doesn't perform any stunts, Sammy dons a pint-sized uniform emblazoned with the red circle to help out with the show, and he dreams of inheriting the prowess of his three dads. *Daredevils* clings to the sound serial's ground rules for pathos by isolating it in the first few episodes and efficiently converting it into heroic motivation. The film innovates by making the boy adventurer, a surefire figure of empathy for juvenile viewers, 39013's first and only individuated victim.

Witney and English depict Sammy's demise in two scenes. First, flames set by the villains to burn the amusement park to the ground close in on Sammy while he screams Gene's name. Tuffie, the trio's trusted dog, alerts the heroes just as the boy is crushed under a falling lamppost. Tiny lifts the post and Gene carries the boy from the conflagration, commanding, "We've got to get to a hospital, quick!" The dog-and-hero team performs admirably. Witney stages the next scene in a devastatingly simple single take. The camera begins on Tuffie, lying pathetically on the hospital floor, and pans rightward to reveal the Daredevils gathered beside Sammy's bed.[15] Kneeling by the bandaged child, Gene reassures his brother (and viewers): "You're going to be all right, Sammy. The doctor says that in a couple of days you'll be as good as new." William Lava's score of hopeful strings, uncharacteristic for any serial, lends Gene's words the air of promise. At Gene's prompting, Sammy offers a final repetition of his life goals.

> GENE: And remember, when you grow up you're going to be as strong as Tiny and as fast as Bert, remember?

SAMMY: Yeah. I'm going to have a lot of brains like you, Gene. (Sammy winces in pain.)
GENE: What is it?
SAMMY: It hurts!

The doctor puts his stethoscope to Sammy's heart and then nods to the nurse, who covers the boy's body with his blanket. Meanwhile, the camera reframes to a medium shot of Gene, bent over in sadness. Slowly Gene raises his head, fixing his gaze in the distance with determination as the strings rise and the image fades.

The scene stands out in the history of sound serials for both its poignancy and its surprising cruelty. In comforting his brother, Gene misleads the audience, dangling Sammy's full recovery before us. The iconography of Tuffie, the fearless canine companion alongside the stalwart heroes, seals the deal. They are bound to protect their ward under the generic contract of the boy-hood adventure tale. Yet when Sammy passes away, the solemnity of the scene and the lack of surprise in the room reveal that this has been a deathwatch all along. We are meant to feel the loss, but only briefly. That the writers use Sammy's death as an opportunity to repeat the heroes' traits and skills testifies to the form's calculated narrative economy. Similarly, the directors' decision to treat the scene in a single take exposes the serial's true priorities. The plot must move on; no time for tears. The Daredevils' first recue is an abject failure, but serial heroes do not linger over loss. They resolve to fight.

Gene's quest to avenge Sammy's death is more a catalyst than an ongoing motivation. In the next scene, the trio asks Granville for the job of tracking 39013. With the encouragement of his granddaughter Blanche (Carole Landis), whom they saved from the carnival fire, and aided by a mystery figure known as the Red Circle, they take up residence in the estate as a full-fledged security team. From this point, heroism is essentially their calling, and they are driven by the simple desire to do what is right: stop the bad guy. Even so, the situation powerfully triggers the recognition of innocence through its violation, emotionally amplifying the necessary melodramatic moral binaries. Within ten minutes, *Daredevils* achieves the clarity of a straightforward single-hero premise. The filmmakers creatively meet the challenge of intelligibility and direction using physical operations and functional pathos. *Daredevils* and *Nyoka* innovate from within conventional plot structures, setting and solving problems by mining the tradition; together they illustrate the generative potential of sound-serial story conventions at the height of the era.

A Surplus of Action, an Abundance of Ideas: Plotting the Chapter

These serials stand apart from the norm because they seem unusually busy and eventful. Broad plot structures help organize a serial's attractions and impart rudimentary unity, but sound serials are designed to deliver a frantic, action-filled present. Viewers engage with chapters first and foremost, while filmmakers concentrate their energies on crafting a cascade of compelling moments. *Daredevils* and *Nyoka* excel at small-scale narration, strategically fulfilling, departing from, and experimenting with the five-part format. In doing so, they deploy strategies to increase the apparent action in each chapter.

The master criminal and the weenie hunt create new opportunities at the chapter level. Cliffhangers and take-outs are fixed features, and alternation between exposition and action remains paramount. In *Daredevils* and *Nyoka*, these constants help filmmakers define their tasks by narrowing and focusing the field for innovation. Treating middle actions with the care of cliffhangers, multiplying the fatal gestures within the perils, combining or compressing expositional sequences, layering operational attractions, and jamming action scenes together all enliven the formula without straying from it.

Nyoka, for example, cycles through all five parts in nine of its chapters but renews the format by keeping characters in near-constant transit. *Nyoka*'s spatial narrative encourages middle-action ambushes, in which villains anticipate and interrupt the heroes' trajectory. In five chapters, after a brief bout of exposition (part b), Cassib or the Tuaregs lie in wait for Nyoka and Larry. They spring their trap at about the eight-minute mark and chase and/or capture a hero. If these traps necessarily frustrate any real progress along the trail of the weenie, they motivate scenes of escape and evasion that nonetheless maintain momentum. In episode 2, *Death's Chariot*, for instance, Cassib captures Nyoka after a two-minute and three-stunt chase (part C), Vultura interrogates her during part d, and our hero escapes, only to race Vultura's chariot off a cliff in part E. Alternatively, failed ambushes can provide an inconsequential middle action on the way to the inevitable peril. In chapter 4, *Ascending Doom*, the Tuaregs set up an interception (C) that forces the heroes to retreat, wait, and discuss their options (d) but ultimately find themselves ensnared in a deadly spike trap (part E).

It is a sturdy pattern that resembles the routine cycle of hostage taking and rescue in Columbia's Batman and Superman serials, but adapted to a kinetic spatialized plot. The doubled villains help further enliven the regular pattern because even proximate goals require travel. As the heroes race between Vultura's temple and Cassib's village to confront their enemies, they leave themselves open to a midpoint or cliffhanger ambuscade.

Nyoka's large-scale quest also pays off at the chapter level by mitigating static exposition; characters rarely stand still to make their plans. The grand hunt for the Tablets entails scenes of infiltration that fill stretches between major action sequences with scattered chases and takedowns. Heroes sneak into enemy strongholds (usually caves) for reconnaissance, rescues, and pursuit of the prize in eight of the chapters (1, 5–9, 13, and 14). Not content to repeat the device, *Nyoka's* screenwriters push it to the edge of parody. In chapter 6, *Human Sacrifice*, Jitters, Red's capuchin monkey, infiltrates Vultura's compound. He stealthily evades guards to deliver Nyoka and Larry a pencil and a tiny roll of paper, which they use to send a message back to Red. The entire operation takes four minutes and turns into the middle action when Jitters is chased and caught on his return trip. The little monkey's brave mission comes to naught, but it fills time with a novel approximation of suspense. By keeping characters on the move, and on the sneak, *Nyoka* vivifies the formulaic rotation through exposition and action.

The impression of raw energy evinced by *Nyoka* and *Daredevils* also derives from the Republic unit's intervention in chapter structure. More often than other serials, they extend, excise, and combine parts. Jamming situations together creates an overabundance of action. In *Daredevils*, chapters 2, 4, 7, and 9 expand the opening or closing action (A or E) and eliminate one of the regular expositional passages (b or d), a tactic aimed squarely at the restless juvenile audience. After Gene escapes the flooding tunnel in chapter 2, for example, he immediately raids the enemy operations on a nearby drilling platform, and this action carries on until the midpoint.

Even more unusual, chapters pile on urgent crises but resolve them offscreen. At the start of chapter 9, having escaped a burning oil platform in the take-out, the trio learns they must immediately deliver gas to the city plant by truck because the fire has shut down a pipeline. An unexplained disaster looms if the plant fails to ignite its furnaces before it depletes the rapidly dwindling fuel reserve. The Daredevils spring into action, commandeering a truck and racing toward the city. Henchmen counter by cutting supports to a bridge along the way, but Tiny holds the beams in place as Gene's truck passes overhead. The gas-plant emergency, with its forceful procedural itinerary and ticking clock, could blossom into a full-blown cliffhanger on its own. Instead, *Daredevils* embeds it as an extension of the chapter's take-out and then quickly dispenses with it. After the bridge peril, the story jumps to an exposition scene in Granville's office where Gene announces that trucks are now making regular gas deliveries, and the problem has been solved. The episode signals a problem space but elides its full resolution (the feverish race to beat the oil delivery deadline). This tactic reaches its apex in chapter 7 when henchmen trap Blanche in a flooding mine shaft. In chapter 8, her rescue is accomplished off-screen and mentioned in passing. En route back to the mansion she offers, "I'm all right, just a little wet," and the matter is dropped. All serials have incident-packed narrative compression, but *Daredevils* magnifies the effect by suggesting more action than it can show.

In chapter 3, *The Devil's Crucible*, *Nyoka* achieves the same thing by building the middle action into a cliffhanger-grade set piece and collapsing subsequent exposition. Cassib's troops attempt to ambush Nyoka and Larry on their way to the Lair of the Eagles, but they are swiftly outgunned. Our heroes give chase, only to find that the villains have beat them across a treacherous rope bridge and are now sawing away at the main support line. The falling rope bridge is a venerable cliffhanger situation, appearing in *Zorro's Fighting Legion*, *Winners of the West* (Beebe and Taylor, 1940), *Overland Mail* (Beebe and Rawlins, 1942), and *Jack Armstrong* (Fox, 1947) among many others. *Nyoka* rather flamboyantly expends the gag in a middle action. Witney elaborates the peril as fully as any cliffhanger with cutaways to the fraying and snapping rope, dynamic angles of the bridge from below and receding into the distance, and tight close-ups of Nyoka's terrified reaction. Five shots depict the catastrophic moment (see figure 17):

1) The rope gives way.
2) Nyoka's face drops out of the frame.
3) The bridge falls away from the camera with Nyoka holding tight in long shot.

FIGURE 17 The middle action of chapter 3 of *Perils of Nyoka* (1942) is elaborated like a cliffhanger. Top row: The rope snaps and Nyoka (Kay Aldridge) falls out of frame. Bottom row: Three shots depict the bridge's collapse and Nyoka's survival.

4) The bridge collapses again and swings out of frame in a low angle.
5) Nyoka hits the cliff wall, still gripping the bridge, in another low angle.

The first four shots vigorously depict an apparently fatal trap. The fifth shot works like a take-out; a previously unseen angle reveals that our hero survives by bouncing feet first against the cliff. The sequence condenses calamitous demise and miraculous escape into a few seconds.

Having expanded and intensified the middle action, *The Devil's Crucible* all but eliminates the usual expositional sequence (part d) and rushes into the cliffhanger. Cassib might well be speaking for the filmmakers when he tells his men "we have lost much time" immediately after the bridge sequence. Leaving one guard at the mouth of the cave, the villains investigate the Tunnel of Bubbling Death (a set recognizable from *Zorro's Fighting Legion*). The brief scene demonstrates the hazards of this problem space when an explosion blows one of Cassib's men to the cave floor. Our expectations are confirmed moments later when Larry and Nyoka enter the perilous chamber. Two minutes after Nyoka scrambles from the collapsed bridge, gunfire rings out as she and Larry confront a henchman. Larry declares, "This is going to be dangerous!" and Cassib and his men attack. Jets of flame and steam embellish the fracas, which climaxes with Nyoka apparently plunging into an exploding pit.

Both movies achieve distinction among serials by selectively reconfiguring the standard formula to disperse action across the chapter. *Daredevils* and *Nyoka* feather exposition into fights and chases to create unusually long stretches of conflict. *Nyoka's* fifth chapter, *Fatal Seconds*, illustrates Republic's aptitude for handling the form. *Fatal Seconds* stuffs part b with machinations and largely dispenses with part d, the second expositional sequence. During the early exposition Vultura initiates the Tuareg attack, which forms the middle action, while the chief sets the cliffhanger trap. Vultura "calls down the wrath of our great fire god" amid sacramental blazes and tribal drumming in the Tuareg chamber, and the chief (Nyoka's amnesiac father), suspicious of the "goddess," secretly places a bomb to protect the sacred inscriptions. The middle action arrives somewhat late (near the ten-minute mark), by which point Fang and Jitters have teamed up to warn our heroes of the Tuaregs' assault. The ensuing fight (C) flows directly into the cliffhanger (E) with exposition seeded along the way.

As her team exchanges fire with the Tuaregs, Nyoka announces her plan to infiltrate the caves while the warriors are distracted. Mort Glickman's brassy theme pounds away as she restates her goals and motivations between gunshots: "The papyrus says the inscription room is behind the lion statue in a Tuareg cave corridor. This is my chance to get it. . . . I must find my father, and the inscription may lead me to him." On her race to the cave, Nyoka slays two pursuers (one with a spear) and dives onto the Tuareg sentry (stunt courtesy of David Sharpe in a Nyoka costume). A single-shot crosscut of Vultura ordering Cassib and Maghreb to find the inscription primes viewers for confrontation. In place of stolid conversation, the sequence is paced for action, firing off exposition on the run.

Fatal Seconds climaxes with a cascade of potential cliffhangers. In the final two minutes Cassib seizes Nyoka outside the secret chamber, and Vultura orders Maghreb to silence her screams. As Maghreb raises his arm to strike her down, Larry interrupts the fatal gesture, the peril resolved. When Nyoka investigates the chamber she unknowingly ignites the bomb fuse. Meanwhile, Larry fires his last shot and enters a life-or-death struggle with the knife-wielding heavy. Maghreb throws Larry back on a rock and, towering over him, lunges off-frame with his blade. A cut reveals Larry dodging away in the nick of time. Nyoka discovers the inscription just as the fuse runs out and, bang, rubble pelts the camera. The serial teases viewers by building Nyoka's capture and Larry's near-stabbing into vivid hair's-breadth escapes. Where other serials labor to produce a single climactic peril, *Fatal Seconds* throws two away en route to the bomb blast.

The sound serial's narrative locomotive runs on a five-part schedule, making regular stops between stretches of action. Republic's writers rearranged the track. Always an economical formula for delivering three situations per chapter, the five-part format provided a basis for originality. Tight budgeting, flat-fee distribution, and a predictable audience lowered the risks of production; serials could reliably generate a modest profit for the studios. Such stability would seem to limit the value of product differentiation beyond basic premise or presold property. Once exhibitors had signed up for *Superman* or *Batman*, there was little reason to experiment. Indeed, serial artistry tends toward refinement rather than invention. Yet in the late 1930s and 1940s, Republic exceeded commercial requirements by honing formulas into exceptionally engaging movies. Serial form ensures that chapters travel efficiently between situations, and *Daredevils* and *Nyoka* breeze through the stations, gathering momentum along a sloping track that ends on the edge of a cliff.

Creative Imperilment and Narrative Revision: Two Innovative Sequences

Without ever breaking the rules, *Daredevils* and *Nyoka* present distinctively complex situations. Our discussion has focused on patterns of storytelling, but both films construct bravura stand-alone sequences as well. This kind of innovation doesn't easily translate into repeatable practice, but it speaks to the way convention spurs creativity. Two final examples illustrate this inventiveness.

Chapter 10 of *Nyoka* stages an intricate, high-stakes, dilemma, and chapter 11 of *Daredevils* wages an ostentatious game of narration that affects our understanding of the grand story.

In the usually innocuous part b, *Treacherous Trail* introduces a startlingly vivid situation drawn from the tradition of medical melodrama. Having rescued Nyoka and her father from a burning tent, Larry, in his all-but-forgotten capacity as a medical doctor, diagnoses the injured Professor Gordon. Typically frank and clear-cut dialogue establishes the parameters of the problem:

> LARRY: It's a complicated case. The old fracture left a bone fragment pressing on the brain. That causes loss of memory. Now this injury has increased the pressure until he is practically paralyzed. . . .
>
> NYOKA: Can you do anything for him?
>
> LARRY: Yes, I'll operate as soon as he recovers from the shock. I can remove the bone fragment. That should restore his memory up to the time of his first injury.
>
> PROF. CAMPBELL: Do you suppose he will be able to remember everything that happened during the time he was with the Tuaregs?
>
> LARRY: No, I'm afraid that part of his life will be a complete blank.
>
> TORINI: But then he won't remember where the tablets are.
>
> LARRY: No, but I could give him an injection of adrenaline before I operate. That might revive him enough to let him talk. The shock might prove fatal.

The others swiftly reject endangering Nyoka's father, and Larry prepares an operating room in the back of the cave. Efficiency heightens the situation's straight-faced preposterousness. As a melodramatic convention, amnesia conveniently combines narrative obstacle with pathos and the enigma of past trauma. Mervyn LeRoy's adaptation of the popular novel *Random Harvest* (1942), for instance, uses the situation where restoration of one set of memories entails the loss of another to weave a superbly affective romantic melodrama. *Nyoka* impetuously employs the plot device not to explore the emotional potential of forgotten love but to momentarily obstruct the treasure hunt. The situation is gloriously bald.

Nyoka conceives of the human brain as a cliffhanger trap. Larry, whose medical background hasn't been mentioned since a passing comment in the first episode, faces the surgical equivalent of a problem space: saving the patient means sacrificing the cure for cancer and unspeakable riches. The ethical quandary doesn't occur to any of the characters, for their world is black and white. Only Torini (Tristram Coffin), Vultura's agent who has infiltrated the heroes' ranks, values treasure more than life. He secretly administers the potentially lethal dose of adrenaline and learns of the Tomb of the Moon God.

The drama of Professor Gordon's brain injury is a screenwriting flourish merited in part by the overarching story. The situation leads to the next clue in the hunt, to the revelation of Torini's treachery and his subsequent death, and to the return of Nyoka's father. The chapter temporarily foregrounds long-range story elements. As usual, though, moment-to-moment action rules the world. *Treacherous Trail*'s expanded b is balanced by dropping d, that is, moving directly from the middle action into the cliffhanger. Gordon's operation is not depicted. Though it is potent with suspense, an extended surgery scene with emotional repercussions lies well outside the sound serial's lexis. Instead, action arrives ten minutes into the chapter when Red and Jitters disarm and fight Torini. As the turncoat flees, Larry abandons his patient on the operating table and joins the pursuit. Torini's demise in the cliffhanger car wreck results in momentary narrational complexity, as no one apart from the viewer knows about the Tomb of the Moon God. This shift in the hierarchy of knowledge, a tool for suspense and mystery, is almost immediately abandoned at the start of episode 11, *Unknown Peril*. Upon reviving, Gordon recalls the last thing he saw before losing his memory: an inscription with the words "Tomb of the Moon God." Gordon is well, the clue is revealed, and the game resets as another spy reports the location to Vultura. The amnesia plot, a melodramatic nugget, briefly boosts narrative momentum only to be resolved and forgotten within a few minutes of screen time. In its creative eclecticism (brain surgery interrupted by a horse-and-car chase), *Nyoka* exhibits the interplay of ambition and limitation embodied by the best serials.

Daredevils saves its most flamboyant storytelling for the penultimate episode, a chapter dominated by flashbacks to previous adventures. Usually the bane of serial fans, economy or retrospect chapters stretch stories by repeating footage from earlier episodes as the characters find an occasion to reminisce. Because of their speed and fluidity, the fights and stunts in *Daredevils* actually merit repeating, which makes recycling more forgivable. In this instance, the flashback format also becomes an occasion for solving enigmas. As in the sequences from *Batman* and *Batman and Robin* discussed at the start of this chapter, *Daredevils* develops narrative complexity from the serial's tendency to reframe and revise events. But where the Columbia serial isolates its experiment, *Daredevils* weaves it into a long-range pattern. In chapter 10, Tuffie attacks and unmasks 39013, who goes into hiding while the Daredevils rescue the real Granville from his cell. Chapter 11, *The Red Circle Speaks*, finds the heroes relaxing, discussing events. After Gene recounts the first episode, he announces: "One thing more, however, still remains a mystery. The identity of the Red Circle." Since their arrival at the Granville estate, a cloaked figure has been helping the trio by leaving clues and warnings marked with the Daredevils' own trademark, a red circle. Blanche solves the mystery. Through a flashback to previously unseen events, she explains that shortly after the

Daredevils arrived she detected 39013's disguise. In a final variation on the transformation scene, the criminal removes his makeup while seated at his desk, the camera panning away and cutting to Blanche's reaction shot to cover the substitution. After blindfolding her and driving her around to obscure the location of his cell, 39013 brings Blanche to visit her grandfather. The criminal secures her silence by displaying his gas-pellet device and threatening to kill Granville should she reveal her secret. The film returns to the present, and Blanche earnestly explains: "I knew I had to help and realized I must do so in such a manner that even 39013 wouldn't suspect it was I. That's how I came to use your own symbol and became the mysterious Red Circle."

By feature standards, Blanche's flashback revelation is remarkably free of psychological development; it is a purely expositional exercise. But for serial audiences it is a highly unusual moment for several reasons. For one, the mystery figure turns out to be a major character, the serial girl no less, with whom we are well acquainted. In contrast to the usually anonymous character actor or indistinguishable member of a roster of suspects (as in *The Lone Ranger* and *Zorro's Fighting Legion*), Blanche has been front and center. For another, the flashback encourages us to reimagine far-flung events. At very least we can search back through our memory of the series to find a plausible moment for her discovery and confrontation with 39013. Attentive viewers are cued to reconstruct her actions as the Red Circle.

The filmmakers have reinforced the enigma throughout the serial's run, highlighting the mystery. In chapter 9, 39013 attempts to trap the Red Circle by planting a false plan, but she delivers her note using a mousetrap contraption that rings the kitchen buzzer while she is with the trio in Granville's security office. Such scenes flag narrative gaps and information withheld, drawing attention to questions that Blanche's confession now plausibly answers. Of course, this risks throwing inconsistencies into relief. Why, for instance, doesn't Blanche confide to the trio when they are away from the house? Why would she fecklessly enter traps that she should easily foresee? The mass of serials, protected by the enormity of their incoherence, never tempt such questions. That *Daredevils* fails to match the sophistication of a feature-film whodunit should surprise no one. But in seeding information across the long haul, *Daredevils* foregrounds narrational processes and engages skills of comprehension rare to the sound serial. By planting this embellishment in an economy episode, the emptiest of all serial conventions, the screenwriters once again demonstrate the kinship of routine craft and artfulness.

Daredevils of the Red Circle is a standout Republic serial, but it is by no means a perfect film. Its most unforgivable defect is its treatment of Snowflake (both the character name and stage name of the African American character actor Fred Toones). A demeaning stereotype, Snowflake is the Granville estate's butler and all-around comic simpleton. His presence helps throw into relief how lily-white the world of serial heroes really is. Racist stereotypes were not rare in serials, but they were rarely so gratuitously mean. As melodramas, serials regularly employ racial typing as shorthand for Manichaeism (Middleton's orientalist portrayal of Ming the Merciless and Henry Brandon's Fu Manchu are blatant and famous examples). Perhaps because comic characters are dispensable accessories to the serial world, Snowflake's stereotyped antics seem even more offensive. Derived from vaudeville and minstrelsy more than from melodrama, his character is never subsumed to the project of moral legibility. Instead, he is a dispensable object of ridicule, a joke. In the film's final image, Snowflake catches his head in a sliding door while the white heroes laugh at him. It is an uncanny moment for the contemporary viewer in the way it dissolves our empathy for and alignment with the heroes. What was a routine unfunny gag in 1939 has become an alienating parting shot, a glaring reminder of the ubiquity of American racism, and serials' participation in it.

Conclusion

Through detailed discussion of serial plotting in a few standout productions, this chapter indicates something of the form's range and depth. *Daredevils* and *Nyoka* conform to the conventions that ensure minimal coherence and maximum excitement in most serials. They also exploit the potential of this formula to move beyond rudimentary storytelling. At their best, these films reveal a group of filmmakers setting challenges for themselves and arriving at novel solutions. They strive for the impression of narrative unity without hobbling situational plotting, complicate networks of characters while maintaining clarity, and fold necessary exposition into extended stretches of action. The sound serial's narrowly repetitive form, which throws variation into striking relief, might have helped encourage invention and refinement. Viewers schooled in conventions at weekly matinees could perhaps recognize a game well played, and appreciate the storyteller's work, while having their expectations seamlessly satisfied. A similar dynamic informs film style in the serial. Directors, editors, stunt choreographers, and other production personnel generally shaped action according to functional standards, but they could also configure image and sound into powerfully engaging cinematic moments.

6

Film Style and the
Art of Formula

• •

The sound serial's storytelling conventions helped producers grind out products that offered a nominal degree of action and excitement, but these same formulas held specific potentials and challenges for ambitious filmmakers. Conventions of film style were similar. The great majority of sound serials are formally undistinguished; they cling to the minimal adequacies of studio-era continuity. Dialogue exposition scenes tend to be sparse affairs, built from as few camera setups as feasible. In scenes of action and peril, however, serials could be breathtakingly original. Unlike most of their feature-film colleagues, serial makers were under constant pressure to deliver vivid fights, chases, cliffhangers, and rescues. Working intensively on a narrow set of cinematic problems encouraged specific areas of formal refinement and set the conditions for experimentation and finesse.

The baseline of serial film form for conversations and dramatic scenes is well illustrated by Larry and Nyoka's first meeting in chapter 1 of *Perils of Nyoka*, *Desert Intrigue*. Witney crams all seven members of the "good side" into a tight master shot with conversing characters near the foreground. He offers a cut-in to medium shot when Nyoka addresses the group, but this composition does double duty when Larry enters the frame to respond. Lacking the time or budget for a standard over-the-shoulder shot/reverse-shot conversation scene, Witney simply maintains the medium framing as the two characters stare vaguely in one another's direction and deliver their lines. The scene has none of the nuance or dramatic rhythm that an interchange of close-ups between leads might offer.

The third camera position is reserved for medium shots of shifty-eyed Torini, to remind us that he is Vultura's mole. Witney sticks to this pattern (master shots with cut-ins to Torini) for most of the heroes' exposition scenes until the traitor is exposed in episode 10. Serial filmmakers aim for passable craft; they seem content to deliver information cleanly and without elaboration.

We should expect little more from a production trend that habituated artists to cheap efficiency. As noted in the first chapter, serial production schedules ran only four to six weeks, with directors getting shots for multiple episodes on a single set at any one time.[1] There would be no time to shape performance, lighting, or composition to the storytelling aim of each scene. The circumstances required proficiency. Against this backdrop, even modestly expressive style becomes prominent. Most serials mix rough-and-ready competence with occasional scenes of formal flair, made all the more impressive by production constraints. Isolated sequences remind us that serial directors were not poor filmmakers by any stretch. Vultura's introduction in *Nyoka*, for instance, merits five camera setups and twelve shots, including some mobile framing. Witney and his art director, Russell Kimball, stretch the space of an imposing establishing shot through the simple device of placing a desk and chair in the foreground, seemingly yards away from Vultura's platform at the rear. A match-on-action cut sweeps the viewer forward to a medium shot of Vultura rising into the frame, the neck of her dress ornamented by a bejeweled snake. This conventional piece of scene dissection contrasts with the all-purpose master shot style. Both the expansive view of the throne room and the details of Vultura's costume reflect pomposity and power (see figure 18).

Witney then offers a quick three-shot interchange between Vultura and her pet gorilla, Satan, as she chastises him for pulling at his chain. Cutting imbues their relationship with more intimacy than Nyoka and Larry's talky introduction. The vivid revelation of Vultura and her hench-ape are serial attractions, and so merit more care in crafting.

FIGURE 18 A simple but effective cut inward communicates Vultura's (Lorna Gray) power and pomposity in *Perils of Nyoka* (1942).

Occasionally expressive passages might help offset a chapterplay's threadbare style, but the form was capable of much more. Serial filmmakers show themselves to be at least as innovative as their feature-film colleagues in specialized areas. Through close analysis of cinematic technique in cliffhangers and action sequences, this chapter makes the case that serial formula supported artistic achievement. As in the previous chapter, *Daredevils of the Red Circle* and *Perils of Nyoka* serve as prime examples of Republic's facility with convention and demonstrate the serial's creative potentials. Stylistic sophistication, however, was not limited to a single producer. Though Columbia's "golden age" entries rarely rise above practical standards, the Universal unit achieved unmatched proficiency in a practice peculiar to the form: reediting stock footage. Before returning to our case studies, we first explore the remarkable work of Universal's editors.

Dexterous Bricolage: Appropriation in *The Great Alaskan Mystery*

Recycling and appropriation are endemic to the serial. Reediting cliffhangers for take-outs required filmmakers, and perhaps viewers, to approach situations as malleable, open to revision. At the same time, stock footage helped ease the severe discrepancy between depicted action and production resources. Altered and repurposed, identical events and images recur from chapter to chapter and serial to serial. Both practices validate speed and vividness at the price of originality. All three producers exploited this flexibility to their advantage, but Universal's expansive storehouse of production materials made the studio unparalleled in the aesthetic of appropriation. Even the high-budget blockbuster *Flash Gordon* retreads sets from *Frankenstein* (James Whale, 1931) and *The Mummy* (Karl Freund, 1932) and footage of Charles Lindbergh's landing in Paris and other newsreels. Universal reached beyond its studio walls to borrow both props and footage from the Fox sci-fi feature *Just Imagine* (David Butler, 1930), including the serial's most bizarre spectacle, Ming's Oracle of Teyo. Featured in the opening credits of every chapter, and shoehorned into the plot of episode 2, the Oracle consists of a master shot of thirty scantily clad chorines cavorting around a vaguely Asian demon statue that lifts dancers into the air. Editors display the dance on Ming's spaceograph screens and bind it to the characters' environment using eyeline matches. It ornaments an already stylized production design, embellishing Mongo with yet another bit of visual strangeness. However, the studio's dexterity with rearranging stock elements was most important to lower-budget, run-of-the-mill efforts, where they provide the very foundation of the action.

The Great Alaskan Mystery (Collins and Taylor, 1944) stands at the apex of Universal's experiments in bricolage. In chapter 2, *Thundering Doom*, the editing team, supervised by Norman Cerf, displays mastery of a little-noted area of formal achievement. Rather than draw on the stock library to flesh out standard situations with explosions or car crashes, the filmmakers construct their story around the spectacular footage of another film. Deemed "fair" by the *Exhibitor*, *Alaskan Mystery* offers a serviceable weenie-plot with hero John Hudson (Milburn Stone) protecting Dr. Miller's (Ralph Morgan) paratron ray from Nazi agents.[2] After the third chapter, most action is set in and around a radium mine in Saskatch, Alaska, which features the conventional assortment of standing sets and studio-ranch locations. *Thundering Doom*, by contrast, takes place on forbidding arctic tundra and in glacial waters. Shipwrecked on an iceberg at the chapter's start (which uses footage from Frank Borzage's 1937 *History Is Made at Night*), the heroes brave the elements in search of civilization. They pilot an ice floe through freezing water, rescue their sled dog from one hungry polar bear, and lose a team member to the claws of another. Meanwhile, the Nazis narrowly escape a spectacular cave-in that consumes their sled and dogs. Fortunately, the skilled aviator Ruth Miller (Marjorie Weaver), the professor's daughter, locates the stranded crew and alerts nearby Inuit villagers who scramble to the rescue on a flotilla of kayaks. Unfortunately, the imperiled heroes' iceberg calves and flips just before they can be reached.

The chapter's location work, breathtaking by any standard and simply astonishing for a sound serial, derives from *S.O.S. Iceberg* (Tay Garnett, 1933), a feature that Universal coproduced with German interests as part of the short-lived Deutsche Universal-Film corporation. Famous for being Leni Riefenstahl's last film as an actress, the German version, *S.O.S. Eisberg* (Arnold Franck), and the English-language version were produced simultaneously, shooting in Umanak on the west coast of Greenland and in Switzerland and Berlin. Though they share all but one actor, the two are quite different films. Franck poetically sets the explorers' privation against a majestic, lyrical treatment of the landscape, while Garnett weaves a more straightforward, action-packed, adventure yarn. The Greenland footage had already received two distinctive treatments before *Alaskan Mystery* shuffled it once again.

The job of matching *S.O.S. Iceberg* dominates every aspect of the chapter. Maurice Tombragel and George Plympton, the screenwriters, pen *Thundering Doom* around the footage, compressing spectacular and sweeping action into an eighteen-minute chronology. Since the *S.O.S. Iceberg* expedition features four main characters, the serial's heroes, Jim Hudson and Dr. Miller, fill out their party with Bosun (Edgar Kennedy), the ship's boatswain, and a self-proclaimed "greenhorn businessman" named Grey (William Ruhl). Neither character continues beyond the next episode. Grey wears a beard that helps him resemble Max Holzboer's character in the original, while Bosun cuts a hefty profile similar to Gibson Gowland's. Grey also outfits the group to match the feature, providing heavy furs and a dogsled that he happens to have in his cabin aboard the sinking ship. The directors, Lewis Collins and Ray Taylor, stage reaction shots and brief conversation scenes of the principals before rear-screen projection and on a soundstage with artificial snowdrifts. Norman Cerf's editing team achieves continuity between the parts using eyeline matches, matches on action, and other conventions of scene dissection.

The serial's editors rarely lift unaltered sequences of shots from *S.O.S. Iceberg*, even when stretches of original footage might efficiently suit their needs. For instance, when Inuit villagers react to Ruth's plane as she comes in for a landing, *Thundering Doom* serves up twenty shots from the feature film's equivalent sequence, but they have been trimmed and reordered. Where the original presents four quick reaction shots of people on the ground, followed by the plane making a banking turn, the serial offers two of the reactions and a shot of the plane from just slightly earlier in the feature, creating a new eyeline match and reinforcing the point-of-view structure. The serial then picks up the remaining reactions but trims off the first half of the banking-plane shot to pick up the pace. Six more identical shots of villagers follow, with one elimination and three trims. The editors compress the already fast-tempo original to fit the serial's hectic rhythm. *Thundering Doom* then drops two very brief shots, keeps two, drops three, keeps two more, then drops another two. This squeezes a fifty-three-second montage down to twenty-four seconds and makes the alternation between seaplane and shore more insistent by streamlining reaction shots. The editors could have easily imported a single portion of the original, especially in a passage without any recognizable characters, but instead they sift and rearrange. For Universal's editing staff, the task of appropriation involved continuous and fine-grained reshaping.

The chapter's most ambitious sequences insert serial characters directly into the feature's situations. Coordinated production design and careful framing help blend the actions, allowing editors to craft new continuity. The filmmakers never rest with simply replacing shots; they restructure action rather than borrow it. Where *S.O.S. Iceberg* lingers in long shot as the cast laconically performs seemingly dangerous feats, *Thundering Doom* redundantly identifies characters and clarifies their actions. The feature's two-minute sequence of the team piloting an ice floe offers a scant four lines of dialogue and builds suspense by cutting between the passengers and a hungry polar bear. The serial reduces the event to fifty-three seconds and adds exposition. Upon reaching the ice, our heroes swiftly state their predicament and their plans:

HUDSON: It looks like all we can do is try to make shore on one of these floes.
GREY: The ice will melt from under us. We haven't got a chance without a boat.
HUDSON: Well, we've got to try; we can't stay here.

Where the feature's characters act, the serial's also explain. In lieu of the polar bear, *Thundering Doom* manufactures tension by restating the basic situation. Midway through the trip, Collins and Taylor stage this exchange:

GREY: This floe is about ready to crack to pieces, we'll never make it.
HUDSON: We better make it. Look, we head for that big iceberg right over there.

Dialogue economically transforms the footage into a serial situation and intensifies repetition. These brief conversations, both framed in medium long shot in high-key light before rear projection, also better individuate the characters than *S.O.S. Iceberg*. The feature suggests layers of motivation and tension among the explorers by leaving concerns and proximate aims unstated. The serial spells out goals point by point, keeping viewers alert to the pattern of problem and solution.

The same is true for purely visual events. Cerf's staff breaks up stunts from *S.O.S. Iceberg* with cut-ins that detail character action. When the heroes are forced to leap a gap in the ice, the feature is actually more efficient, delivering three shots compared to the serial's six. *Thundering Doom*'s elaboration emphasizes physical procedure, problem solving, and individual performers. The original handles the event with a master take broken by a single cutaway. The expedition leader, played by Sepp Rist, jumps across the breach in long shot, and then Holzboer's character, still on the bank and framed in long shot, tosses a ski off-frame, which Rist catches, via match on action, in a return to the first composition. The director holds on this take until Holzboer also clears the gap (see figure 19).

In contrast, the serial breaks the master shot three times. First, editors replace Holzboer's ski toss with a closer shot of Grey, who extends the simple action by swinging his arms in a wider arc. Instead of returning to the master, we move to a medium shot of Hudson catching the ski and turning away. This matches expertly with a return to the feature's master shot in which the leader

FIGURE 19 Characters leap across ice floes in three shots, shown in these four frames from *S.O.S. Iceberg* (1933).

completes his turn and plunges the ski into the snow. The serial then cuts once more to Grey, picking up his ski pole and crossing out of the shot, before completing the take from the feature depicting the second leap. In multiplying perspectives, the serial unit turns a passing, if spectacular, obstacle into a fully articulated and tactile process (see figure 20). The method for moving equipment between floes, and Grey's repurposing of his ski pole as a tool to stabilize his landing, are transformed into crisp procedural details. The chapter more fully embodies steps of throwing, catching, jumping, and landing, shaping them into imitable actions. Once again, the Universal staff refines a cost-saving technique into engaging, rhythmic serial filmmaking.

Thundering Doom's cliffhanger climax provides a final example of masterly constructive editing. Each version of the film concludes with Inuit kayakers rescuing the stranded heroes from their iceberg, but they develop the situation differently. Franck's *S.O.S. Eisberg*, in keeping with its more somber and majestic approach, offers spectacular views of the kayaks speeding toward the berg and brief scenes showing the survivors' relief. They then watch the berg calve and flip from the safety of a rescue boat. *S.O.S. Iceberg* frames a race to the rescue by intercutting the kayaks with views of the calving berg and the survivors in a collapsing cave. *Variety* identified the melodramatic situation as "a duplication of the chase in *Birth of a Nation*" and complained that it bore "no relationship to the utter simplicity and conviction of the prior action."[3] For serial filmmakers, this melodrama becomes a point of departure, a situation to be amplified. Ruth joins the Inuit, guiding them to the survivors in her plane. Our heroes verbalize their dilemma and its possible solution:

> DR. MILLER: We're turning over! (*Shot of calving iceberg.*)
> HUDSON: A piece breaks off like that, we're goners.
> BOSUN: Oh, I hope them Eskimos have speedboats.

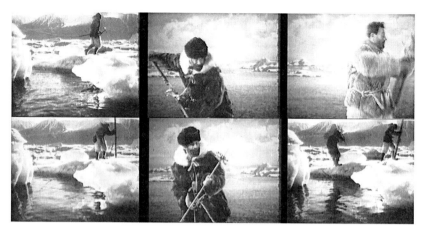

FIGURE 20 The *S.O.S. Iceberg* (1933) leap becomes a six-shot sequence in *The Great Alaskan Mystery* (1944). Top row: A shot from the original film is followed by cuts showing Grey (William Ruhl) throwing and Hudson (Milburn Stone) catching a ski. Bottom row: A shot from the original film is interrupted by a shot of Grey preparing to make the jump.

With a problem space vividly established, the editors assemble shots of the kayak fleet, of the German flyer Ernst Udet's airplane from *S.O.S. Iceberg*, and of Ruth piloting in front of a rear-screen sky. High-angle shots of the boats seamlessly transform into point-of-view shots from Ruth's perspective. Cutting brings together footage from across the feature of various icebergs splitting and turning, and closer views of the heroes falling out of the frame, to convey the cataclysm. At the start of chapter 3, *Battle in the Clouds*, the filmmakers repurpose the feature's earlier scene of Udet pulling Rist from his ill-fated swim as Ruth's timely rescue of Hudson at the very moment the Inuit reach the others. In constructing a new crisis from received footage, editors cleverly consolidate events and create multiple lines of simultaneous action. Where *S.O.S. Iceberg* gives us a straightforward race to the rescue, the serial expands it into a hyperbolic double climax. Recutting stock footage, rightly regarded as a bargain-basement B-film technique, was raised to virtuosic heights at Universal.

Fighting with Distinction: Republic's Stunt Team

Like Universal, Republic excelled in a distinctive area of serial filmmaking. Where *The Great Alaskan Mystery*, at least in its opening episodes, leveraged the studio's collection of high-budget footage to forge scenes of unusual grandeur, Republic's unit worked within tighter limits to achieve spectacle on a human scale. Perhaps the studio's greatest asset was its stunt team, which allowed directors and editors to construct the movement of bodies in space with consummate grace. *Daredevils*, with its three heroes who act in unison, reveals fine-grained

mastery of a formula staple: the fistfight. Fisticuffs were an obligatory component of almost every serial. Columbia and Universal tended to cede pacing and
presentation of fights to casually organized stuntmen, covered by a more or less
distant camera, but Republic, especially in films directed by Witney and English,
developed the form into a precise articulation of force and agility.

Ford Beebe and Ray Taylor's *The Green Hornet* (1939) offers a good example of Universal's fighting style. The serial as a whole places less emphasis on
fisticuffs as an attraction. Beebe and Taylor tend to stage brief scuffles that
interrupt standoffs or lead to car chases. When the Green Hornet (Gordon
Jones) and Kato (Keye Luke) fight, they tend to struggle with henchmen in
close formation in long to medium-long shots. For instance, in chapter 5, *Time
Bomb*, the hero fights three racketeers in a garage as (unbeknownst to the
Green Hornet) the clock runs out on a bomb in a nearby car. The Green Hornet punches out two assailants; then a third, armed with a wrench, attacks. As
they struggle, Kato rushes toward the garage, and a gun heavy revives enough
to take aim at the Green Hornet. Kato arrives just in time to blast the heavy
with his gas gun. The Green Hornet overpowers the wrench heavy just before
the garage clock reaches 11:00 and the car explodes.

Beebe and Taylor cover the fifty-second fight in twenty-six shots, for an
average shot length of just under two seconds. The speed of cutting, though,
does not guarantee kinetic engagement. Most of these cuts are away from the
fight to intensifying details like the garage clock inching its way to the deadline, a heavy preparing to enter the fray, or Kato rushing to the rescue. The
physical struggle between the Green Hornet and the henchmen receives little cinematic elaboration. Beebe and Taylor film the action from three camera positions: one long and two mediums. Shot scale is dictated by practical
concerns. When the Green Hornet grapples with a single assailant, medium
shots prevail. If a third participant should enter the frame, or the action occurs
closer to the ground, the editor selects a long shot.

Since the camera constantly reframes during the fight, the dominant impression is that cinematographers are working just to capture the staged event in
an efficient and legible way (see figure 21). Only three cuts lend punctuation .

FIGURE 21 Three frames from a single shot in *The Green Hornet* (1939), which show the
camera tilting and panning to keep up with the action.

and emphasis to moments in the fight. When the Green Hornet swings two of his attackers to the ground in medium shot, a match on action to long shot allows us to follow movement to the floor, and the graphic change accentuates the fight's development. More effective is a cut from medium to long shot that punctuates the Green Hornet's left hook to a heavy's chin. The edit is timed with an audible snap on the Foley sound effects track, and it is one of the few affective moments in the fracas. The third articulating edit is something of a jump cut. When the wrench heavy enters the frame and raises his weapon to strike, we move suddenly from a long shot to a medium shot that brings both figures closer, obscuring his attack but amplifying it nonetheless. The hand-to-hand combat isn't wholly uninteresting, but it reflects Universal's priorities. The editors are more precise when cutting between contiguous spaces. When Kato fires his gas gun and his target collapses, we are treated to two distinct bursts of action in two shots, each with its own beat. Action within the frame is treated as so much filler, quickly staged and roughly captured.

Columbia serials follow much the same model; cinematography and editing tend to keep up with the staged event. In an effort to inject dynamism into fairly rote dustups, the Columbia unit uses more undercranking (running the camera at a slow speed so that the resulting footage appears fast) than other producers. The effect is at the forefront of James Horne's *Captain Midnight* (1942). Horne, who previously worked in slapstick, treats henchmen as bumbling comic relief characters, and though his fight scenes are "straight," the fast motion lends the action a light quality. For example, when Ivan Shark (James Craven) and three of his henchmen set upon Midnight (Dave O'Brien) on a country roadside in chapter 9, Horne sticks to long and medium shots, cutting away for comic asides, and shifting shot scale to accommodate the action.

Columbia's stunt team stages the fight more broadly than *The Green Hornet*, and they pack several combinations into each shot. One shot begins with a henchman clocking Midnight with a right hook, continues as Midnight returns the blow, throwing his assailant out of the frame, then pans left to follow our hero as he grabs a second heavy by the shoulders, tosses him rightward, and spins to face a third henchman who surprises him from the rear. A cut back to a long shot opens room for Midnight to fall on his back from the punch and then catch his attacker with his feet, flipping him over his head. Just as Midnight stands up, another heavy enters and pulls him into striking range before finishing his punch in the next, closer, shot. Each take delivers two or three small stunts and sets up an action that bridges the next edit (see figure 22).

Undercranking speeds up the choreography and helps mask the contrived staging that sets the stuntmen up for each gag. The fighters broadcast the punches they throw by swinging out from their shoulders and exaggerate the impacts they receive with a good deal of tumbling and rolling. Overall, they

FIGURE 22 Three frames from a single shot in *Captain Midnight* (1942), which show the arrangement of small stunts in a continuous take. Characters use broad gestures, while speeding up the film helps hide the contrived staging of the flip.

tend to use more space within the frame than their Universal counterparts. Later Columbia serials, produced by the infamously cut-rate Sam Katzman, retain the undercranking for even looser choreography. In *Jack Armstrong* (Fox, 1947) and *Blackhawk* (Bennet and Sears, 1952), the stunt teams stage group fights with multiple assailants and defenders within a single frame. Fast motion and constant movement give the fights a free-for-all quality that degenerates into disorganized flailing. This is the fighting style lampooned by William Dozier's camp *Batman and Robin* television series in 1966.

The fights and stunts at Republic, and particularly in *Daredevils*, achieve a level of craft polish well beyond the competitors. Witney takes credit for innovating a new style of shooting the sequences in his memoir. In a description that well suits the Universal style, Witney writes: "I was never satisfied with the way movie fights were shot. . . . The stuntmen staged the fights, and they stunk. . . . The fights always seemed to be okay for the first punch. Then the stuntmen were always out of place for the next punch. By the time three or four minutes had passed, the stuntmen were out of breath, scattered all over the set and seemed to be staggering around waiting for someone to hit them." Witney was inspired by a visit to the Warner Bros. lot around 1937, where he watched Busby Berkeley at work. Berkeley had broken a long dance into short segments and intensively rehearsed sequences of steps. Once the forty dancers had mastered the steps to the point "you could have shot a bullet down the line and not hit anyone," they were sent to wardrobe and makeup while Berkeley's assistant "shot a close-up of one of the leads doing the same dance steps that the other girls had done." Witney and English decided to bring the "rehearse, break, close-up" method to Republic's stages. Hurst suggests that *Daredevils* was the first serial for which Witney choreographed his own fights in this manner, though he offers no citation. Witney describes the process thusly:

> Each cut might be only fifteen seconds: a punch, cut, a fall over a chair, cut, a charge into someone over a desk, cut. Each time you saw "cut" in the lines above represents a close-up of one of the leads.

The stunt people caught on fast. It made their work easier. A fall over a table could be done with precision and without the chance of being off balance as they hit the table.... And after a few walk-throughs, everyone knew exactly where they should be at all times. There was no more wandering around the set looking for someone to hit them so they could fall down.[4]

Witney's technique roughly resembles "segment shooting," which David Bordwell identifies with Hong Kong martial arts cinema from the 1960s on. Facing small budgets, short schedules, and high demand, Chinese directors found it more efficient to rehearse and film combat in short segments, setting camera angles and constructing the fight as they went. As Bordwell notes, this method is labor intensive, requiring long continuous workdays from the crew, but it yielded more "tangible benefits" than spending equal time on story construction and screenwriting. The Republic fights are not as painstakingly precise as those of the Hong Kong masters, and it is almost certain that schedules were even tighter for serials than for kung fu films. Still, one senses a kindred "kinesthetic artistry" in the work of Republic's stunt team.[5]

The studio's stunt crew originally developed around Yakima Canutt, who worked for Mascot when Republic formed. Though he continued to stunt and direct for Republic, by the late 1930s Canutt was in high demand and already considered Hollywood's premier stuntman. In 1939 alone he appeared in *Stagecoach* (John Ford), *Young Mr. Lincoln* (John Ford), *Dodge City* (Michael Curtiz), *Gone with the Wind* (Victor Fleming), and sixteen other productions. His protégé at Republic was a former vaudeville acrobat, juggler, and national tumbling champion, David Sharpe. Sharpe took leadership of the Republic team between 1939 and the start of World War II.[6] In industry parlance, the lead stuntman was known as the "ramrod," a crew chief who organized the other performers as instructed by the director.

Cast as a lead (Bert) in *Daredevils*, and therefore indispensable to the production, Sharpe was himself doubled in the film by Jimmy Fawcett, another vaudeville acrobat who started at Republic that year.[7] Still, *Daredevils* owes some of its dynamism to the fact that Republic's ramrod was a major player. Sharpe brings physical panache to routine exposition, as in chapter 3 when he sits down to the breakfast table by effortlessly leaping over the back of his chair. The other stunt doubles on *Daredevils* included the veteran professionals Cy Slocum and George DeNormand (for Gene) and Ted Mapes (Tiny). Mapes had been with Republic from the beginning, working as a grip, extra, and stunt performer (he also doubled for Brix the year before in *Hawk of the Wilderness* [Witney and English, 1938]), DeNormand was a freelancer who appeared in serials from all three studios (including *The Green Hornet*) from the 1930s through the mid-1950s, and Slocum began his career doubling for Oliver Hardy at the Hal Roach studios (which Mascot occupied after 1930) and was a regular at Republic through the 1940s. Together, they created gag-packed energetic routines in which each hero is fully individuated.

Many of the Daredevils' fights develop into wide-ranging chases as each of the trio engages a fleeing henchman or two. The dustup in chapter 6, *Thirty Seconds to Live*, is contained to a single room and so offers a nice comparison to the Universal and Columbia sequences. The trio has been dispatched to investigate Professor Seldon (Stanley Price), who supplies scientific secrets to 39013. Seldon tricks the three and locks them in a storeroom from which they almost immediately escape. In the meantime, four of 39013's henchmen interrogate Seldon and threaten to eliminate him. To hold his assailants at bay, Seldon reveals a contact switch bolted to the edge of his desk and announces: "There's a time bomb planted in this room, and in just thirty seconds after I throw this switch, it will blow up." One of the henchmen (a gun heavy) shoots Seldon in the stomach, and he falls to the ground. The Daredevils have been spying on this confrontation from the doorway, and they immediately burst into action.

Twenty-nine shots fly by in sixty-three seconds as Gene, Bert, and Tiny engage the four henchmen. Unlike the *Green Hornet* example, only two shots might be called "cutaways," a medium shot of Seldon writhing on the ground and a quick close-up of a heavy knocking the contact switch closed. All of the remaining shots feature the heroes punching, flipping, and wrestling the heavies, and this action is covered from thirteen different camera positions. Clearly, Witney and English invest more time and creative energy in their brawl than their Universal and Columbia counterparts.

Professor Seldon's laboratory is a simple three-sided set with his desk near a window at the far left and a doorway on the opposite wall at right. The rear wall is lined with what appears to be radio equipment, and a second desk is placed near the doorway. This wide set design affords plenty of floor space in its center, as well as desks, chairs, and cabinets for the stuntmen to knock into. When our trio burst through the door, they have room to race leftward in a panning long shot, picking up momentum as they near the heavies at Seldon's desk. All three leap into the air at precisely the same time. In a flamboyant opening maneuver, Bert uses his running start to dive over the desk and bounce across the back of a thug on the other side. Bert's (in this shot played by Jimmy Fawcett) altitude is breathtaking; he clears the desk, a tall lamp, and a henchman standing beside the desk in a full shot that rules out any hidden trampolines or springboards. As Bert lands at the left, Tiny punches two heavies down to the floor in the background, beyond the desk, while Gene drags a foreground thug off-frame by his leg to the right. In a single fluid movement and in under two seconds, the Daredevils have floored all four thugs (see figure 23).

Choreography distributes action across all areas of the frame. Bert's leap activates the air above the desk and pushes our attention leftward; at the same time, Tiny uses the background to sweep his thugs downward, and in the foreground

FIGURE 23 Three frames from a single shot in *Daredevils of the Red Circle* (1939) in which Bert (stuntman Jimmy Fawcett) leaps over a desk while his partners take down heavies in the foreground and rear.

Gene whisks his target in the opposite direction. The timing is immaculate. The camera pans back right as Bert on the left and Gene on the right rise upward in symmetry to reengage their opponents. The entire shot runs just under five seconds, and in that time the viewer's attention courses first to the left, then toward the background, and finally is pulled between two synchronized foreground actions at either edge of the frame. It may be too swift for us to track each individual, but the flurry of action high and low, left and right, fore and back, engages us in a smooth kinetic movement and promotes muscular empathy.

This wide shot works as a master—a camera position that takes in all of the action from a distance by panning and reframing—but it is not an all-purpose composition. The framing of the opening leap is too precise for that, and set furnishings have been adjusted for maximal clarity and dynamism in this shot. Four shots later, when we cut back to a seemingly identical wide composition, a large worktable loaded with electrical equipment suddenly appears in the middle of the room, between Seldon's desk and the door. The table materializes just in time for Gene to crash into it, reeling from a thug's right hook. Rather than shooting coverage of the entire sequence and then inserting a series of close-ups, Witney and English have broken things down into discrete units that allow fine control of each frame.

Even so, their work isn't flawless. When Bert and Gene each rise on either edge of the composition, the camera operator does not pan far enough right and Gene steps out of the frame, so we miss the punch he throws at his opponent. In the next shot, a heavy falls backward against a radio on the far wall, but since we haven't seen the strike, his relation to the larger fight is unclear. It is a momentary incoherence that reflects the editor's practice of covering gaps in action with closer shots of random thugs falling down (a nearly identical example can be found in the first fight in chapter 1). The two shots would have proper continuity if the first were reframed just a little. The filmmakers seem to have recognized the error, because they eliminate the cut when the fight is replayed at the start of the next episode. As a form, serials are invariably marked by the compromises and contingencies of quick production. The choreography of *Daredevils* represents considerable achievements within those constraints.

The fight is constructed around the individual struggles of our heroes, mostly Bert and Tiny, in tighter shots, followed by wide compositions that allow the combatants to interact. Small stunts can occur within single frames, or cutting can punctuate a blow. Toward the end of the sequence, for example, Bert blocks a thug's jab and returns a right hook in a medium shot. A ninety-degree cut to long shot reveals new space near the doorway, a desk chair, and another worktable against the wall. In a match on action, Bert completes his punch and the thug careens backward, knocking the chair and table away. Cutting does not follow action so much as create it; the sudden widening of the frame and revelation of new space carries the force of Bert's punch. The new composition has been arranged to accommodate the stuntman's fall, allowing him to spectacularly (and safely) hit his mark. This simple articulating cut achieves elegance when the shot continues to facilitate a second stunt. While Bert's thug is still crashing into the table, our hero races back into the frame, picks up another heavy, and tosses him leftward as the camera pans with him. The single take organizes two distinct beats, foreground and background (see figure 24).

Witney and English vary this method in the shot of Gene crashing into the surprise worktable described above. While Gene is socking his thug in the corner, a cutaway shows Bert rolling a heavy across Seldon's desk and landing with him on the floor. When Gene is propelled into the table, Bert has been well placed at the foot of Seldon's desk. As the thug steps forward to finish Gene off, Bert bounces up from the floor and intercepts him, plowing him into the back of the frame. Action surges forward and then backward as the two lines interconnect in a single shot. The rough-and-tumble clash achieves the grace of dance (see figure 25).

In this way, phases of action flow into one another and overlap. The filmmakers pack the short sequence with flips, leaps, and falls, and these tend to cohere into larger units of action. The first seven shots follow Bert's opening leap through his defense of Gene just described. Shots eight through thirteen generally focus on Tiny and his struggle against two heavies. When one of them lifts a desk chair to bash Tiny, Gene appears and disarms him. All three lines again intersect in the fourteenth shot, a wide composition in which Gene is tackled by the chair heavy, Tiny knocks his opponent over Seldon's desk, and Bert punches down another assailant. The next seven shots alternate between Tiny battling a tough near Seldon's desk and Bert fending off his attacker near the door. The editors blend Tiny's and Bert's separate scuffles by carrying the direction of action across cuts. When Bert throws a henchman off toward the left, a cut to Tiny punching his thug leftward against a cabinet creates continuous motion. Organizing the larger fight into smaller sets of action lends the whole a sense of progress as we shift among characters encountering and solving physical problems; it gives a perceptible structure to what might have been an aimless free-for-all. Viewers gain precise impressions of sharply defined moves, all the better for

FIGURE 24 A cut from medium to long shot articulates Bert's (David Sharpe in medium shot, stuntman Jimmy Fawcett in long shot) punch. Then, while the heavy crashes down, Bert races to the back of the set, where he engages another henchman in *Daredevils of the Red Circle* (1939).

re-creation in the schoolyard. The emphasis, though, is on process rather than goal. As if playing a self-sustaining game of tag, combatants appear ceaselessly capable of leaping back up to throw another punch; no end is in sight.

The deftly woven series of stunts comes to a sudden halt when Tiny knocks his thug into Seldon's contact switch (an action depicted in four continuous shots). The thug pulls a gun, and everyone freezes when he announces: "Hold it! We gotta scram outta here. I closed the contact!" It is a chance interruption. Fighting could have continued indefinitely or been halted at any moment that this henchman remembered he was carrying a gun. The punch-up is an intricately choreographed, neatly designed end in itself. Republic's crew mastered a particular brand of kinetically entertaining physical storytelling. In place of an undefined melee, viewers follow a flowing series of defined but interconnected physical feats. Frames are filled with speed and motion, so details like suit color (the three stuntmen wear contrasting shades), fighting style (Bert leaps and tumbles; Tiny prefers to fight two bad guys at once), and the distinct cracks and thwacks on the Foley track keep things legible. The immediate stakes and the status of the combatants are always clear. This is a sophisticated form, crafted from space, frame, movement, and tempo.

FIGURE 25 Action flows forward and rear as Gene (stuntman George DeNormand) crashes into the table and Bert (stuntman Jimmy Fawcett) pulls his assailant back for a punch in *Daredevils of the Red Circle* (1939).

Chasing and Climbing: Games in the Industrial Playground

Republic refined and emphasized fights and stunts more than other studios, forging an unusually powerful kind of viewer engagement. Focusing the serial's operational aesthetic on the stunt performer's movement through space primes spectators to assimilate the film's rhythms and anticipate actions and their outcomes. We get caught up in a flow of human-scale bodily problem solving conceived as a fight. In *Daredevils* Witney and English extend this aesthetic to lengthy action sequences, transferring stunt choreography from a three-walled set to an ongoing world. The chemical plants, gas plants, electric powerhouses, oil fields, and secret scientific facilities in Horace Granville's empire provide 39013 a choice selection of arenas to test the Daredevils.

The various industrial sites that crop up in eight episodes are actually filmed on one or two locations, a convenience that undoubtedly helped the unit stay on schedule. Beyond squeezing potential from available resources, this mise-en-scène opens new formal possibilities. Catwalks, steel towers, and refinery tanks are visually novel but more or less indistinguishable, which frees editors to create rough continuities between different spaces. Meanwhile, the cinematographer, William Nobles, finds unusually dynamic compositions by placing the camera on walkways above or below the action, an inexpensive source of visual flair. The industrial settings allow directors to choreograph action on a broader scale, and the machinery and scaffolding give stunt performers a vertical dimension to explore. Spectacle remains that of bodily speed and agility, the stuntman's fundamental tools, but played across a synthetic unfolding cinematic space. The factory fight and chase is a logical extension of Republic's house style. It expands the action without diluting coherence. Equally, the form extends action's playability by bringing the studio's brand of viewer engagement to a more fully realized ludic space, the industrial playground.

These fights and chases form the serial's spine, collapsing the distance between storytelling and action, and between narrative and play. As stuntmen, Gene, Tiny, and Bert play for a living, and their individual specialties align character and body. Factory fights piggyback on established folk games like tag, base games, and hide-and-seek while providing a kinetic experience of character and space. The sequences draw from the reservoir of "the golden age of unstructured play" that the historian Howard Chudacoff locates in the early twentieth century. Chudacoff notes that before the 1950s, children "adapted formal games and created new ones, incorporating the built environment and the objects they found there." Empty lots, sidewalks, and construction sites were more appealing than supervised parks and playgrounds, and "urban structures were an essential and challenging component of hide and chase games."[8] The landscape of *Daredevils* is compatible with the recreation space of many 1930s urban youth, and with the world of physical play more generally. In pursuit of justice, the heroes scale, swing, and leap among concrete blocks and iron girders. Caverns of piping and multilevel buildings form an all-purpose obstacle course. Under pressure of a chase or fight, the industrial jungle gym becomes a narrative architecture in which the heroes struggle for spatial mastery.

Each sequence quickly defines a physical goal that sets the game in motion. In chapters 2 and 9, Gene directs Tiny and Bert to break off in pursuit of different thugs, activating a session of tag. Chapter 4 stages a contest resembling capture-the-flag, as Bert and Tiny divert gashouse heavies on a wild goose chase while Gene climbs and zip lines his way to a safety valve that will prevent a catastrophic explosion. Characters reveal themselves through their game play. In chapter 9, when Tiny's thug blockades himself in a storeroom, instead of breaking down the door the strongman finds an open window through which to deliver a knockout punch. The gag is simple, but it shows Tiny solving his problem with cleverness rather than brute strength. Meanwhile, when Bert discovers that his target has climbed into a different building, he quickly finds a rope and swings from one structure into the other, races down a flight of stairs, and executes a cartwheel that ends with the thug in a headlock between his legs. The routine marks him as a resourceful gamer, able to repurpose his surroundings with speed and ingenuity. In chapter 6, the clever Professor Seldon combines tag with hide-and-seek to gain an advantage. He hides from the heroes after dropping a metal chest on them and lures them into a trap. Creativity comes from mixing games together, exchanging rule sets.

This emphasis on individual actions in dynamic spaces invites what Jennifer Barker calls "muscular empathy," or embodied engagement. From the perspective of phenomenological film studies, film form addresses the viewer's body, encouraging it to ingest and respond to cinematic rhythms. Something like Barker's "passionate investment" in movement seems at work in chapter 2, for instance, when Bert climbs across machinery, vaults over railings, and swings himself up to a catwalk to catch a henchman who opted to take the sensible, but slower, route via the staircase (see figure 26). In a single, fluidly unfolding shot, Bert's command of space contrasts the henchman's confinement to convention: an embodied lesson in cutting an unanticipated path, converting

FIGURE 26 Six frames from a single shot from *Daredevils of the Red Circle* (1939). Bert (stuntman Jimmy Fawcett) converts obstacles into an unanticipated path in pursuit of a henchman.

obstacles into implements for traversing space. As Barker observes, such depictions bid the viewer to "become momentarily as graceful or powerful as the film's body."[9] Republic's refinement of physical dexterity narrows the distance between watching and playing. *Daredevils* shapes serial action into a primer for problem solving on the corporeal level.

Narrative progress takes a backseat to the articulation of physical problems and solutions in these sequences. Neither apprehension nor interrogation of the thugs seems to be on the Daredevils' agenda. They engage fleeing heavies and knock them cold, then run on to face more pressing threats. Story serves as an occasion for demonstrating spatial proficiency; it is merely the launching point for an ongoing series of discrete material challenges and acts of inconsequential violence. Factory fights, like the punch-up in Seldon's office, could be infinitely extended. Henchmen tend to materialize as needed to keep the action moving, and in chapter 4 it appears that every worker in the gas plant is on 39013's payroll. As on the playground, the game doesn't reach closure so much as it is interrupted. Eventually Gene faces an obstacle he cannot surmount, launching the cliffhanger. In chapter 2 he is knocked from a catwalk into a water tank covered with burning oil, in chapter 4 the release valve apparently explodes, and in chapter 9 his ladder is tipped from the top of a skyscraping tower. The sudden halt in screen action leaves viewers to carry the game's momentum forward for a week, until the catastrophe is reversed and the situation reset by the start of the next chapter.

Stylistic Set Pieces: Form in the Cliffhanger

Serial filmmakers concentrated their creative energies on the cliffhanger. The commercial importance of each chapter's ending put a premium on vividness and novelty. Even a lackluster production might distinguish itself through the straightforward presentation of a clever design. Columbia's 1942 *Captain Midnight*, for instance, reaches delirious heights in the display of mechanical contrivance, though the film as a whole lacks any formal ambition. Whenever Ivan Shark has the opportunity to easily dispatch his enemy, he insists instead on activating some new elaborate apparatus. In the final episode, Captain Midnight's entire crew is trapped in a crushing room with electrified walls, but chapter 10, *The Hidden Bomb*, puts the pinnacle of Shark's engineering on display.

Shark pulls his henchmen off of Midnight, explaining, "This is what I've been waiting for," and throws the hero into a small cell behind a steel door. The only object in the windowless chamber is a large cylindrical column running floor to ceiling in its center. Shark retreats to his control room, where he will watch the event through an electric periscope-like viewer, and flicks a switch. The apparatus is revealed in stages, each more menacing than the last. First, the cell floor begins rotating around the center spindle, forcing Midnight to fight for his balance. Next, Shark pulls a control lever and the walls of the cell rise off-screen, showing the floor to be a large turntable supported by the spindle in the center of a much larger concrete vault. In a feat of showmanship aimed squarely at the viewer, the camera dollies backward, revealing a fire raging beneath the turntable. Midnight clings to the spindle for his life, battling the centrifugal force that will propel him off the edge and into the furnace below. Shark has one more feature to engage. When he pulls a second lever, a giant crushing metal plate the same size as the floor begins slowly to slide down the column toward the turntable. If Midnight manages to hang on

FIGURE 27 The four-stage revelation of the death chamber in chapter 10 of *Captain Midnight* (1942). First the hero begins to spin; then the walls rise and the platform retracts, revealing the pit of fire. Finally a crushing weight descends from the ceiling.

and avoid being burned alive, he will surely be squashed flat by the descending press. With each revelation, the death chamber becomes more spectacular and less escapable (see figure 27).

Ivan Shark's literal infernal machine attains the schematic clarity of the best cliffhangers. Danger comes from above and below, while the usual points of egress (through a door or a secret passage in a wall) are simply removed from play. This is astonishingly inefficient malevolence, but its vividness in the heat of the moment justifies its absurdity. Murderous gadgetry, though rarely developed on this magnitude, condenses several appeals of the serial. It is wildly implausible but physically precise, fascinating in its complicated operation but simple in its function, and unabashedly presentational. In successively laying out the parameters of the trap, *Captain Midnight* gives the viewer a seemingly unfathomable puzzle to mull in the intervening week. The downside, of course, is that putting the hero in such a tight spot almost inevitably requires a disappointing or cheated resolution. In chapter 11, we learn that Shark's boneheaded henchmen, blindly following the boss's orders to destroy all the evidence, cut the compound's power and halted the device. Midnight is spared to fight another day, and the serial speeds ahead to the next peril.

In contrast to Columbia's occasional accomplishments in gag design, *Daredevils* and *Nyoka* explore the cinematic elaboration of cliffhangers. They define and complicate suspenseful problem spaces through editing, staging, and cinematography. Though each has its share of off-the-rack perils, in key instances they fully demonstrate the Republic serial's potential for stylistic sophistication. The remainder of this chapter analyzes two exemplary cliffhangers: the flooding-tunnel climax in the opening chapter of *Daredevils*, *The Monstrous Plot*, and the ritual execution that closes *Nyoka*'s sixth episode, *Human Sacrifice*. Together these sequences reveal a depth of cinematic craft rarely associated with the form and testify to the aesthetic value of convention.

At the close of *The Monstrous Plot*, 39013 sabotages the grand opening of Granville's channel tunnel, connecting St. Alicia Island to the California mainland. The screenwriters fashion a tight situation that imperils both the hero and a carload of innocents through a precisely metered chain of events. In his Granville disguise, the villain sends Blanche in the first car across the tunnel as a gesture of faith in its safety. 39013's henchmen, manning an offshore oil platform nearby, pierce the tunnel with their drill and time its collapse to coincide with Blanche's ride. Meanwhile, Gene patrols the tunnel on his motorcycle, riding toward Blanche's car. In an impressive display of Howard and Theodore Lydecker's ingenuity with miniatures, the tunnel is breached and Gene tries to outrace an all-consuming wall of water. English and Witney intercut shots of a flooding model tunnel with dynamic compositions of Gene on his bike, and rear projection composites, to give the commanding impression that the rushing torrent overtakes our hero.

Republic had recently staged a flooded-tunnel cliffhanger in *Zorro's Fighting Legion* (1939), but *Daredevils* tops it in scale, speed, and intricacy. Tunnel traps are notable for their aggressive linearity. They are labyrinths stripped of blind turns, dead ends, and the hope of escape: powerfully simple problem spaces. By restricting character movement to a single vector, the tunnel hamstrings the serial hero's free exploration of space, putting all emphasis on forward momentum. Meanwhile, the approaching water or fire (as in *Spy Smasher* [1942], *Zorro's Black Whip* [1944], or *The Black Widow* [Bennet and Brannon, 1947]) marks time by devouring space.

Daredevils depicts the destructive mechanism with uncommon clarity by connecting the slow leak and then inundation to actions on the drilling platform. On his first trip through the tunnel, Gene stops to investigate a dull grinding and thumping sound, which motivates a short expositional sequence on the rig. Three minutes and one fight later, as Gene mounts his cycle to travel back through the tunnel, Witney, English, and Republic's editing team signal the cliffhanger's onset with a cut back to the drilling platform. The process has been thoroughly explained, and now the viewer has only to watch it play out. *The Monstrous Plot* efficiently implies elaborate operations from nominal material. Tight and low-angle shots around the derrick eliminate the background, probably the Baldwin Hills oil field featured in chapter 8.[10] In the entire sequence there isn't a single image of the channel. Our visual knowledge of the exterior space is limited to a brief shot of a beach, and one stock shot of an oil platform inserted twice early into the proceedings. In constructing the problem space from telling fragments, filmmakers make a virtue of economy.

Our first glimpse of the platform at sea comes as part of a radio broadcaster's exposition about the grand opening. Listening to the radio in Granville's cell, 39013 takes the opportunity to show his hostage a diagram illustrating the well and its procedure for "drilling at offset" to pierce the tunnel. His description leads to a graphically matched dissolve to our second and final glimpse of the platform. From here on, the connection between the drill and the outside of the tunnel is suggested with minimal means. Gene's glance at the tunnel ceiling when he initially hears the sound is followed by a shot on the platform. After the henchmen restart the drill, the editors alternate a shot of the derrick with a close-up of a crack on the tunnel ceiling, and reintroduce the thumping and grinding sound over a rear-projection shot of Gene speeding through the tunnel. Witney and English manage to impart a vivid understanding of the mechanism through sound and editing. One of the great pleasures of *Daredevils,* and of serials in general, lies in recognizing the distance between the catastrophic events depicted and the means of depiction.

The scale of the *Daredevils* tunnel trap is far grander than its immediate predecessor's, and the Republic staff further embellishes the situation by introducing Blanche's unwitting movement toward the deluge. This doubles the tension, and the opportunities for crosscutting, as we now follow two lines of action on a collision course. As Gene speeds away from the water to save himself, he is also rushing forward to warn Blanche of her rapidly approaching demise. The episode climaxes when Blanche screams in terror and the camera lens sinks below the waterline (see figure 28). Gene's solution in the take-out is to engage an emergency watertight door by spinning a valve at the side of the tunnel. The safety mechanism was heretofore unknown, but immediately understood and commonsensical. Witney and English attain their customary procedural clarity with a rear-projection shot of Gene

FIGURE 28 Six shots from the cliffhanger of chapter 1 of *Daredevils of the Red Circle* (1939). Top row: Cutting between an oil rig, a crack in the ceiling, and Gene (Charles Quigley) on his motorcycle suggests clear cause and effect. Bottom row: As Gene speeds away from a rear-projected miniature flood, Blanche (Carol Landis) screams at the impending deluge and the camera dips below the waterline.

spinning the valve in front of the model door closing off the Lydecker brothers' miniature flood.

The channel-tunnel sequence is a masterpiece of functional intelligibility, and an almost perfect marriage between basic suspense structures, operational aesthetics, and visual expediency. Where a direct presentation of the underwater sabotage would be prohibitive, Witney and English reveal 39013's hand-drawn diagram. Sound and cutting imply causal links in the operational chain, while model work worthy of Universal lends the affair authenticity. The impossibility of directly presenting the trap's physical contours in the manner of Ivan Shark's killing room led the Republic unit to craft a veritable meditation on direction and velocity through constructive montage. To a large extent, the cliffhanger was an editor's art, but few productions developed or refined the standard methods of crosscutting. In delineating three lines of action, none of which represent hope for escape, *Daredevils* magnifies suspense without sacrificing speed or dynamism.

Nyoka's cliffhanger in *Human Sacrifice* takes a different tack. The episode embellishes a relatively static cliffhanger situation through an elongated cutting pattern, stylized camera work, and emphatic score. The result is a less kinetic but more nuanced interaction of style and narration than in *Daredevils*. In it we can grasp a fine-grained control of time and space to shape viewer response. The climax of *Human Sacrifice* encourages and rewards close analysis more than any other single sequence discussed in this book.

The situation crystallizes when the Tuaregs capture Nyoka, and Vultura, in her Sun Goddess outfit, orders up a ritual sacrifice. The Tuareg chief, now recognized by Nyoka as her amnesiac father, is suspicious of Vultura but goes along with her plan nonetheless. Rube Goldberg has apparently inspired Tuareg ritual, and the operational aesthetic is in full force. Nyoka is bound and hoisted by a rope running through a pulley on the cave ceiling. Beneath her, the Tuaregs ignite a crater full of oil. The other end of the rope is anchored to the floor at the far side of the cavern near the "sun idol," a relief sculpture with a mirrored lens in its center. Upon Vultura's command, a Tuareg uses his key to open a window on the wall above Nyoka. Light streams in across the cavern and strikes the lens at the center of the idol. The lens magnifies and directs the light to slowly burn the rope. In the final moments of the chapter, the rope snaps, plunging Nyoka toward the pool of fire.

The mechanism is designed for suspense. The first several steps of the ritual (binding, hoisting, igniting the fire pit, opening the window) progressively reveal the exact fate that awaits Nyoka. Once the machine is set in motion we can only wait for the light beam to burn through the rope, an event open to delay given its largely indeterminate length. Witney and his editors, Tony Martinelli and Edward Todd, stretch the event out across fifty-five shots and three minutes and five seconds of screen time. The editing cycles through details of the situation including medium shots of Nyoka struggling (eleven shots), close-ups of the burning oil (four shots), Vultura and the chief surveying the scene (four shots), and the smoking rope (six shots from two camera setups) (see figure 29). This heavy decoupage is anchored by a regularly returning master shot of the entire cavern, which repeats eight times. Action expands beyond the confines of the cavern only once in a quick four-shot sequence showing Larry and Red scaling the exterior cliff. This line of action is cited and dropped about thirty seconds into the scene; instead of generating suspense, the parallel editing dutifully marks Larry's progress and is discontinued.

Intensified analytical cutting among a few repeated elements within the cavern proves a practical way of enlivening a fairly slow process. Having opted not to follow Larry's more dynamic efforts to rescue Nyoka, the filmmakers fashion a kinetic effect by shuffling between details. Film form rearticulates the parameters of the trap and in doing so narrows the apparent problem space. The editing, abetted by Mort Glickman's driving score, engages the viewer in an accelerating rhythmic structure that culminates in a series of twenty-two shots, each trimmed to two seconds or less. The scene achieves an affective charge, which channels attention away from potential rescues and toward the small set of ever-closing options within the cavern. To be sure, the sequence bears evidence of a sound serial's rushed and low-budget production. Continuity errors are common during cutting between the master and detail shots; Tuaregs change position quite a bit, and Nyoka turns suddenly around from shot to shot. Compositions tend to be inexact, and awkward reframing mars several of Reggie Lanning's tilting and panning shots. Nonetheless, *Perils of Nyoka* is unusually ambitious.

All together, the sequence boasts fifteen camera positions in the cavern, an extraordinary number of setups for a single serial set. After establishing the basic series of compositions (the master shot, a low-angle medium shot of Nyoka, a shot of the fire, etc.), the editors progressively add intensifying details. For example, though Nyoka and the fire are legible in the master, shot 23 dynamizes the situation by reframing beneath and behind her so that her legs

FIGURE 29 Three shots from the cliffhanger of chapter 6 of *Perils of Nyoka* (1942). The sequence alternates between Nyoka (Kay Aldridge), the fiery pit, the burning rope, and other details.

extend from the top of the frame over the flame. The composition also introduces four drummers in the background as their ritual rhythm is imposed
on the score, an exceptional level of cooperation between sound and image.
This shot is slotted into a regular pattern, repeating four times in the sequence.
Shot 28 further reframes the drummers in an emphatic medium composition
that adds no new information but provides another rhythmic element; it is
repeated three times (see figure 30).

Other camera positions accumulate, including closer shots of the rope and
a tighter medium shot of the Tuareg chief, but two framings stand out. The
first, shot 34, is a high-angle long shot from above Nyoka pointing down into
the cavern (see figure 31). The vertiginous composition packs in nearly all the
major elements: Nyoka, the fire, and the drummers, as well as Vultura and
the chief in the background. Lanning manages a directional lighting scheme
with the fire pit motivating highlights in the lower right and a torch illuminating the upper left. Lighting, combined with the high angle that contrasts the
low shot of Nyoka in the next image, creates the kind of mannered expression-
ism celebrated in the Universal horror films of the 1930s. This shot is also the
scene's last image to be held more than two seconds; it launches the episode's
final stretch of furious editing, which packs twenty-two shots into half a minute. It is a moment of perceptual novelty offered at the cusp of a rapid, inevitable climax.

The second outstanding composition is the scene's most daring, a repeated
extreme close-up of Vultura's eyes as she watches the sacrifice (see figure 32).
Serial scenes were commonly built out of long to medium shots, which could
be quickly filmed without precision lighting. Thus Vultura's close-up comes as
a double surprise, both as a new image introduced so late in the cutting pattern (in shot 38) and as a rare tight shot. The camera position is repeated in
shots 46 and 51, and each time it registers a microgesture. In the first, Vultura
raises her eyes upward to engage with well-defined eye-lights reflected near

FIGURE 30 Editors add intensifying details as time runs out for Nyoka (Kay Aldridge) in the
climax of chapter 6 of *Perils of Nyoka* (1942).

FIGURE 31 An unusually expressive high-angle shot from the climax of chapter 6 of *Perils of Nyoka* (1942).

her pupils. In the second, she glances downward, moving out of the reflective highlights. In the third, she is looking up again, but her eyes widen with excitement just before the rope snaps and Nyoka falls. The care in crafting the shot is obvious, and it confers a fleeting individuation to Vultura's character. It grants viewers psychological access to the villain as she savors the cruel spectacle.

In the climax to *Human Sacrifice*, *Nyoka* rises well above the sound serial's generally pedestrian aesthetics. Dwelling within a single space and following one line of action deepens cliffhanger form beyond crosscutting and achieves novelty through film style. Editing and composition fulfill the standard requirements of clarifying the trap and delaying its actualization, but they do so in a fresh way. As soon as Vultura commands the Tuaregs to light the fire pit (and

FIGURE 32 Three close-ups of Vultura (Lorna Gray) as she reacts to Nyoka's (Kay Aldridge) plight. Eye-lights and shot scale reveal unexpected craft.

likely before this), viewers recognize that the chapter has reached its final impasse. There will be no further revelation of story information, and the hero will not escape. Film style, at this point, comes forward; it draws viewers into the tense unfolding of a predetermined course of events. We are swept up in a torrent of details as the rope burns and the drums sound. Camera positions seem to cover the action from every angle, assuring us, against our certainty, that there is no way out. If the scene works, it is because rhythmic and graphic embellishment overtakes our interest in solving the problem. In cognitivist terms, formal structures place viewers alongside the character, outstripping deliberative thought. For a phenomenologist, the cutting binds the viewer's body to the film, ensuring our visceral engagement. The sequence reminds us of the generative possibilities of a genre that seldom produced more than adequate stylistics.

This cliffhanger's resolution illustrates the power of the rhythmic decoupage that has been built up. As usual, the narrative deception depends on recasting information in a previously unavailable frame. The recap cleverly revises our understanding of events by reordering them. The four-shot sequence of Larry's progress, inserted early in the proceedings of the cliffhanger so that it could be quickly forgotten, is moved later in the recap.[11] After rerunning shots 14 through 23 of the original cliffhanger, the resolution repeats shots 9 through 12, which show Larry and Red climbing the mountain.

This temporal adjustment is subtle but important, since it reminds us of the rescuers' activities even as the Tuareg ritual passes the point of no return. The remaining crosscutting is impressively efficient. Fourteen shots later, a single image of Larry unhooking his rope from the rock he had lassoed assures us of his continued progress. Once again the scene returns to the cavern, where eight more shots are replayed, bringing us up to the moment when the burning rope snaps its second strand (originally shot 48). Larry and Red answer the crisis point with a burst of action. In two punctual shots that match the rhythm of the cut with action in the frame, they clear a hillside, race forward, and peer over a boulder. The next shot closes the knowledge gap and signals the means of escape. The steep high-angle perspective of Nyoka and the cavern below repeats, but this time as an eyeline match from Larry and Red's position (see figure 33). This revision, to use Branigan's language, draws a new epistemological boundary around the image of Nyoka as it is transformed into a subjective view.[12] The unusual angle that gave the shot salience in its first iteration is now attributed to the heroes' vantage through the sun-window above Nyoka's head. The window, which had been functionally fixed as part of the trap, is reconfigured as a potential solution. An expressive composition retroactively becomes the revelation of Nyoka's escape hatch.

In a resourceful touch, Larry throws his rope, the very tool that he demonstrated while scaling the mountain, to Nyoka and commands her to grab on just before she takes the plunge. Vultura's close-up, formerly a look of sadistic

FIGURE 33 Chapter 7 of *Perils of Nyoka* (1942) revises the high angle as the rescuers' point of view.

glee, is revealed to be one of eye-widening surprise as Nyoka catches the rescue line. Reframing old data and repurposing tools help bind and conflate the new version of events with our previous understanding. These transformations pave the way for more brazenly revisionist narration in the final moments of the recap. Nyoka's plunge, originally covered in the regular master shot, is framed from a new camera position, an extreme long shot from the other side of the fire pit, directly facing the sun-window. As she falls, a Tuareg worshipper stands up and blocks our view, obscuring Nyoka's landing, which was more conclusively fatal in the previous episode. This restaging is exceptionally subtle, and the rapid editing and varied camera positions that energized the cliffhanger further help to cover the revision (see figure 34).

In the strict sense, this resolution is a "cheat" because it depends on restaging events, effectively changing the evidence. But *Nyoka* embeds the change in a deluge of reframings and transformations of earlier depictions, immersing the viewer in a serial-specific version of film narration's constant regulation and alteration of knowledge. If classical narration tends to affirm first impressions

FIGURE 34 Two versions of Nyoka's (Kay Aldridge) fall. At the end of chapter 6 of *Perils of Nyoka* (1942), she plunges into the flames. At the start of chapter 7, a change in angle and staging obscures her fall.

and trace causes to effects in a linear fashion, the sound-serial cliffhanger almost always dissimulates, changing the world to suit its conventional ends. *Nyoka* shows that the cheat need not always be cheap or easy. Rather, serial narration could achieve elegance and complexity rivaling a classical feature, but within a decidedly different framework.

Conclusion

Our consideration of storytelling and style in this chapter and the previous reveals the creative returns of craft forged from poverty. Aside from the occasional Universal "super-production," sound serials were never marked by an ambition to rise above their station. Pretension was not an issue. Perhaps this explains why the smallest of the three studios produced the most rigorous and inventive examples of the form. Film historians rarely direct their attention beyond the feature film, especially in cases of aesthetic study. Looking so closely at a marginal form exposes the limitations of this historical bias. Sound serials could never approach the A feature in causal elegance, character individuation, or dramatic subtlety. But those are feature-film standards for which serials have little use. Intense visual situations delivered at regular intervals and with force: this defines the sound serial's mission. To grasp the chapter-play's achievement, we must attend to matters of formula, to the aesthetics of melodrama, and to unheralded areas of expertise like reediting stock footage and staging the studio-era fight and chase scene. On these terms, the films stand tall.

The art of formula lies in achieving conventional tasks with economy and grace. Strict constraints rule out radical experiment. Instead, the industry's intensive and focused production model encouraged incremental innovation. Screenwriters, directors, editors, stunt performers, effects crews, and others mined the same narrow formula week after week and year-round. They honed techniques to serve the serial's well-defined goals. While filmmakers could get the job done by following a template, they occasionally attended to their craft with surprising precision and ingenuity. The form's melodramatic nature makes it amenable to bursts of creativity and spectacularly realized moments in routine or barely passable films. Some areas, like cliffhangers and middle actions, receive more attention than others, and this creates the possibility for small-scale artistry in nearly every film. *Daredevils* and *Nyoka* are rare in their consistency, but neither challenges norms. Instead, they achieve sophistication within and through convention.

Above all, serial artistry is viewer centered and practical. In her cultural study of serial narrative in literature, comics, and soap opera, Jennifer Hayward emphasizes the form's potential for creative interaction between reader and author. She characterizes the serial as a "collaborative narrative experience."[13]

Serial fans, often dismissed as naïve, could not avoid becoming conversant in the conventions of so repetitive a form, especially one that encouraged them to carry situations beyond the theater and to judge deceptions when they returned. Knowing that most of their viewers recognize the rules encourages popular filmmakers to play the game with care. Sound serials present audiences with pressurized experiences of problem solving, and kinetic engagement with physical space. The craft refinements we have discussed in these chapters all aspire to this goal. They provide viewers with legible domains for play and channel their collaborative experience into backyards, schoolyards, empty lots, sidewalks, and open fields. The sound serial's highest aim is to occupy its audience.

7

Cliffhanger Legacies

● ● ● ● ● ● ● ● ● ● ● ● ● ● ● ● ● ● ● ●

After 1956, the practices of conceiving and shooting long films quickly for distribution as chapters, and the intensive refinement of the serials' narrow range
of cinematic routines, were lost to American cinema. So too was the predictable but reassuring rhythm of exposition, action, and cataclysm packed into a
standardized weekly timeline. Serials, like B films generally, fell victim to the
decline of the studio system and the rise of alternative entertainments, especially television.[1] But serial-style physical procedures, problem spaces, and narrow escapes did not simply vanish. Audiences, future filmmakers among them,
had been raised on the form and its pool of expectations. Syndicated broadcast
in the 1950s and 1960s kept chapterplays alive as a reference point, if a minor
one, for another generation.

Serials left a pool of conventions that some action and adventure films
absorbed and revised. The most overt poachers parlayed the tradition into
popular and financial success scarcely dreamed of in the old serial units. This
chapter traces the persistence and transformation of serial conventions in
Hollywood film, using *Raiders of the Lost Ark* (Stephen Spielberg, 1981) as its
central case study. However, *Raiders* and the Hollywood action blockbuster
in general owe their serial heritage to an earlier franchise: the James Bond
films. Bond appropriated and transformed serial conventions for a new and
broader audience, while *Raiders* adapted and paid homage to the formula with
ingenuity and care. Making the case for the serial's legacy returns us to questions of Hollywood classicism and melodrama noted at the start of this book,
framed around the issue of "postclassical" film. Finally, the Jason Bourne films
illustrate the flexible durability of serial pleasures in a contemporary franchise

that has been acclaimed for character development and realism. This chapter does not attempt an exhaustive accounting of the sound serial's influences on contemporary cinema, but it opens the discussion with regard to Hollywood's most popular and influential franchises.

James Bond's Serial Inheritance

Perhaps the first and certainly the most commercially successful and influential inheritor of serial convention was Albert Broccoli and Harry Saltzman's James Bond series launched in 1962, six years after the last sound serial. The first generation of James Bond fans was also the last to grow up with serials. Broccoli and Saltzman built their series from Ian Fleming's best-selling run of spy novels beginning in 1952, and the producers quickly refined a resilient cinematic formula that has returned a profit for over fifty years. Though they are adult oriented and lavishly produced, the Bond films share an unmistakable kinship with the chapterplay. The critic and historian Alexander Walker observed that the Bond formula "was a return to those Saturday afternoon serials. People who went to see the Bond films henceforth knew the game and anticipated playing it and even working at it as the filmmakers fed them the clues." That game involved self-contained action sequences, which the producers called "bumps," placed at regular intervals, operational gimmickry, and taut situations.[2] Bond's villains, like Dr. No (Joseph Wiseman), Auric Goldfinger (Gert Fröbe), or Ernst Stavro Blofeld (Donald Pleasence), mix ambition for world domination with elaborate methods of extermination.[3] When Bond (Sean Connery) finds himself on Goldfinger's industrial-laser cutting table, he faces the same peril as Mary Randolph (Luana Walters), who is threatened by a concentrated beam of sunlight burning a fatal path in her direction in chapter 9 of *Drums of Fu Manchu*. James Bond gave serial melodrama a new life.

You Only Live Twice (Lewis Gilbert, 1967) displays the fully developed Bond formula and its reworking of serial norms. The fifth film in the series was the first to more or less abandon Fleming's original plot. Roald Dahl, who wrote the screenplay, recalled the novel as "Ian Fleming's worst book, with no plot in it which would even make a movie," and so he constructed the story around the structure used in *Dr. No*.[4] The film's pace is on par with serial standards. Bond packs twenty-eight sequences of action into just under two hours, with only two stretches of over ten minutes between fights, chases, or enemy attack. Serial situations abound. Bond's false execution in the prologue recalls the firing-squad cliffhanger in *The Three Musketeers*, while his subsequent delivery to the coast of Japan by way of a submarine's torpedo tube replays a device from *Spy Smasher*. The sudden knifing of an informant just before he can name a key suspect echoes a common scene from *Zorro's Fighting Legion*, and the floor trap that Aki (Akiko Wakabayashi) triggers as Bond chases her down a corridor resembles one in *Perils of Nyoka* and any number of other serials. Helga Brandt's (Karin Dor) entrapment of Bond in an unmanned airplane conjures *Ace Drummond*, *Captain Midnight*, and *Sky Raiders*, among other aviator serials. Blofeld's office piranha pond mirrors Dr. Daka's crocodile pit in Columbia's *Batman*, while his rocket base hidden inside a volcano imitates Dr. Grood's island lair in *Jack Armstrong*. More generally, Tiger Tanaka's (Tetsuro Tamba) and Mr. Osato's (Teru Shimada) pervasive television surveillance systems have the same seemingly panoptic powers as those in Murania, on Planet Mongo, or in the relatively realistic worlds of *Spy Smasher* and *Batman and Robin*.

Adapting serial thrills to a new demographic required adjustment. Broccoli and Saltzman countered the formula's juvenile reputation with two significant additions: sex and humor. The Bond world is as artificially sexual as the serial world is chaste. A regular Bond screenwriter, Richard Maibaum, inspired by Fleming, established the "three-girl format," which quickly became convention. Dahl describes the structure with brutal clarity: "Bond has three women through the film: . . . the first gets killed, the second gets killed, and the third gets a fond embrace during the closing sequence. And that's the formula. They found it's cast-iron. So, you have to kill two of them off after he has screwed them a few times."[5] The emphasis on sexuality departs from sound-serial concerns, but its treatment obeys familiar episodic logic, plugging a series of liaisons into the plot at regular intervals. Though the three-girl format entails rituals of desire and loss, the action's forward momentum prevents the exercise of pathos. Bond, like a serial hero, cannot linger over consequences when another chase or fight is just around the corner.

Broccoli and Saltzman also buffer serial absurdity with a layer of self-conscious humor. When Bond explains that he carries a gun because of his "slight inferiority complex," and then puns "Shocking, positively shocking" after electrocuting an assassin in *Goldfinger*'s prologue, he signals the film's awareness of artifice.[6] Bond's humor would be out of place in the earnest world of the sound serial. Buster Crabbe's Flash Gordon occasionally makes wry remarks, and James Horne's Columbia productions might feature bumbling henchmen and sidekicks, but jokes at the expense of action were rare. In his memoirs, Witney recalls the Republic producer Moe Siegel objecting to the pun "The trail is getting hot" delivered by a hero following a smoking line left by dripping acid. Siegel exclaimed, "What are you trying to do, kid the serials?" and ordered the joke dubbed over at some expense.[7] By acknowledging silliness, humor risks undermining the stakes of adventure, but it also deflects reproach and extends the audience. In the Bond franchise, serial pleasures maintain their juvenile appeals while explicit sexuality and self-deflating comedy tailor adventure to a knowing adult audience. Broccoli and Saltzman's marketing of their property through both *Playboy* pictorials and the licensing of children's toys bears troubling testimony to the success of this formula.[8]

The Bond films carved a sustainable niche for serial situations in mainstream action cinema and set a model for high-budget franchise production. Other series followed, most of them short-lived variations on Bond. One exception was the producer Arthur P. Jacobs's *Planet of the Apes* (Franklin Schaffner, 1968), which launched a five-film series. The *Apes* films became increasingly juvenile across their run, returning serial-styled adventure to the junior set and supporting the merchandising of role-playing toys.[9] But the serial tradition surged to the forefront of Hollywood production in the late 1970s and early 1980s. In *Star Wars* (1977) and *Raiders of the Lost Ark*, George Lucas and Stephen Spielberg mined serial storytelling to forge the contemporary Hollywood blockbuster. The phenomenal success of these films and their subsequent franchise installments helped reorient popular American cinema toward action and laid the groundwork for a pervasive adoption of serial conventions. If the sound serial has any contemporary relevance beyond Bond's orbit of influence, it is by way of Lucas's and Spielberg's appropriations.

Lucas, Spielberg, and Blockbuster Form

In *Star Wars*, the invocation of serials begins before the first spaceship enters the frame, as Universal-style opening titles crawl from the foreground into depth and recap an unseen previous chapter. Lucas originally pitched his idea for a space adventure as an "updated *Flash Gordon*," and the resulting franchise draws deeply from the sound serial's conglomeration of sword fights and alien worlds, as well as on specific details like the Lightning's helmet in *The Fighting Devil Dogs*, which served as a model for Darth Vader's. As the franchise developed into a veritable industry, however, neither the creative team nor its critics dwelled on its serial origins, preferring instead to highlight Lucas's creation of a complete fantasy world. In the context of our study, the serial influence on *Star Wars* comes boldly forward, but Lucas has successfully deemphasized this lineage by blending it with elements from the fairy tale, the historical adventure, the Western, and "the hero myth" as described by Joseph Campbell.

Where *Star Wars* conceals its inheritance, *Raiders* celebrates it. The sound serial casts a long shadow over blockbuster cinema generally, but *Raiders* presents a rare and significant case of conscious and acknowledged influence. Setting it during the 1930s, and reviving such foundational structures as the weenie hunt and the deathtrap, Spielberg (as director), Lucas (as producer), and Lawrence Kasdan (as screenwriter) explicitly rework serial formulas. Lucas opened his story conference with Spielberg and Kasdan by evoking the chapterplay: "Generally, the concept is a serial idea. Done like the Republic serials. As a thirties serial. Which is where a lot of stuff comes from anyway. One of the main ideas was to have, depending on whether it would be every ten minutes or every twenty minutes, a sort of cliffhanger situation that we get our hero into."[10] Spielberg recalls that Lucas first pitched him the idea during the phenomenal opening run of *Star Wars*. When Spielberg expressed his desire to "make a James Bond–style adventure thriller," Lucas proposed the story of Indiana Smith (later changed to Jones): "Sure enough, there were all the 'Bonding' elements, but without the hardware and the gimmickry, which is what appealed to me." Inspired by revivals of Saturday matinees he frequented as a youngster in Phoenix, Spielberg set out to reawaken "the genre of the outdoor adventure: of narrow misses and close calls."[11] This book has often measured the chapterplay against the feature, but the case of *Raiders* reverses the equation: it is a feature emulation of the serial.

Tracing continuities between the sound serial and contemporary cinema brings us once more to the debates about classicism. As we have noted, situational dramaturgy and seriality ride against standards of unity so often identified in studio-era feature films. The debate, represented by Bordwell and Altman in chapter 1, over whether these standards adequately capture the nature of Hollywood storytelling is paralleled in recent disputes about "postclassical" contemporary film. Postclassical criticism argues that, for a variety of reasons, popular American cinema since *Star Wars* has replaced studio-era coherence and unity with eclectic packages of appeals and attractions. The serial's marginal status during the studio era allowed it to develop an alternative set of storytelling practices, which we have argued are based in melodrama and distinct from classicism. To the extent that they appropriate serial tendencies, contemporary blockbusters move formerly peripheral practices to the center of popular cinema. This brings our study into contact with ongoing discussions about Hollywood storytelling and, in particular, its relationship to studio-era norms.

Warren Buckland uses *Raiders* as a case study to test the validity of postclassicism, which he characterizes as the argument that "films are not structured in terms of a psychologically motivated cause-effect narrative logic, but in terms of loosely linked, self-sustaining action sequences built around spectacular stunts, stars and special effects." He frames the film in relation to the sound serial, splitting it into six episodes, "each of which is relatively self-contained, and each of which ends in a series of rapid dramatic actions and/or in an unresolved cliff-hanging sequence." Buckland argues that motifs, parallels, and the manipulation of viewer and character knowledge offset the episodic qualities of Spielberg's blockbuster. Instead of dismantling classical standards, he claims, *Raiders* integrates serial elements into a unified structure and achieves the marks of classical storytelling.[12] Buckland maintains that fundamental studio-era standards remain in force.

Buckland's conclusion is convincing, but in seeking to disprove the post-classical thesis, his analysis only broadly addresses the sound serial. Our interest is less to establish narrative sophistication of *Raiders*, which in comparison to a serial seems blatantly obvious, but to understand the trade-offs and transformations involved in adaptation. A close look at the film reveals points of overlap and distinction between the blockbuster and the serial. *Raiders* nego-tiates traditions, reinforcing shared tactics and finding ways to emulate serial qualities within a feature. Lucas, Spielberg, and Kasdan undertook a process of translation rather than re-creation: a process that inevitably leaves much of the original language unspoken but develops a vocabulary for the contemporary action adventure.

Raiders of the Lost Ark: Plotting the Serial in Three Acts

Raiders takes openly from Republic's catalog. Indy's (Harrison Ford) facility with a bullwhip derives from the Zorro serials, the opening jungle chase to an awaiting seaplane from *Jungle Girl*, and elements of archaeology and desert intrigue from *Perils of Nyoka*, among others. But the film just as readily appropriates from studio-era feature-length programmers like *China* (John Farrow, 1943) and *Secret of the Incas* (Jerry Hopper, 1954) (likely sources for Indiana Jones's costume) and from canonized classics including *Casablanca* (Michael Curtiz, 1942), *The Treasure of the Sierra Madre* (John Huston, 1948), and even *Citizen Kane* (Orson Welles, 1941). However, something more fundamental supports these surface similarities and direct quotations: the adoption of storytelling built out of "narrow misses and close calls." Lucas, Spielberg, and Kasdan's appropriations are neither superficial borrowings nor simple thefts.

The story's essentials are standard serial issue: heroes and villains pursue a weenie. Reaching back to World War II–era serials like *Spy Smasher, Adventures of Smilin' Jack* (Collins and Taylor, 1942), *Secret Service in Darkest Africa* (Bennet, 1943), and *Jungle Queen*, *Raiders* handily activates "good war" Manichaeism. The Nazis, and Belloq (Paul Freeman) by association, are irredeemably evil and in thrall to their unseen overlord bent on world domination. Nazi plans to wield the Ark of the Covenant as a superweapon capable of "leveling mountains and laying waste to entire regions" set the plot in motion and give our protagonists a heroic goal. The trail of the Ark is not quite as extended as that of the Tablets of Hippocrates, but it establishes a clear itinerary. In a lengthy exposition scene set in a lecture hall, we learn that Indy must obtain the headpiece of the Staff of Ra and bring it to the map room in Tanis, which will reveal the location of the Well of Souls where the Ark has been hidden. The weenie hunt organizes the film's first half, after which the Ark trades hands between the Nazis and Indy. Ultimately, like the Scorpion and Don del Oro, the villains fall prey to their own device. In a self-conscious twist, the

Ark is literally a machine of God, powered not by radium or some mysterious ray but by Old Testament righteousness. That our heroes are spared the wrath confirms their unquestioned moral superiority.

The contest between heroes and villains plays out as a series of physical challenges and confrontations, but *Raiders* modifies serial components to fit feature-film proportions. It is comparatively light in the chase and fight departments. Indy engages in five major brawls and pursuits, and one very brief punch-up. His serial counterpart would encounter about twelve in a similar running time. *Raiders* offers up three instances of entrapment and escape, spaced at the start (the South American cave), the middle (the Well of Souls), and the end (the Ark ceremony), and two cycles of hostage taking and liberation (when Marion is abducted in Cairo and then again aboard the cargo ship). Assuming the two-hour feature is roughly equivalent to five chapters, we would safely expect a serial to churn out six cliffhangers and up to five middle-action imperilments and rescues. Aware of this from the very start of their story conference, Lucas advised his collaborators that a cliffhanger situation every ten minutes would yield twelve situations, which he warned "may be a little much. Six times is plenty."[13]

Buckland proposes breaking the film down into six sections, based on location and the protagonist's goals. Following his lead, we might identify six "chapters" buried within the feature:

Chapter 1: We are introduced to Indy during his hunt for a golden idol in South America, which is taken from him by his nemesis, a rival archaeologist named Belloq (Paul Freeman) [20 minutes].

Chapter 2: Indy returns to his job as a university professor and is drafted by government officials to acquire the Ark of the Covenant before Belloq and the Nazis claim it for the Reich. Indy travels to Nepal, reunites with his estranged girlfriend and fellow adventurer Marion Ravenwood (Karen Allen), and battles Nazis over the headpiece of the Staff of Ra, a clue to the Ark's resting place. [21 minutes]

Chapter 3: Indy and Marion reach Cairo and contact Sallah (John Rhys-Davies), who has been following the Nazis' activities. Marion is kidnapped, Indy confronts Belloq but evades capture, and he and Sallah learn how to use the headpiece. [15 minutes]

Chapter 4: At the Nazis' archaeological dig in Tanis, Sallah and Indy discover both Marion and the Ark, but Belloq gets the drop on the heroes. The episode climaxes in a cliffhanger with Indy and Marion sealed in the Well of Souls—a snake-filled tomb. [21 minutes]

Chapter 5: Indy and Marion escape from the tomb, blow up a Nazi airplane, and reacquire the Ark in an extended truck chase. They attempt to smuggle the Ark to England aboard the *Bantu Wind*, a cargo ship, but are intercepted by a Nazi U-boat. Marion and the Ark again fall into enemy hands, while Indy hides aboard the submarine. [26 minutes]

Chapter 6: The final chapter begins on the secret island where Belloq and the Nazis plan to open the Ark. Indy is captured once again and forced to witness the ceremony, but the Ark unleashes the wrath of God upon the Nazis, killing them all. Marion and Indy are spared because they avert their gaze from the Ark. In the epilogue, upon returning to America, Indy learns that the authorities have confiscated the Ark, and he takes Marion's arm, confirming their romance. The final shot, in homage to the last scene in *Citizen Kane*, shows workers storing the Ark in a vast warehouse filled with hundreds of similar crates. [17 minutes]

These divisions more or less capture the plot's speedy movement among locations and action sequences.[14] Each chapter contains a well-defined melodramatic situation, which is resolved through physical problem solving and/or spectacle. The varied lengths of the episodes, ranging from fifteen to twenty-six minutes, and a surprising lack of cliffhanger endings in this analysis, suggest that *Raiders* does not so much retread serial structure as evoke it within the limits of contemporary norms.

Raiders also conforms to the most widely recognized formula for the mainstream American screenplay: the three-act structure. This format, popularly advocated by the screenwriting guru Syd Field in his book *Screenplay: The Foundations of Screenwriting* (1979), is something of an industry standard. In a typical two-hour film with each page translating into about a minute of screen time, the first act should last thirty pages, the second act sixty, and the third another thirty. Bordwell explains that this template is actually more rigid than those associated with studio-era Hollywood production, but it has become a standard formula for mass-market films since the 1980s.[15] This 30/60/30 division encourages scripts with unified action split between setup (act 1), complication (act 2), and climax (act 3). *Raiders* breaks into the following acts:

Act 1: Within the first thirty-three minutes, *Raiders* introduces the main characters, their goals, and the stakes. This concludes when Marion and Indy join forces as the Raven bar burns to the ground.

Act 2: Conventionally this act accounts for about one-half of the total running time, and in *Raiders* it lasts just over an hour. It opens when Indy and Marion arrive in Cairo and culminates with Marion's recapture just after she and Indy have reignited their romance aboard the *Bantu Wind*.

Act 3: The final act coincides with the sixth episode, beginning when Indy and the Nazi U-boat arrive at the secret island and ending with his and

Marion's reunion in Washington, DC. It efficiently packs the climax and epilogue into an unusually succinct seventeen minutes.[16]

Laid out this way, *Raiders* confirms Bordwell's observation that contemporary action films are "more tightly woven than they need to be" and that the "industry's ideal action movie is as formally strict as a minuet."[17] Where the chapter breakdown emphasizes discrete melodramatic situations, the act structure foregrounds character relationships and classical balance. Indy and Marion are cynical former lovers at the end of act 1. Throughout act 2, they learn to work as a team, falling into one another's arms aboard the *Bantu Wind*. In act 3, Indy's pursuits of the Ark and of Marion fully align, and though he loses the weenie to the American government, he gains a romantic partner. The romantic subplot, foreign to serials but a staple of the Hollywood feature, cements episodes together into acts and gives them closure.

As noted in chapter 1, debates about classicism oppose unity and coherence to the ad hoc accretion of situations. The two blueprints for *Raiders*, however, suggest that melodramatic and causal plot construction need not be fundamentally at odds. The film welds serial situations to the three-act framework, which imposes a quasi-Aristotelian composition of beginning, middle, and end, while also supporting an episodic model. In this sense, *Raiders* answers to both classical and nonclassical or postclassical readings. The boundary between melodrama and classicism could be porous. In their study of the early feature film, Brewster and Jacobs observe that well-motivated situations can give melodrama the appearance of strong causality. Even Georges Polti, author of *The Thirty-six Dramatic Situations*, warns against relying on noticeable coincidence to resolve situations, and he rejects overly familiar devices because they make melodramatic contrivance too obvious. For instance, according to Polti, the public had grown weary of the thirty-fifth situation, Recovery of a Lost One, because of "the fortuitous coincidences with which it has too generously been interlarded."[18] The successful melodramatist could combine episodes with enough care that the play has the look and feel of a classically unified story, save for the fact that it is constructed from preexisting situations that carry with them spectacular potentials. *Raiders* and many other contemporary action films take this approach by finding opportunities within the three-act structure to fit situations together, tempering coincidence and marking out character development.

In terms of plotting, the film's strongest tie to the chapterplay resides in the weenie hunt, a serial method of suggesting unity while arranging situations. The Ark of the Covenant's closest serial relative is probably the Sacred Scepter from the lost tomb of Genghis Khan, which structures the plot of *Drums of Fu Manchu* (Witney and English, 1940). The Scepter may not have the Ark's supernatural punch, but it is buried in a hidden chamber somewhere in a distant land (vaguely described as "the Orient") and grants its owner the status of a new messiah. Its possession is the key to Fu Manchu's quest for world domination. Yet where the Ark's discovery requires two steps (acquire the headpiece, go to the map room), the Scepter's requires six. The two sides first battle over the Dalai Plaque and then over a secret papyrus hidden within the plaque. The papyrus requires translation, and it points to the Kardac Segment, a sort of code cipher. Fu Manchu acquires the segment, but the heroes make a cast from an impression left when it dropped into the mud, much like the impression of the staff head burned into Major Toht's (Ronald Lacey) hand. Heroes and villains race to Asia to find the Temple of the Blind Dragon, where the segment fits into an altar. First they must discover that this temple is now called the Temple of the Sun, and once there Fu Manchu uses the Segment to ignite a crystal-powered laser-beam sacrificial altar. Only in chapter 10 do the characters learn the location of Genghis Khan's tomb, and they acquire the Scepter in chapter 11. Each clue in the hunt for the Scepter entails a cliffhanger trap and/or deadly confrontation with Fu Manchu and his army of Dacoit henchmen.

In comparison, the quest in *Raiders* is positively minimal: an express route to the prize. There are no dead ends, and Indy's map points directly to the weenie, rather than to another set of obscure inscriptions. The weenie itself is self-contained, and once discovered it is fully functional. Streamlining helps *Raiders* maintain coherence and internal plausibility, keeping viewers oriented to a clear causal chain. Still, in both serial and feature the weenie hunt serves the same purpose: it provides a framework for situations. The Cairo sequence features a chase and fight concluding in Marion's abduction. It also provides two last-minute rescues: first when Sallah sends street urchins to interrupt the Nazi agents holding Indy at gunpoint, and second when he stops our hero from eating a poisoned date. Once the action moves to the archaeological site at Tanis, Lucas, Kasdan and Spielberg contrive a race against time as Indy and Sallah infiltrate the map room before the sun passes, and a fatal entrapment when Indy and Marion are sealed in the Well of Souls. Once the heroes escape, the plot passes beyond the initial itinerary laid out in the exposition scene and focuses on the direct struggle for possession of the Ark. The story mirrors the last four chapters of *Drums of Fu Manchu*, but with more unifying touches. In a serial, the weenie offers a method for joining together otherwise disparate situations; it provides a kind of forced appearance of unity. In the feature, with the three-act structure and character relationships helping to ensure classical causality, the weenie is more important as a framework for thrills.

The simplified weenie hunt reduces the need for detailed reiteration of goals and rapid movement from point to point along the map. This helps the itinerary mesh with the aim of providing viewers a coherent emotional experience by opening room for character development. Lucas, Kasdan and Spielberg fill longer nonaction stretches with exposition and travel, as in the serial, but they also offer scenes that sketch character relationships, backstory, beliefs, and emotional stakes. Indy's brief chat with Marcus, for example, underlines the importance of the Ark and its power but also brings up our hero's lack of faith: "I don't believe in magic, a lot of superstitious hocus-pocus. I'm going after a find of incredible historical significance; you're talking about the boogey-man." Though a minor thread in the film, this first-act exchange sets up character development for Indy when in the third act he experiences the hocus-pocus firsthand and averts his eyes. Similarly, Belloq takes the opportunity to observe: "You and I are very much alike. Archaeology is our religion, yet we have both fallen from the pure faith. . . . I am a shadowy reflection of you." The none-too-subtle parallel of hero and villain may be an action-film cliché, but it is starkly opposed to the serial's moral clarity. The third act ties up both the Belloq parallel and the romance when the Ark annihilates the villain, and Indy saves Marion. Spielberg reaches toward the kind of elegant efficiency of the studio-era films that he reveres. This fluid weave of theme and emotional texture throws the austerity of serial exposition into strong relief. Serial writers had little incentive to spend valuable time developing characters when that might muddy the moral dichotomies, make them less appropriable to play, and task actors with charting character change. For the blockbuster, character exposition bridges situational melodrama and classical causality.

The three-act structure also facilitates a more flexible rhythm. In place of the chapterplay's unrelenting schedule, the pulse of events in *Raiders* appears to be set within the story world by character needs and actions, rather than externally imposed running times. Ironically, the act structure's variability allows *Raiders* to exaggerate serial pacing. Just after the film's midpoint, Spielberg piles action sequences on top of one another, barely breaking to reorient viewers. Intervals of scarcely two minutes separate the escape from the Well of Souls, the fight on the German airstrip, and the horse-and-truck chase. Though few serial episodes could afford this stretch of wall-to-wall action, it is the sequence that most strongly evokes sound-serial momentum. Our heroes encounter and navigate disparate problem spaces in quick succession. Stunts abound: in the tomb, Indy topples a huge statue to reveal the hidden passage; on the tarmac, Marion uses the airplane's guns to ignite a gas explosion while Indy exploits the propeller to defeat the Nazi thug; and when he is thrown through the windshield during the chase, Indy climbs along the speeding truck's undercarriage, pulls himself to the roof, and reenters the cab. The truck stunt, a tribute to Yakima Canutt's stagecoach stunt in *Zorro's Fighting Legion*, itself replayed in *Stagecoach* (John Ford, 1939), is *Raiders of the Lost Ark*'s greatest showpiece of spectacle on a human scale. It caps a run of action situations drawn from the serial repertoire, but it is a run that would be impossible in an actual chapterplay. Where serial filmmakers would revert to an exposition scene, here action can crest and recede in time with plot developments. The three-act structure can reach fever pitch where the serial moves in steady lockstep.

Emulating the Cliffhanger: Three Sequences from *Raiders*

Raiders aims to harness serial pleasures, but while a high-budget, self-contained story can excel at both spectacle and character individuation, it must rule out the cliffhanger. Sound serials give viewers arrested scenarios, reversible catastrophes, and parameters for play. The feature film necessarily anchors and closes situations, leaving Lucas, Spielberg, and Kasdan to seek equivalents within the confines of three acts. Contrary to the postclassical argument, it appears that *Raiders* must work to make room for serial sensations. The film continuously offers suspense scenes, some of them contained within action sequences (as in the conflagration of the Raven bar) and others merely hinted at and then dropped (as in Toht's truncated interrogation of Marion at the excavation site). Three sequences stand out as fully realized variations on serial situations: the prologue in South America, Indy and Marion's entrapment in the Well of Souls, and Marion's capture and liberation at the film's climax. Each merits discussion for the way it emulates the cliffhanger within an ongoing narrative.

The modular action prologue, vaguely connected to the main narrative, is a generic adaptation of serial convention. James Bond films standardized the practice. Each installment reintroduces the titular spy at the climax of a dangerous mission, like a serial episode that opens by resolving the previous week's cliffhanger. Because they so rarely have direct causal implications for the events that follow, action prologues offer prime situational real estate. Filmmakers can spring life-or-death traps with little exposition or consequence. In the Bond films, the modular openings also suggest a continuing story; they encourage viewers to imagine the unseen adventure that brought the hero to a point of crisis.

Indy's retrieval of the golden idol at the opening of *Raiders* capitalizes on the action prologue's implied seriality. Spielberg introduces Jones as a serial figure, withholding individuation for three minutes while the camera follows his trek through the forest. The revealing close-up comes after Indy strikes the gun from an assassin's hand with his bullwhip in a cutting-and-sound pattern borrowed from *Zorro's Fighting Legion*. Milieu, costume, and signature weapon announce Jones as a fully formed and physically defined explorer in the midst of his latest adventure. Action prologues resemble serials in that they equate the character with an identifiable narrative architecture, inhabitable by any number of actors, stuntmen, or imaginative film fans.

Raiders intensifies this kinship to seriality by multiplying potential cliff-hangers. Indy runs a gauntlet of fatal traps, any of which might have been interrupted by the close of a previous episode. His partner (Alfred Molina) deserts Indy on the wrong side of a bottomless pit across from a slowly closing stone door. It is a crystal-clear problem space requiring our hero to leap over the pit and slide under the door in the nick of time. When his jump falls short and he scrambles for a handhold only to discover that the root he grabs is not anchored, Indy begins to slip into the pit and the door inches downward. All is lost. A cut back to Indy reveals that the root has in fact held his weight, allowing him to scramble to safety. Spielberg fluidly joins cliffhanger and take-out, protracting the moment of suspense via cutting but then rapidly resolving the problem.

Moments later Spielberg springs the film's most famous trap, an eighty-ton boulder that careers down the tunnel toward Indy. The situation is admirably vivid, recalling Gene's attempt to outrun the wall of rushing water on his motorcycle in *Daredevils of the Red Circle*. Spielberg and Lucas borrowed the device from *The Seven Cities of Cibola*, an Uncle Scrooge comic published in 1954, but the boulder trap also evokes *Goddess of the Far West*, the second episode of *Perils of Pauline* (Gasnier and MacKenzie, 1914).[19] Seven shots show the boulder closing in on Indy as he races through the cavern. The first exposes the rock bearing down from above and behind him as he whisks out of frame in the foreground. The second shot seals Indy's fate by framing the action from behind the rock as it rolls down in front of the camera, blotting out our view of the hero. It is reminiscent of the final frame of the first episode of *Daredevils*, in which the torrent overtakes the camera. But *Raiders* cannot pause. Instead a cut farther down the tunnel reveals Indy continuing toward the camera with the boulder at his heels. In the fourth shot, he stumbles but regains momentum just before he is crushed. In the sixth shot, Douglas Slocombe's telephoto lens provides persuasive evidence of Indy's certain demise by exaggerating the boulder's proximity to our hero. The stunt delivers a cliffhanger's operational clarity and catastrophic inevitability. Spielberg formally elaborates the stunts in the manner of a William Witney showstopper. Images that seem to guarantee Indy's demise would be right at home as the final frame of a Republic serial chapter. True to form, Indy escapes the rock by leaping through an undetected opening in the cave, only to be held at knife and arrow point by a tribe of warriors. The prologue's concatenation of narrow misses announces the film's generic affiliation in no uncertain terms. It also sets the terms of our relationship with this world: we will follow an unambiguous hero through perilous labyrinths, which he surmounts with physical mastery and luck.

Indy's cave adventure needs little setup beyond the swift definition of character and goal, and, as in a serial, situational immediacy secures our investment. But the nature of the device changes when appended to a first act. In features, in-medias-res openings help mask the artifice of storytelling. Action prologues plunge viewers into the ongoing flow of an apparently continuous diegesis: a world in progress. By contrast, cliffhanger resolutions emphasize the narrator's hand. Episode recaps directly addresses viewers either by text or voice-over, and the take-outs highlight the act of telling by rearranging and cheating events. Serials acknowledge their viewers with overt and arbitrary narration, where most features seek to absorb them into a seamlessly unfolding story world. The visual miscues that seem to depict Indy's demise beneath the onrushing rock are the remnants of serial discontinuity in a continuous film. Narration can mislead viewers at the level of basic perception, but not for long, and not at the cost of breaking the diegesis.

The second act of *Raiders* builds to the film's most vivid cliffhanger situation: Belloq and the Nazis seal Marion and Indy in the Well of Souls. Spielberg crafts the scene with an air of finality. Belloq, framed from a low and distant angle as though viewed from the depths of the pit, basks in his triumph: "What a fitting end to your life's pursuits. You're about to become a permanent addition to this archaeological find." Once Marion is tossed into the hole and lands face-to-face with a king cobra, Belloq bids Indy "adieu," and we witness the heavy stone cover sliding into place. It casts a shadow over our heroes, and Marion's screams are muffled and then silenced as workers close the chamber. Sallah, held at gunpoint, lowers his head in grief. *Raiders* is full of potential cliffhangers: deadlocks showcased and resolved in a continual flow of action. The Well of Souls is different. Spielberg lingers on details and extends the moment into a brief pause, allowing the parameters of the trap to crystallize, the hopelessness to sink in. It is an extraordinarily focused predicament. The heroes are captured, the weenie is secured by the villain, and all is now very definitely lost.

The three-act feature reshapes the serial's routine climaxes into a larger-scale arc of tension and release. Serial cliffhangers can be gloriously capricious, but *Raiders* takes care to line the hero, innocent, weenie, and villain up in this way only at the midpoint and the climax. Its pride of place distinguishes the Well of Souls from perils in a serial, where all cliffhangers appear equally catastrophic and their regularity creates an oddly reassuring rhythm of anomalous suspense. Kasdan has further integrated the situation with motifs: this is the second time that Belloq appropriates Indy's discovery, a point underscored by dialogue; it mirrors Indy's abandonment on the wrong side of the bottomless pit at the film's start; and it brings to fruition his fear of snakes. The viewers, and Indy, are back where they started in South America, and this time things are even worse.

Indy and Marion's fatal entrapment calls on many of the same viewing protocols as an actual cliffhanger. To the extent that we have internalized the three-act rhythm of a feature, we recognize that death and defeat are unlikely outcomes at this juncture. In this sense, all suspense in genre films might be weakly anomalous. *Raiders*, though, has stacked the deck by creating a single, externally defined serial-style hero and by constructing a world marked by studio-era references and clichés. This is not the kind of a hero who loses, nor the kind of a world that allows him to. But if we know that Indy will survive, Lucas, Spielberg, and Kasdan can delight in sealing the problem space. Nearly ten pages of the story conference transcript are devoted to working out this situation. Lost in a secret chamber that had protected the Ark for centuries, Indy and Marion are surrounded by venomous snakes as their torches burn low. The take-out appears particularly tight because the threat reveals the solution. If the snakes have survived for so long in this chamber, they must have means of egress. Indy discovers that they are coming into the chamber from behind a wall. He quickly makes use of the conspicuously tall statue that Spielberg has twice before called attention to (when it terrifies Sallah and when it breaks Marion's fall). Crashing the statue through the wall reveals a hidden passage and a way out. Indy's physical problem solving opens a seemingly inescapable space and delivers something close to the pleasure of a well-made serial.

As in a serial, the weenie changes hands and the hero finds himself back where he started, despite a breakneck pace of action. Where the chapterplay might repeat the pattern ad infinitum, Spielberg faces a different kind of formal constraint. He must escalate action toward a strongly anticipated climax within a single showing. The serial can spin out countless episodes, but the feature must progress. *Raiders* delivers a viewer experience somewhere between those provided by a very short serial and a very long episode.

Typically the third act of an action film, which Bordwell describes as "a continuous climax, often a race against time," offers the most likely place to develop and resolve a melodramatic situation.[20] Here, contemporary action films almost invariably deploy races to the rescue, hostage situations, or chases with specific tangible deadlines and pyrotechnic displays. The fact that the third act and the sixth chapter of *Raiders* are coterminous suggests an affinity between serials and feature climaxes generally. Hostage situations have a long melodramatic lineage. The basic structure is a variation on what Polti calls Deliverance, and Crime Pursued by Vengeance (his situations 2 and 3), and serials regularly avail themselves of the situation, sometimes repeatedly in a single episode. In features the device is especially useful for climactic confrontations because it aligns romantic and action goals. In *Adventures of Robin Hood* and countless contemporary action films from *Die Hard* (John McTiernan, 1988) to *Speed* (Jan de Bont, 1994) to *Spiderman 2* (Sam Raimi, 2004), the third-act hostage situation facilitates both victory over the villain and romantic closure.

Marion's final abduction swings the film into its final act, which restages the central conflict in stark terms. Kasdan and Spielberg complicate the hostage situation when they introduce a standoff over the Ark. The standoff between heroes and villains arranged as a deadlock such that neither party can strike is another situation directly inherited from nineteenth-century melodrama, but this one lacks a satisfying resolution.[21] Climbing atop an embankment with a bazooka, Indy halts the soldiers who are carrying the Ark through the island's interior. He threatens to blow up the Ark unless Belloq and Toht free Marion. Indy's gamble suggests character development. The hero who earlier had left Marion tied up in the enemy's tent will now sacrifice the weenie for love. Belloq, however, calls Indy's bluff, offers him a clear shot at the Ark, and appeals to the archaeologists' professional code: "You and I are passing through history. This [*gesturing to the Ark*] . . . this is history." Indy breaks the stalemate, lowering his weapon and surrendering to his captors.

The moment is irreconcilable with serial principles. Belloq traps Indy by placing the hero's two goals in tension, creating a psychological dilemma. For a comparison, recall Nyoka and Larry's choice in chapter 10: administer a potentially lethal dose of adrenaline to her unconscious father in order to reveal the location of the weenie, or elect surgery that will restore his memory but erase his knowledge of the lost tablets. Nyoka's dilemma is more contrived than Indy's but no less fraught. The trail of the Tablets of Hippocrates led Nyoka to discover her father, but the Tablets also contain the cure for cancer and other dread diseases. Larry, if anyone, should be entrapped by this impossible choice. His professional code (named for the very Tablets he seeks) requires him to do good or at least to do no harm. Is risking the life of one elderly professor who mistakes himself for a tribal leader worth the cure for cancer? In *Nyoka* the answer is an immediate and unambiguous no. The heroes barely acknowledge the question; being right is always a clear choice. In refusing to shoot the Ark, by contrast, Indy admits crippling ethical ambivalence. Serials take place in a morally determined and legible universe, but Lucas, Spielberg, and Kasdan devise a cliffhanger with no take-out. Belloq wins; Indy is helpless.

This truncated cliffhanger prepares the way for the big climax. Where serials invest in each cliffhanger equally, *Raiders* promises a spectacular revelation. Lucas, Spielberg, and Kasdan must escalate perils toward the end. From the lecture-hall exposition scene in which Indy produces an illuminated manuscript depicting the Ark's blinding light through intimations of its power suggested through the score, mysterious wind, and a shot of the swastika burning off the shipping crate aboard the cargo ship, *Raiders* systematically builds expectations. We are very curious. Serial viewers, upon reaching a final episode, are prepared for the adventure to stop, but not necessarily to reach a satisfying conclusion. The three-act structure, because of its familiarity as a norm, also signals the approaching end, but with the promise of meaningful closure. Viewers can fully expect that the plot elements will align themselves in the final half hour to facilitate a speedy resolution, and this buys the filmmakers room to tease them with an unwinnable dilemma. In his plea to Indy, Belloq holds out the enticement of spectacle: "Inside the Ark are treasures beyond your wildest aspirations. You want to see it open as well as I." Our hero's inability to behave heroically may be impossible in a serial and disappointing in a feature, but it also protects our anticipated narrative and visual pleasures.

In the film's ultimate problem space, the Nazis have tied Indy and Marion to a lamppost on a ridge overlooking field operations set up for opening the Ark. The hero and heroine bound to a post, like Nyoka and her father in Cassib's burning tent, are helpless innocents at the mercy of the merciless. The villains follow serial protocol in setting a dramatic tableau. Portable lights ring a dais carved into the rock face surrounded by the deep darkness of the desert night. Belloq, in ceremonial garb, mumbles sacred incantations as ranks of armed soldiers look on. The ritual has the air of a sacrifice, with Indy and Marion perched precariously on the perimeter. For the first time since the midpoint, heroes, villains, and weenie are arrayed with schematic clarity. Spielberg, however, does not create the suspense of an ineluctably encroaching threat: no fires, buzz saws, or laser beams have been trained on our protagonists; no rescuers have been left conveniently unattended on the periphery of the action, and our victims do not struggle to escape. The Nazis, focused on the Ark, pay their hostages no mind. Indy and Marion are mere witnesses, "passing through history." Tense anticipation of spectacle rather than fear for survival drives the scene. The blockbuster transmutes the cliffhanger into a situation that resembles Spielberg's climax to *Close Encounters of the Third Kind* (1977) more than a serial confrontation. Viewers and characters are united by the simple desire to see what comes next.

When Belloq inadvertently unleashes the Ark's pyrotechnic power, *Raiders* delivers a sensation scene that mixes elements of horror (wraiths, melting faces, and an exploding head), science fiction (a fiery death ray reminiscent of George Pal's 1953 *War of the Worlds*), and religious spectacle (a pillar of fire reaching to the heavens). It is a combination of Polti's second and thirty-first situations: deliverance comes in the form of "punishment for contempt of a god."[22] *Raiders* pulls out all the stops to resolve the final hostage situation, meeting improbability with blinding spectacle. God's wrath prevents catastrophe with a whirlwind of visual effects.

The climax shares the sound serial's enthusiasm for arbitrary victory. Indy and Marion survive by averting their gaze, as the ancient power of God cuts their bonds and vaporizes the enemy. Indy saves Marion's life with simple and direct advice: "Don't look at it, no matter what happens." The fact that this means of escape has not been previously planted in the story lends it the appearance of a cheat: a secret passage conveniently discovered at the last minute.[23] For critics of melodrama, the scene must be an affront to the ideals of causal storytelling. Not only does the hand of God dispatch the bad guys, it also more or less invalidates the hero's causal agency. Indy's efforts to keep the Ark out of Nazi hands do not clearly change the course of events. In resting on spectacle rather than character action, this third-act climax borrows a serial situation for a blockbuster end. It would seem to confirm Richard Schickel's oft-quoted lambast that contemporary action-adventures "offer a succession of undifferentiated sensations, lucky or unlucky accidents, that have little or nothing to do with whatever went before or is about to come next."[24] But as melodrama, the ending is fittingly spectacular. Causality takes a distant third place behind sensation and the emotional recognition of virtue.

Finally, then, the climax of *Raiders* substantially modifies serial characteristics but also occupies common ground with them. The passive, conflicted hero and the lack of a concretely specified impending threat to the hostages are alien to the world of the chapterplay. So too are Lucas, Spielberg, and Kasdan's efforts to unify the story with motifs, patterns of narration, and a romantic backstory. The intimations of the Ark's power and the three-act structure's tendency to escalate and intensify central conflicts help mask and motivate plot contrivances, something most serials seem unconcerned with. But imagery, situation, and the minimal, arbitrary means by which Indy survives are firmly in the serial's wheelhouse. Commenting on contemporary narrative structures, Murray Smith notes that trends in popular Hollywood film are "traceable to serials, B-adventures, and episodic melodramas" of the studio era.[25] *Raiders* plainly borrows from the serial, and even its climax, which deviates from the form in the name of blockbuster showmanship, remains rooted in situational dramaturgy.

Conclusion and the Serial Re-Bourne

The Bond films and *Raiders* demonstrate the influence of serials on popular action and adventure cinema in different ways. Broccoli and Saltzman searched the serial storehouse for gimmicks and situations that they could update for an older audience. In blending serial elements with Fleming's spy narrative and other generalized pulp-thriller ingredients, the Bond series formulated a resilient model for action films, *Raiders* among them. Its borrowings are largely unacknowledged, in part because of the shift in demographics, and because the franchise quickly eclipsed the serial in worldwide popularity. Lucas's and Spielberg's debt to the serial is more conscious and specific. For them, the serial was an archive of ideas, a nostalgic reference point, and a model of viewer involvement. *Star Wars* and *Raiders* emerged from Lucas's and Spielberg's desire to recreate their childhood experiences of studio-era cinema.

In overtly and successfully emulating the sound serial, *Raiders* reveals both continuities and distinctions. Foremost, it displays the contemporary action film's accommodation of melodramatic principles. Situations and sensation scenes, from the one-reel era forward, have been the building blocks of action and adventure cinema. Like the early features that Brewster and Jacobs study, serials import situational dramaturgy to generate engaging narratives that emphasize immediate and flamboyant suspense over unity or coherence. Serials were the studio era's purest avatars of action melodrama, which also informed some feature genres like the historical adventure, the crime film, and the Western. In stark contrast to the sound serial's marginal role in the cinema marketplace, *Raiders* was a defining exemplar of the Hollywood blockbuster.

Yet *Raiders* does not attempt to ape either the five-part formula of an episode nor the meandering path of a whole serial. Rather, it breaks out identifiable components of the serial form (stunts, cliffhangers, the weenie hunt, suspense situations) and redistributes them across three acts. This structure may be no less artificial than a serial's, but it affords time to construct internal plausibility. Without the pressure to deliver physical situations every five minutes, Kasdan's screenplay can let tension build or action explode, as events seem to merit. Widely viewed as advantages, gains in plausibility and organic rhythm also involve a loss. Feature films tame the serial's wild and distinctive mix of predictable formula and unbounded inventiveness, its freedom to elevate the vivid over the credible while still keeping to an itinerary.

Since the early 1980s the blockbuster action film has solidified into one of Hollywood's sturdiest tent poles. Lavishly produced adventures, released in the summer and aimed toward younger audiences, support the industry as a whole. Many bear resemblance to sound serials in premise and to *Raiders* in structure. Marvel Studios' superhero cycle, for instance, seems an obvious inheritor of the chapterplay's ethos. But few films throw the cliffhanger's legacy into relief better than the Jason Bourne trilogy. Where it is easy to trace correspondences between Republic's *Captain America* (English and Clifton, 1944) and Marvel's (Joe Johnston, 2011), the Bourne franchise reveals how conventions have wended their way into more "mature" branches of the action genre. We close this chapter by considering the persistence of serial elements in a transformed state.

Films from the Jason Bourne franchise helped renew the flagging secret-agent formula by reconfiguring conventions. Between 2002 and 2007, the producer Pat Crowley and the screenwriter Tony Gilroy, along with a large and shifting group of collaborators, developed three films based on Robert Ludlum's character and starring Matt Damon: *The Bourne Identity* (Doug Liman, 2002); *The Bourne Supremacy* (Paul Greengrass, 2004); and *The Bourne Ultimatum* (Paul Greengrass, 2007). All three received strong critical praise for character depth and realism, a striking departure from discourse around Bond.

Todd McCarthy called *Identity* "cold-bloodedly realistic" and "a character piece," David Edelstein praised *Supremacy's* "vérité charge" and its "bravura cliffhangers," and Carina Chocano concluded that *Ultimatum* is "ultimately a movie about self-discovery. It moves fast but its real momentum is internal."[26] Each film presents a convoluted conspiracy plot in which the amnesiac secret agent of the title must piece together a traumatic event and expose the powers responsible. Bourne's memory loss leaves him with fleeting images of past events that he investigates, leading to a new revelation about his training and work as a government assassin. The premise and plotting would seem ill suited to the situational clarity demanded by the serial tradition.

In fact, the Bourne films share a great deal with Bond, *Raiders*, and serials. Bourne's amnesia is a melodramatic chestnut. It conveniently concretizes the character's internal struggle, turning his past into something like a weenie that he must repeatedly chase. Journeys of self-discovery may be antithetical to the chapterplay, but in repeating the same character arc in each film, the franchise offers a formulaic version of psychological development that meshes with serial convention; Bourne is instantly legible and predictable, even in his personal growth. The trilogy's attempt at complex narration also summons up serial technique. In perhaps the most elaborate possible variation on a serial recap, almost all of the action in *Ultimatum* takes place during an ellipsis passed over at the end of *Supremacy*. These similarities suggest that Bourne and serials play related games, but they also traffic in similar pleasures.

Each film puts Bourne through a series of chases, fights, entrapments, and escapes, as he seeks to unravel a clearly set enigma. The apparent complexities of the conspiracy plots, which are further obscured by Greengrass's formal abstractions in the later two films, place pressure on the filmmakers to vividly define each action situation. As in a serial, the whole makes little sense, but the parts are powerfully lucid. Bourne is a physical problem solver exploiting his surroundings to defeat a steady stream of henchmen. Greengrass's film style, greeted by critics as realistic, renders action as a barrage of fragments, broken by accelerated editing and a juddering camera. Specific actions may be blurred, but situations deliver schematic parameters of hero, villain, and challenge. The central pleasure of the franchise involves witnessing the hero liberate himself from seemingly airtight situations. In each film, the government shadow organization activates "assets," instantly recognizable henchmen that Bourne must evade and kill, sets ambushes and traps that he must navigate, and deploys city police forces to chase him. He is caught in a serial's narrative architecture.

Bourne cleverly masters these problem spaces with detached efficiency. Amnesia provides an internal struggle and motivates bouts of subjective stylization, but it also empties Bourne of complexity, or even apparent thought, in the heat of action. Unable to recall how or why he is so lethally skilled, Bourne moves with the certainty and clean transparency of a serial hero.

When he appears cornered in a tiny interrogation room by a field agent and security guard in *Supremacy*, escape is a foregone conclusion. The field agent's ineffectual attempts to get Bourne to speak provide viewers with the chance to examine the physical situation (four walls, three men, a table and chair) and to anticipate his eventual repurposing of it. This fixes our attention on Bourne's procedure: the swift ease with which he floors the agent and guard, then obtains the agent's gun and clones his cell phone before locking the men, unconscious, in the cell. In the relative absence of technological gimmickry, the hero's movements engage operational aesthetics.

Bourne's foot chase through the streets and across the rooftops of Tangier in *Ultimatum* illustrates the franchise's investment in depicting and resolving problem spaces. Greengrass achieves novelty by shuffling conventions. The scenario elaborates pursuit and rescue into a triple chase: police pursue Bourne, who races to intercept the hit man Desh (Joey Ansah) before he reaches his fleeing target, Nicky Parsons (Julia Stiles). Greengrass places increasingly severe obstacles in Bourne's path, sometimes signaling solutions before identifying problems. When our speeding hero grabs laundry from a rooftop clothesline and wraps his hands, he introduces a momentary question answered by a quick shot of a wall lined with shards of broken glass. Bourne vaults effortlessly over the obstruction, leaving the police behind. Revealing the solution before the problem drives attention to in-the-moment procedures.

As Desh closes in on Nicky, Bourne must leap ever-widening gaps between buildings, culminating in his breathtaking jump through a closed window, which the handheld camera follows through the air. Bourne clears the first three chasms with ease, the camera barely discovering the obstacle as he navigates it. The appearance of the fourth and final window briefly halts him, allowing us to size it up and prepare for the leap. Greengrass broadcasts the approaching difficulty and sharply emphasizes its daring resolution. Bourne's abilities having been established in the previous jumps, a series of five shots covering this stunt directs viewers to procedure and process: the camera tracks quickly backward before the advancing hero, echoing his speed; a static shot allows him to rush through the frame; a cut-in presents Bourne's shoe striking the balcony railing; a low-angle long shot reveals the distance between the buildings. Constructive montage shows how rather than simply what. The fifth shot, which follows the hero over the edge and through the air, further invites spectators to share an embodied experience of physical problem solving. These cinematic goals are closely aligned with those of the sound serial. Bert's fluid navigation of industrial landscape to tackle a henchman in *Daredevils* delivers an equivalent kinetic charge, and anticipates Bourne by nearly seventy years.

Further removed from the tradition than the Bond series and lacking Spielberg's conscious emulation, the Bourne films may represent the outermost edge of the sound serial's range of influence. Indeed, if serials have shaped this franchise, it is by way of the Bond movies' appropriation of them. Bourne updates the formula by developing the hero's internal struggle and trimming back technological gimmickry: two choices that attenuate the appearance of serial melodrama. This has precedent in Broccoli and Saltzman's attempt to shift Bond in a more mature and legitimately dramatic direction during the climax of *On Her Majesty's Secret Service* (Peter Hunt, 1969), in which they allow the "third girl," who is Bond's new wife (Diana Rigg), to die. Bourne returns the favor by providing a model for Bond's darker, reflective reboot in *Casino Royale* (Martin Campbell, 2006). All cases resemble the late nineteenth-century modified melodramas identified by Neale in that they soften stock characterizations to raise the form's critical profile. Nonetheless, each is built on a sturdy situational framework that delivers regularly spaced requisite action. Like the contemporary action film generally, the Bourne movies participate in a cinematic practice vigorously constituted by studio-era serials. That is, they blend melodrama with forceful articulations of physical procedure in scenes of pursuit, entrapment, and confrontation. Causal unity and character depth are not essential to these pleasures.

8

Conclusion

● ●

This book argues that the sound serial is a unique popular cinematic art. Constructing stories on a five-part, chapter-by-chapter framework orients viewers to the passing moment and promotes the part over the whole. Characters and conflicts, built with the resources of melodrama, tend to be well defined, serving as unchanging vehicles for exciting happenstance and compelling operations. In place of the studio-era feature film's narrative progression, serials linger on cyclical process. Serial worlds, though fraught with constant peril, are also reassuringly predictable. They offer viewers regular return to physically navigable spaces, and they provide projectable situations. The chapterplay works like an efficient machine, churning through exposition and action, then suddenly stopping, reversing, and restarting. Viewers caught up in this mechanical rhythm are primed to continue its cognitive and physical processes, as though by inertia.

Cliffhangers, with their layered narrational address, discontinuities, and deceptions, are the sound serial's defining attribute. A compelling peril demands the clear and vivid depiction of physical inevitability. The specialized areas of serial craft, including stunt work, constructive editing, and repurposing footage, were honed in these scenes of certain catastrophe. Chapterplays are not known for narrative complexity, but weekly take-outs required withholding, reframing, and reordering information. In this way, cliffhangers exercise narrative competencies in anticipating unseen events, contemplating resolutions to apparently unsolvable predicaments, and detecting gaps in knowledge. Sundering action at the height of engagement transforms situations into puzzles and scenarios for play. Through the cliffhanger, serials seek to occupy spectators during the span between chapters, extending the experience of cinema beyond the matinee. The serial's highest aim was to entertain a return audience, but its invitation to dwell within the story could also serve as a training ground for cinematic thinking.

The serial's rigid parameters enabled speedy and cheap production. At first glance serials can appear poorly made, hardly worth the self-respecting film historian's attention. Though many of them are only adequate affairs, this should not blind us to their potential for refinement and virtuosity. Historical poetics sensitizes us to practical goals, norms, and variations. It illuminates the way formula can narrow problems and intensify creative focus. Neither *Daredevils* nor *Nyoka* set out to challenge or transcend convention; in fact, they cling to tried-and-true plot patterns and stock actions. Yet they also reveal the possibilities for innovation and achievement in formula filmmaking. The art of the serial lies not in formal unity or dramatic nuance but in balancing the five-part format toward action, multiplying the possible perils, and shaping film style into a means of kinetic engagement.

Aimed at a juvenile audience, and consumed by adults as well, sound serials presented the cinematic intersection of melodrama and play. Screenwriters built plots from the stockpile of action-oriented situations already defined by the one-reel melodrama and the silent serial. The chapterplay was home to powerfully visual depictions of innocence and villainy throughout the studio era, delivering a weekly dose of moral clarity to viewers of all ages. At the same time, sound serials promoted the operational aesthetic, exploiting the pleasures of concrete visible systems, which also found cultural expression in magic acts, *Popular Mechanics*, construction toys, slapstick comedy, and the silent serial. Crossed with conventions of play, these appeals took on practical significance for children. Sound serials offered inhabitable figures and portable scenarios, modeling the creative repurposing of material and space. Melodrama was conditioned by its value to play, with pathos subordinated to imitable action. Instead of loss and amplified emotion, sound serials gave their viewers fantasies of physical mastery in a world defined by intelligible (if implausible) problems and solutions. In the face of an ever-looming "too late," they rehearsed endlessly reassuring variations on "in the nick of time."

Continuities between the sound serial and the contemporary action film suggest that we should not view melodrama and classicism as mutually exclusive forces. In *Raiders of the Lost Ark,* Spielberg's narrative chugs along in continuity, plugging holes and closing gaps within a single showing, but it manages to evoke, if not duplicate, the sound serial's allure. Perhaps something like the serial dynamic inspired the repeat audiences who kept the new Hollywood blockbusters playing for extended runs and fueled the participatory culture of fandom that thrives among adults who attend conventions and children who buy toys. In drawing their situations so vividly, and in multiplying them, Spielberg and Lucas gave viewers a reason to reexperience the adventure. As in a serial, knowing how it all turns out is no impediment to the pleasure of the moment.

This book indicates a path from nineteenth-century sensational melodrama through one-reel films and early features, and into the heart of the studio era via the sound serial. This historical trajectory gives some credence to Elizabeth Cowie's proposal that "unhooking classical narrative and classical Hollywood as equivalents is . . . an important step in enabling the difference between 'classical' and 'post-classical' American cinema to be properly assessed."[1] For, rather than view either the serial or the action film as a radical departure from classical conventions, we might well understand them both in light of melodrama's legacy; they elaborate structures that helped define the early life of the feature film. Sound serials existed side by side with Hollywood's features, offering a narrative experience that should encourage us to expand our account of studio-era entertainment.

We have focused on the sound serial as a historically specific mode of cinema. The historical poetics approach can discourage generalization in favor of the concrete accounting of proximate contexts. But the study of sound serials opens onto wider concerns because they participate in broad, ongoing traditions of melodrama, seriality, and play. The relationship between the sound serial and early television, for example, deserves further scrutiny. From the early 1950s on, juvenile viewers have found their adventures on the domestic screen. Where matinee serials relied on situational force to keep their worlds alive between chapters, television brought the adventure directly into the home, making it a daily part of lived experience.

The dominant televisual mode, inherited from radio, was the stand-alone episode. *The Lone Ranger* (ABC, 1949–1957), filmed on the same locations as the serial, adopted the episodic series format, as did *Superman* (syndicated, 1952–1958), *Flash Gordon* (syndicated, 1954–1955), and other properties. Cliffhangers briefly reappeared in Irwin Allen's *Lost in Space* (CBS, 1965–1968), which shifted the first act of the next episode to the end of the previous, and in William Dozier's production *Batman* (ABC, 1966–1968), which utilized and parodied serial form, breaking episodes in half for the first season.[2] These shows derived their cliffhangers by modifying the norms of episodic containment. In general, though, interruption and curiosity migrated from the end of an episode to the commercial break, where a fatal gesture could ensure that viewers stayed tuned in. Commercial breaks are short-term affairs, distinct from the vividly wrought problem spaces that serials left with viewers for a week, and television did not take up the same rhythm of action and exposition, narrative compression, repetition, or situational intensity. As with contemporary action films, television's inheritance was a matter of translation: of finding equivalents to serial effects within a distinct form.

Rather than seek the sound serial's direct influence on subsequent media, we might think even more broadly of it as encompassed by a larger ludic tradition. Television shows and chapterplays are historically proximate serial forms, but both resonate with contemporary gameplay. For instance, Henry Jenkins hints at continuity between digital gaming and folk play when he describes video game consoles as "machines for generating compelling spaces, that . . . have helped to compensate for the declining place of the traditional backyard in contemporary boy culture."[3] The sound serial's parallel relationship to the playground suggests a kinship between these historically disconnected media.

In "Digital Seriality: On the Serial Aesthetics and Practice of Digital Games," Shane Denson and Andreas Jahn-Sudmann call for "a serious consideration of both the specificities of game-based serialities and the common ground they share with other media-cultural practices and aesthetic forms."[4] They hope to catalyze research into the serial nature of digital gaming by drawing attention to affinities between seriality and play: "Play itself, we must recall, is an essentially serial activity, characterized by ritualistic practices of repetition and variation." In a sense, this book heeds Denson and Jahn-Sudmann's call, albeit in reverse. If the concept of play can illuminate serial qualities of digital games, then perhaps earlier, analog serial forms should be regarded in terms of their ludic potentials. In bringing this perspective to the history of sound serials, we have cast them as part of a continuum to which digital gaming also belongs.

The relevance of a film mode that ceased production fifty years ago to digital gaming may at first blush seem slim. Certainly there does not appear to be any direct connection between the two forms, beyond their predilection for sci-fi, and the coincidence that both have produced painfully inadequate superhero franchise adaptations. The sound serial's relationship to gaming is one of prehistory; it presents an earlier example of ludic storytelling, the practice of constructing visual narratives to facilitate play. Serials are virtual domains for confronting and mastering uncertainty: domains experienced corporeally in the cinema and explored as fictional components of physical play. Like digital games, they address our desire to inhabit fictions and run imaginary gauntlets. My claim is not that sound serials are games but that they shadow and assist play. In their design of narrative space, their repetitive situations, and their obsession with physical process, they prefigure the fully ludic fictions of digital games.

Concepts like narrative architecture and the disjunction between story and rule help distinguish fiction from the experience of linear narrative. They help us see how serials generate fictional worlds that revise themselves according to the external logic of formula. Nyoka plunges into the lava pit at the conclusion of *Human Sacrifice* but escapes on Larry's rope at the start of *Monster's Clutch*. The full depiction of a catastrophic problem space requires contradiction in the story world, as in a videogame where the hero dies and respawns during play. Discontinuity creates the possibility of play, though unlike the game, once restarted the serial rushes forward on its preordained path.

We can observe a similar dynamic if we consider how serials and digital games treat time. Denson and Jahn-Sudmann note the collapse of story and plot time in digital gaming because generation of the fiction depends on the player.[5] Jesper Juul clarifies this. He conceives of games as having two temporal registers: play time and fictional time. Unlike watching a film, interacting with a game generates time within the fictional world; the two are interdependent. Juul discusses the relationship in terms of "projection": "Projection means that the player's time and actions are projected onto the game world where they take on a fictional meaning."[6]

The interruptions, revisions, and reversals of cliffhangers entail a similar articulation of time frames. For viewers, the period between peril and escape exists as an elongated present, an atemporal problem space in which to play out alternative eventualities, with the knowledge that the actual solution will itself undo and rewrite time. Cliffhangers introduce ludic ruptures, converting progressive stories into open scenarios and training viewers in their creative navigation. In this sense, "to be continued" evokes game time, an invitation to dwell within a highly structured situation and fill it with rounds of play.[7] But if sound serials in this way anticipate digital gaming's temporal collapse, they nonetheless must regulate access to the story. Synchronicity, the simultaneous availability of the story and world in their entirety, which Denson and Jahn-Sudmann also associate with digital media, would short-circuit the enforced break between episodes and ameliorate the play space.[8] Only by imposing a cessation of the on-screen action can cliffhangers transform narratives into fictional frameworks that enable play. In this sense, serials straddle digital and analog time, bridging pre- and postdigital forms.

This book suggests the value of play and seriality as interconnected historiographical frames. Thinking of narratives as structures with ludic potential might unearth neglected spectatorial avenues in popular cinema. Stories deprived of causal logic and character depth can be rich with inhabitable roles and projectable worlds. Clearly, the ludic perspective suits children's media, especially those with melodramatic tendencies like comic books and radio, television, and film adventures. However, as we've noted of sound serials, demographic boundaries are notoriously porous. Although these forms may be dismissed as unsophisticated, adults have long been avid consumers of them. Melodrama, with its penchant for physicalizing moral struggle in vivid terms, continues to fuel popular storytelling with playable scenarios. Anecdotal evidence of contemporary fiction's ludic potency is available in my local park where tweens play *The Hunger Games* (novel by Suzanne Collins, 2008; film by Gary Ross, 2012) by piling their Nerf swords and guns at the center of a circle and then rushing forward to take arms.

The sound serials' consonance with play might tempt us to cast them as proto-digital, or analog precursors to the digital age: the magic lantern shows of computer gaming's cinema. It is more appropriate, though, to think of both as part of the continuing history of ludic seriality. By its nature, seriality rides against containment and coherence, and this is advantageous to play. When measured against standards of studio-era feature films, sound serials are painfully redundant and narratively inadequate. The very qualities that seem an affront to Hollywood classicism (discontinuity, bare-bones motivations) support the possibilities of narrative architecture, the regular return to an ongoing world of pursuits, fights, and escapes.

Sound serials are an important but not singular point on a spectrum that encompasses digital games. Other forms of serial media also occupy the nexus of narrative and play. Jason Mittell, for instance, brings game studies and television studies together to address "a mode of ludic storytelling that transcends the false dichotomy between game and narrative."[9] It is hard to imagine a kind of story more different from the sound serials than the complex, expansionist transmedial world of *Lost* (ABC, 2004–2010), which Mittell uses as his case study. Producers employed *Lost*'s labyrinthine mythology to launch intermedial extensions including web-based alternate reality games (ARGs) in which participants could solve puzzles and explore the story world. Sound serials, by contrast, are supremely mappable and repetitive; what you see is what you get, again and again. Where *Lost* is populated with emotionally rich and developing characters, serials offer one-note types who behave predictably from start to finish. What the two share, though, is the unfolding of a sometimes incoherent story through repeated spaces with continuing characters and in vividly situational episodes. Both stage regular, ludic breaks in their stories through which curious viewers can take up the world, on the playground or in the ARG. These continuities should embolden those of us studying predigital media forms to take the lessons of ludology seriously, and to recognize the ludic potential of episodic narrative. Huizinga points out, "In nearly all higher forms of play the elements of repetition and alternation . . . are like the warp and woof of a fabric."[10] Seriality makes stories playable.

We began this book with the observation that sound serials are intrinsically interesting but poorly understood. Beyond the lessons they teach us about the studio era, cinematic storytelling, or play, these films deserve attention simply because they so effectively entertain. These pages have attempted to capture some of the form's raw excitement while illuminating its workings. Eighty years after its release, *The Phantom Empire* remains a ceaselessly watchable, instantly involving piece of cinema. Its fundamental bizarreness and brio are crafted from historically specific conventions that, despite their seeming obviousness, supported artistic variety and refinement. The sound serial's scholarly neglect may in part stem from its investment in the passing moment. Without long-range ambitions, pretensions to higher purpose, or even much development, these films fail to provide the common kinds of intellectual purchase. Instead, looking closely at the serial's formulae, aesthetics, and brand of viewer engagement brings us in contact with cinema's power to shape the fleeting present. Serials calculate sound and image to do little more than grip and excite. Ultimately, I hope to have demonstrated the complexity and creative value of such apparently modest aims.

Appendix

Some Sources for Sound Serials

Long the province of specialized collectors, sound serials are more widely available than at any point in their history thanks to digital media. Major distributors have issued a few titles on DVD with high-quality sound and image.

Major studio releases consulted for this book include:

Atom Man vs. Superman (Warner Home Video)
Batman (Sony Pictures Home Entertainment)
Batman and Robin (Sony Pictures Home Entertainment)
Superman (Warner Home Video)

VCI Entertainment, a specialized DVD distributor, offers an extensive catalog of serials, mastered from high-quality materials (http://www.vcientertainment.com/index.php?route=common/home).

VCI titles consulted for this book include:

Ace Drummond
Adventures of Smilin' Jack
Brenda Starr, Reporter
Buck Rogers
Captain Midnight
Dick Tracy (and sequels)
Don Winslow of the Navy
Drums of Fu Manchu

Flash Gordon (and sequels)
The Green Hornet (and sequels)
Holt of the Secret Service
Jack Armstrong
Jungle Girl
Jungle Queen
King of the Royal Mounted
The Last of the Mohicans
Mandrake, the Magician
Perils of Pauline
The Phantom
The Phantom Creeps
The Phantom Empire
Scouts to the Rescue
Secret Agent X-9
S O S Coast Guard
Tailspin Tommy (and sequel)
Terry and the Pirates
Undersea Kingdom
White Eagle
Zorro Rides Again
Zorro's Black Whip
Zorro's Fighting Legion

The Serial Squadron is a website and boutique DVD distribution outlet operated by Eric Stedman (http://www.serialsquadron.com/dvds/). It specializes in rare and public-domain DVDs, mastered from collectors' prints. Image and sound are high quality.

Serial Squadron titles consulted for this book include:

Gang Busters
King of the Mounties
The Lone Ranger (and sequel)
The Phantom Empire
Undersea Kingdom
The Vanishing Legion
Zorro's Black Whip

A multitude of independent online merchants offer extensive sound-serial catalogs in DVD-R format. In many cases, these merchants may be infringing on copyright by selling DVDs of serials that are otherwise unavailable but not public domain. Often, the DVD versions are merely copies of previously marketed VHS or Laserdisc editions. Sound and image tend to be passable.

Independent online merchant titles consulted for this book include:

Adventures of Captain Marvel
Blackhawk
Captain America
Commando Cody: Sky Marshal of the Universe
The Crimson Ghost
Daredevils of the Red Circle
The Fighting Devil Dogs
The Great Alaskan Mystery
Hawk of the Wilderness
The Hurricane Express
Jungle Girl
Junior G-Men
The Lightning Express
Panther Girl of the Kongo
Perils of Nyoka
The Purple Monster Strikes
Radar Men from the Moon
Secret Service in Darkest Africa
Sky Raiders
Spy Smasher
The Tiger Woman

Many serials distributed by small DVD companies are offered by large Internet retailers like Amazon.com. In some cases, these releases may infringe on copyright. Sound and image quality can be quite good.

Small-distributor DVDs consulted for this book and available through Amazon.com include:

Flying Disc Man from Mars
The Hurricane Express
King of the Rocket Men
The Shadow
Sky Raiders
Spy Smasher
The Three Musketeers
Zombies of the Stratosphere

Finally, because many serials have fallen into the public domain, they are available on the nonprofit digital library Internet Archive, founded by Brewster Kahle (https://archive.org/index.php).

Titles consulted for this book available on the Internet Archive include:

Adventures of Captain Marvel
The Crimson Ghost
The Great Alaskan Mystery
The Green Hornet
The Phantom
The Phantom Empire
S O S Coast Guard
Spy Smasher
Zorro's Fighting Legion

Notes

Chapter 1: Serials, Melodrama, and Play

1 "About Popular Seriality," last modified March 13, 2014, http://www.popular seriality.de/en/ueber_uns/index.html.

2 David Bordwell, *Poetics of Cinema* (New York: Routledge, 2008), 11–18, 23.

3 Viktor Shklovsky, "The Resurrection of the Word," *20th Century Studies* 7/8 (1972): 44.

4 See, for instance, Ron Backer, *Gripping Chapters: The Sound Movie Serials* (Albany, GA: BearManor Media, 2010); Michael Bifulco, *Heroes and Villains: Movie Serial Classics* (Woodland Hills, CA: Bifulco Books, 1989); William Cline, *In the Nick of Time: Motion Picture Sound Serials* (Jefferson NC: McFarland, 1984); Jim Harmon and Donald Glut, *The Great Movie Serials: Their Sound and Fury* (Garden City, NY: Doubleday, 1972); R. M. Hays, *The Republic Chapterplays* (Jefferson, NC: McFarland, 1991); Jon Tuska, *The Vanishing Legion: A History of Mascot Pictures, 1927–1935* (Jefferson, NC: McFarland, 1982); Raymond Stedman, *The Serials: Suspense and Drama by Installment* (Norman: University of Oklahoma Press, 1977); and James Van Hise, *Serial Adventures* (Las Vegas: Pioneer Books, 1990).

5 Guy Barefoot, "Who Watched That Masked Man! Hollywood's Serial Audiences in the 1930s," *Historical Journal of Film, Radio and Television* 1, no. 2 (2011): 167–190; Rafael Vela, "With the Parents [*sic*] Consent: Film Serials, Consumerism and the Creation of a Youth Audience, 1913–1938" (PhD diss., University of Wisconsin, Madison, 2000).

6 Bob Moak, "Hollywood Eyes Serial Cycle," *Variety*, November 6, 1940, 21, 23.

7 "Big Grosses in Making Serials," *Variety*, March 27, 1946, 5.

8 "Serials in Marked Comeback," *Variety*, March 6, 1940, 7.

9 Moak, "Hollywood Eyes Serial Cycle," 21.

10 The spans of production varied somewhat by studio. Universal began production during the silent era, and its serial unit continued until the studio's reorganization as Universal International in 1946. Columbia entered the market in 1937, contracting the work to low-budget producers like the Weiss brothers, Larry Darmour, and Sam Katzman but also contributing in-house productions. Columbia was the last serial producer in America, bowing out of the format in 1956. Republic Pictures formed

in 1935 when Herbert Yates merged six Poverty Row producers, including Mascot. The Republic serial unit, which developed out of Mascot's and was widely considered the best in the industry, closed its doors in 1955.

11 Hayes, *Republic Chapterplays*, 6.

12 Jack Mathis, *Valley of the Cliffhangers* (Northbrook, IL: Jack Mathis Advertising, 1975), vii.

13 *The Lone Ranger* Pressbook (New York: Republic Pictures, 1938), Autry National Research Center, Los Angeles, 8f.

14 Royal Cole, William Lively, and Sol Shor, *Ghost of Zorro* Cutting Continuity (New York: Republic Pictures, 1949), Autry National Research Center, Los Angeles.

15 See William Witney, *In a Door, into a Fight, out a Door, into a Chase* (Jefferson, NC: McFarland, 1996), 167, 168.

16 Panel Presentation on Serials, Museum of the Moving Image, April 22, 1989, tape recording.

17 See Witney, *In a Door*, 205.

18 Ibid., 220–221.

19 Mathis, *Valley*, vii.

20 Ibid.

21 Review of *White Eagle, Exhibitor*, February 5, 1941, servisection 4.

22 Review of *Drums of Fu Manchu, Exhibitor*, February 21, 1940, servisection 20.

23 Review of *Riders of Death Valley, Exhibitor*, February 5, 1941, servisection 4.

24 Review of *The Phantom Empire, Exhibitor*, March 15, 1935, servisection 34.

25 Review of *Overland Mail, Exhibitor*, July 29, 1942, servisection 3.

26 Review of *Invisible Monster, Exhibitor*, June 7, 1950, serivisection 5; review of *The Lost Planet, Exhibitor*, June 17, 1953, servisection 6.

27 See Harmon and Glut, *Great Movie Serials*, xvii, Hayes, *Republic Chapterplays*, 5; and Ken Weiss and Ed Goodgold, *To Be Continued* (New York: Crown Publishers, 1972), ix, x.

28 Vela, "With the Parents [*sic*] Consent," 261.

29 *How to Make Money with Serials: A Universal Text Book for Use of Motion Picture Exhibitors* (New York: Universal Pictures Corporation, 1927), 13, 56.

30 Review of *Scouts to the Rescue, Exhibitor*, November 30, 1938, servisection 4; review of *Junior G-Men, Exhibitor*, August 7, 1940, servisection 5.

31 Barefoot, "Masked Man!" 183.

32 Steve Neale, *Genre and Hollywood* (New York: Routledge, 2000), 179, 196, 198–200.

33 Ben Singer, *Melodrama and Modernity: Early Sensational Cinema and Its Contexts* (New York: Columbia University Press, 2001), 44–50.

34 David Bordwell, "The Classical Hollywood Style, 1917–1916," in *The Classical Hollywood Cinema: Film Style and Mode of Production to 1960*, by David Bordwell, Janet Staiger, and Kristin Thompson (New York: Columbia University Press, 1985), 14, 18.

35 Rick Altman, "Dickens, Griffith, and Film Theory Today," in *Classical Hollywood Narrative: The Paradigm Wars*, ed. Jane Gaines (Durham, NC: Duke University Press, 1992), 25–26.

36 Ben Brewster and Lea Jacobs, *Theatre to Cinema* (New York: Oxford University Press, 1997), 19–29.

37 Georges Polti, *The Thirty-six Dramatic Situations* (Boston: The Writer Inc., 1977), 123, 120, 121.

38 Brewster and Jacobs, *Theatre to Cinema*, 24.

39 Ibid., 22.

40 Polti, *Thirty-six Dramatic Situations*, 131.

41 *The Fighting Devil Dogs* Correspondence, MPPDA PCA File, Academy of Motion Picture Arts and Sciences, Margaret Herrick Library.

42 Witney, *In a Door*, 254.

43 Peter Brooks, *The Melodramatic Imagination: Balzac, Henry James, Melodrama, and the Mode of Excess* (New Haven, CT: Yale University Press, 1995), 13, 20.

44 Linda Williams, *Playing the Race Card* (Princeton, NJ: Princeton University Press, 2001), 25, 15.

45 Tom Gunning, *D. W. Griffith and the Origins of the American Narrative Film* (Chicago: University of Illinois Press, 1991), 204.

46 Williams, *Race Card*, 19.

47 Ibid., 20.

48 Janet Murray, "From Game-Story to Cyberdrama," in *First Person: New Media as Story, Performance, and Game*, ed. Noah Wardrip-Fruin and Pat Harrigan (Cambridge, MA: MIT Press, 2004), 2.

49 Shane Denson and Andreas Jahn-Sudmann, "Digital Seriality: On the Serial Aesthetics and Practice of Digital Games," *Eludamos* 7, no. 1 (2013): 6.

50 Jesper Juul, *Half-Real: Video Games between Real Rules and Fictional Worlds* (Cambridge, MA: MIT Press, 2005), 16.

51 Johan Huizinga, *Homo Ludens: A Study of the Play-Element in Culture* (Boston: Beacon Press, 1950), ix, 28, 11, 12, 36, 38, 40.

52 Alice Miller Mitchell, *Children and Movies* (Chicago: University of Chicago Press, 1929), 75–76, 96, 101, 100.

53 Herbert Blumer, *Movies and Conduct* (New York: Macmillan, 1933), 9, 121, 117, 120, 19, 26, 13, 21.

54 Jacob Peter Mayer, *Sociology of Film* (London: Faber and Faber, 1946), 54, 161–162. Phyll Smith brought Mayer's work to my attention.

55 Henry Jenkins, "Game Design as Narrative Architecture," in Wardrip-Fruin and Harrigan, *First Person*, 119, 121, 122, 123–124, 129.

56 Juul, *Half-Real*, 162, 6.

57 Ibid., 135.

58 Herbert Blumer, "The Motion Pictures Autobiographies," in *Children and the Movies: Media Influence and the Payne Fund Controversy*, ed. Garth S. Jowett, Ian C. Jarvie, and Kathryn H. Fuller (New York: Cambridge University Press, 1996), 177.

59 Vivian Sobchack, *Carnal Thoughts: Embodiment and Moving Image Culture* (Berkeley: University of California Press, 2004), 60, 82 (emphasis in original).

60 Mayer, *Sociology of Film*, 62.

61 Jennifer Barker, *The Tactile Eye: Touch and the Cinematic Experience* (Berkeley: University of California Press, 2009), 74, 83.

62 Lisa Purse, *Contemporary Action Cinema* (Edinburgh: Edinburgh University Press, 2011), 45, 48.

63 Brian Sutton-Smith, *The Ambiguity of Play* (Cambridge, MA: Harvard University Press, 1997), 231.

64 Neil Harris, *Humbug: The Art of P. T. Barnum* (Boston: Little, Brown, 1973), 87–88.

Chapter 2: Storytelling on a Schedule

1 *Middle action* was the term used by screenwriters and directors for this portion of a chapter. See Jack Mathis, *Valley of the Cliffhangers* (Northbrook, IL: Jack Mathis Advertising, 1975), 291.
2 Jack Mathis, *Valley of the Cliffhangers Supplement* (Barrington, IL: Jack Mathis Advertising, 1995), 281.
3 The opening chapter runs twenty minutes: a reduction from thirty minutes, which had been standard for first episodes.
4 Mathis, *Supplement*, 84.
5 A year later Republic produced a television show featuring the *Radar Men* characters entitled *Commando Cody: Sky Marshal of the Universe* (Keller, Adreon, and Brannon, 1953) recycling footage from both *Radar Men* and *King of the Rocket Men* (Brannon, 1949). The program did not follow the five-part structure nor the tight serial timeline. Each episode runs a leisurely 26.5 minutes, and each is self-contained. The model appears to have been the half-hour radio adventure rather than Republic's own serial production.
6 David Bordwell, Janet Staiger, and Kristen Thompson, *The Classical Hollywood Cinema: Film Style and Mode of Production to 1960* (New York: Columbia University Press, 1985), 31.
7 Ibid.
8 Ben Brewster and Lea Jacobs, *Theatre to Cinema* (New York: Oxford University Press, 1997), 22–25.
9 *How to Make Money with Serials: A Universal Text Book for Use of Motion Picture Exhibitors* (New York: Universal Pictures Corporation, 1927), 20, 291.
10 Steven Connor, "'I Believe That the World,'" in *Cultural Ways of Worldmaking: Media and Narratives*, ed. Vera Nünning, Ansgar Nünning, and Birgit Neumann (Berlin and New York: De Gruyter, 2010), 22, 23.
11 Brian Taves, *The Romance of Adventure: The Genre of Historical Adventure Movies* (Jackson: University of Mississippi Press, 1993), 4.
12 William Cline, *In the Nick of Time: Motion Picture Sound Serials* (Jefferson, NC: McFarland, 1984), 7.
13 Ibid., 8.
14 Brewster and Jacobs, *Theatre to Cinema*, 26–27.
15 Johan Huizinga, *Homo Ludens: A Study of the Play-Element in Culture* (Boston: Beacon Press, 1950), 10.
16 Ruth Mayer, *Serial Fu Manchu: The Chinese Supervillain and the Spread of Yellow Peril Ideology* (Philadelphia: Temple University Press, 2014), 10.

Chapter 3: The Serial World

1 Neil Harris, *Humbug: The Art of P. T. Barnum* (Boston: Little, Brown, 1973), 57, 75, 81, 86–88.
2 Charles Musser, *The Emergence of Cinema: The American Screen to 1907* (Berkeley: University of California Press, 1990), 354; Tom Gunning, "Crazy Machines in the Garden of Forking Paths: Mischief Gags and the Origins of American Film Comedy," in *Classical Hollywood Comedy*, ed. Kristine Karnick and Henry Jenkins (New York: Routledge, 1994).
3 Gunning, "Crazy Machines," 91, 100–101, 99, 103, 93–97.
4 Ilka Brasch, "Structuring Serial Worlds: New and Fiction Media in Film Serials

of the 1910s," paper presented at the annual meeting of the Society of Cinema and Media Studies, Seattle, WA, March 19–23, 2014.

5   Harris, *Humbug*, 75; Gunning, "Crazy Machines," 101.

6   Gunning, "Crazy Machines," 101.

7   Maaike Lauwaert, *The Place of Play: Toys and Digital Cultures* (Amsterdam: Amsterdam University Press, 2009), 47, 81.

8   Simon Bronner, "Material Culture of Children," in *Children's Folklore: A Sourcebook*, ed. Brian Sutton-Smith, Jay Mechling, Thomas W. Johnson, and Felicia R. McMahon (New York: Garland, 1995), 253, 252.

9   Johan Huizinga, *Homo Ludens: A Study of the Play-Element in Culture* (Boston: Beacon Press, 1950), 8, 10.

10 Iona Opie and Peter Opie, *Children's Games in Street and Playground* (Oxford: Oxford University Press, 1969), 2.

11 Jean Piaget, *Play, Dreams and Imitation in Childhood* (New York: Norton, 1962), 167–168, 171.

12 Huizinga, *Homo Ludens*, 10.

13 Ben Singer, *Melodrama and Modernity: Early Sensational Cinema and Its Contexts* (New York: Columbia University Press, 2001), 208; William Witney, *In a Door, into a Fight, out a Door, into a Chase: Moviemaking Remembered by the Guy at the Door* (Jefferson, NC: McFarland, 1996), 165. Singer uses the spelling "weenie," which I retain, though Witney prefers the spelling "wienie."

14 Brian Sutton-Smith, *Toys as Culture* (New York: Gardner Press, 1986), 250.

15 Not all weenies are so flexible. For instance, the super pursuit plane that foreign agent Felix Lynx (Eduardo Ciannelli) continually fails to steal in Universal's *Sky Raiders* (Beebe and Taylor, 1941) was too one-note to sustain a full run, and the writers dropped it in episode 10 and introduced a new machine, a classified bomb site, in episode 11.

16 Janet Murray, "From Game-Story to Cyberdrama," in *First Person: New Media as Story, Performance, and Game*, ed. Noah Wardrip-Fruin and Pat Harrigan (Cambridge, MA: MIT Press, 2004), 2.

17 Kristin Thompson, *Breaking the Glass Armor* (Princeton, NJ: Princeton University Press, 1988), 43.

18 Jacob Peter Mayer, *Sociology of Film* (London: Faber and Faber, 1946), 62; Mary Parnaby and Maurice Woodhouse, *Children's Cinema Clubs Report* (London: British Film Institute, 1947), 7.

19 Mayer, *Sociology of Film*, 9, 17, 18.

20 Peter Brooks, *The Melodramatic Imagination: Balzac, Henry James, Melodrama, and the Mode of Excess* (New Haven, CT: Yale University Press, 1995), 35.

21 This is not to claim that all Hollywood features offer psychologically complex characters, but many do. Sound serials, as a rule, do not.

22 Brooks, *The Melodramatic Imagination*, 35.

23 Ibid., 33, 38.

24 The Wasp is responding to Mandrake's explanation that he discovered Andre's identity by investigating records from the medical bureau. That investigation is not mentioned earlier in the serial, making this turn of events all the more arbitrary.

25 Brian Taves, *The Romance of Adventure: The Genre of Historical Adventure Movies* (Jackson: University of Mississippi Press, 1993), 137–143, 4, 136, 137, 142.

26 Martin Rubin, *Thrillers* (Cambridge: Cambridge University Press, 1999), 25–30, 32.

27 Linda Williams, *Playing the Race Card* (Princeton, NJ: Princeton University Press, 2001) 30–32.

28 Ibid., 35.
29 *The Fighting Devil Dogs* (Witney and English, 1938) also kills off the hero's father in the first-episode cliffhanger. In that case, though, the father's death results from the Lightning's attack, not a case of self-sacrifice.
30 Witney, *In a Door*, 101.
31 Margaret Thorp, *America at the Movies* (New Haven, CT: Yale University Press, 1939), 11.

Chapter 4: Cliffhanging

1 Ben Singer, *Melodrama and Modernity: Early Sensational Cinema and Its Contexts* (New York: Columbia University Press, 2001), 210.
2 See Tom Gunning, *D. W. Griffith and the Origins of the American Narrative Film* (Chicago: University of Illinois Press, 1991), ch. 3.
3 Singer, *Melodrama and Modernity*, 197.
4 Richard Gerrig, *Experiencing Narrative Worlds* (New Haven, CT: Yale University Press, 1993), 82, 83, 78.
5 Ibid., 84.
6 Gunning, *D. W. Griffith*, 105.
7 Ibid., 190.
8 Meir Sternberg, *Expositional Modes and Temporal Ordering in Fiction* (Bloomington: Indiana University Press, 1993), 54, 181.
9 In Griffith's Biograph films the successful race to the rescue was normative but not always guaranteed (as in *Death's Marathon*). There is only one sound serial that I know of in which the hero actually dies. In *The Phantom Empire*, Gene Autry is fatally wounded in episode 6. However, in episode 7, titled *From Death to Life*, he is brought back to life in the Muranian revival chamber.
10 Sternberg, *Expositional Modes*, 177.
11 Richard Gerrig, "The Resiliency of Suspense," in *Suspense: Conceptualizations, Theoretical Analyses, and Empirical Explorations*, ed. Peter Vorderer, Hans J. Wuff, and Mike Friedrichsen (Mahwah, NJ: Lawrence Erlbaum Associates, 1996), 102–103 (emphasis in original).
12 Ibid.
13 Noel Carroll, "The Paradox of Suspense," in Vorderer, Wuff, and Freidrichsen, *Suspense*, 74, 82, 90.
14 Ibid., 73, 87, 81.
15 Edward Branigan, *Narrative Comprehension and Film* (New York: Routledge, 1992), 96, 113.
16 Linda Williams, *Playing the Race Card* (Princeton: Princeton University Press, 2001), 34.
17 David Bordwell proffers a related explanation of suspense. After reviewing Gerrig and Carroll, Bordwell speculates that different aspects of our cognitive processes are isolated from one another. He hypothesizes that hardwired "fast, mandatory, data-driven pickup," which can generate suspense, is impervious to deliberative thought, the capacity to predict outcomes based on conventions and memory. Bordwell's distinction roughly corresponds to Branigan's levels of narration, but with the additional claim that certain kinds of information processing are automatic and involuntary: "According to this argument, the sight of Eve Kendall dangling from Mount Rushmore will elicit some degree of suspense no matter how many times

you've seen *North by Northwest*, and that feeling will be amplified by the cutting, the close-ups, the music, and so on. Your sensory system can't help but respond. . . . For some part of you, every viewing of a movie *is* the first viewing." One appeal of Bordwell's idea is the way it connects the prospect of involuntary suspense to the workings of film form (cutting, close-ups, music). This aligns with our observations about the longevity of formal routines like accelerated crosscutting and the power of cinematic vividness in producing successful cliffhangers. Given the intricacies of film comprehension, much less general cognition, such a theory remains tentative and highly speculative. Not all cliffhangers are equally effective; a routine plunge from an aircraft in *Captain Midnight* isn't half as engaging as the firing squad in *Three Musketeers*. Things like familiarity or the novelty of execution can apparently limit the power of mandatory suspense. Bordwell's qualification is important: lower-level processing might account for "*some degree* of suspense." Its potency probably hinges on innumerable other factors. David Bordwell, "This Is Your Brain on Movies, Maybe," *Observations on Film Art* blog, March 7, 2007, http://www.davidbordwell.net/blog/2007/03/07/this-is-your-brain-on-movies-maybe/.

18 Gerrig, *Narrative Worlds*, 155. Noel Caroll, *The Philosophy of Horror; or, Paradoxes of the Heart* (New York: Routledge, 1990), 133.

19 Herbert Blumer, *Movies and Conduct* (New York: Macmillan, 1933) 121.

20 Mary Parnaby and Maurice Woodhouse, *Children's Cinema Clubs Report* (London: British Film Institute, 1947), 7.

21 Branigan, *Narrative Comprehension*, 83.

22 Later in the episode, Wayne is shown in a flashback replay of an earlier suspense situation.

23 In this case, the contrivance is even more obvious because it is the third time that *The Lone Ranger* resorts to a fatal plunge (the others being chapters 3 and 12).

24 Carroll, "The Paradox of Suspense," note 16, 88; Carroll, *Philosophy of Horror*, 68–79.

25 Lisa Purse, *Contemporary Action Cinema* (Edinburgh: Edinburgh University Press, 2011), 45.

26 Ron Backer, *Gripping Chapters: The Sound Movie Serial* (Albany, GA: BearManor Media, 2010), 171–213.

27 Also discussed by Backer, *Gripping Chapters*, 242–243, 247–248.

28 See Backer, *Gripping Chapters*; Jim Harmon and Donald Glut, *The Great Movie Serials: Their Sound and Fury* (Garden City, NY: Doubleday, 1972). For an online discussion of serials see *In the Balcony*, http://www.inthebalcony.com/matinee/.

29 Miriam Bratu Hansen, "The Mass Production of the Senses: Classical Cinema as Vernacular Modernism," *Modernism/Modernity* 6, no. 2 (1999): 59–77.

Chapter 5: Narrative and the Art of Formula

1 The three major serial producers issued 9.4 titles on average during the period. Production peaked between 1940 and 1942 with 13 serials per year and then declined to 9 in 1943 and 1944. The Weiss brothers, who produced Stage and Screen serials, were contracted by Columbia in 1937, and Sam Katzman, who produced Victory Pictures, moved to that studio in 1938. Universal halted serial production when it was reorganized as Universal International in 1946, and production declined thereafter.

2 Once Batman has been captured, one of the thugs leads Linda out of the room.

Though she entered in a pine box, once demonstrated she is, apparently, free to walk home.

3   Unlike Ron Backer in *Gripping Chapters*, I do not regard this technique as a "cheat," because it only involves suppression of information rather than the actual revision of a depicted event.

4   The two serials were written by different teams. *Batman* was scribed by Victor McLeod, Leslie Swabacker, and Harry L. Fraser; *Batman and Robin* by George Plympton, Joseph Poland, and Royal Cole. Poland also wrote for *Spy Smasher*, which may account for similarity in costume-switching cliffhangers.

5   For a discussion of the serial's "golden age" of the late 1930s and 1940s, and of Republic's place in it, see Richard M. Hurst, *Republic Studios: Between Poverty Row and the Majors* (Lanham, MD: Scarecrow Press, 2007), 70; Jim Harmon and Donald Glut, *The Great Movie Serials: Their Sound and Fury* (Garden City, NY: Doubleday, 1972), xvii; William Cline, *In the Nick of Time: Motion Picture Sound Serials* (Jefferson, NC: McFarland, 1984), 61; Jack Mathis, *Valley of the Cliffhangers* (Northbrook, IL: Jack Mathis Advertising, 1975), viii.

6   Review of *Perils of Nyoka*, *Exhibitor*, July 1, 1942, servisection 85.

7   Republic's third trend involved military heroes (or "service serials"), primarily represented by *Spy Smasher* and *The Fighting Devil Dogs*, but even these share plots, gimmicks, mise-en-scène, and more generally the "serial world" with our case studies.

8   Peter Brooks, *The Melodramatic Imagination: Balzac, Henry James, Melodrama, and the Mode of Excess* (New Haven, CT: Yale University Press, 1995), 34.

9   Tom Gunning, "An Aesthetic of Astonishment: Early Film and the (In)Credulous Spectator," in *Film Theory and Criticism*, ed. Leo Braudy and Marshall Cohen, 5th ed. (New York: Oxford University Press, 1999), 821.

10   Nyoka is more commonly imperiled in the cliffhangers, but they share the peril in chapters 1 (collapsing room), 8 (an avalanche), and 10 (a car crash). Larry rescues Nyoka from the cliffhangers in seven chapters, but she returns the favor in two climactic episodes, which is highly egalitarian in serial terms. Like Cassib, Larry supports his partner without threatening the spotlight.

11   *Jungle Girl* also had the benefit of Edgar Rice Burroughs's imprimatur, well known from the Tarzan books and movies. The lead character's name, Nyoka, was not part of Burroughs's original property, and this allowed Republic to produce the sequel without paying any rights. For the sake of plausible deniability, the producer, William O'Sullivan, recast the lead role, originally played by Frances Gifford, with a professional model and untested actress from the Fox roster, Kay Aldridge. The character was also altered. In the original *Nyoka* Meredith is the daughter of a white physician who raised her among African tribes. The later character is named Nyoka Gordon, daughter of an explorer who vanished in a fictional area in the North African desert. The result was successful enough to inspire a line of Nyoka comic books, which ran in various guises until the mid-1950s. After the studio released another serial queen chapterplay, *The Tiger Woman*, in 1944, the producers reissued *Perils of Nyoka* under the title *Nyoka and the Tiger Men* (1952), creating a retrospective quasi-trilogy.

12   William Witney, *In a Door, into a Fight, out a Door, into a Chase: Moviemaking Remembered by the Guy at the Door* (Jefferson, NC: McFarland, 1996), 186, 214.

13   Mathis, *Valley*, 112.

14   Witney, *In a Door*, 186.

15   Tuffie's skill in scenes of pathos is also on display near the end of *Trail of the*

Lonesome Pine (Henry Hathaway), Paramount's groundbreaking Technicolor feature of 1936. Here, he crawls heartbreakingly to the foot of young Buddy Tolliver's (Spanky McFarland) casket.

Chapter 6: Film Style and the Art of Formula

1 See William Witney, *In a Door, into a Fight, out a Door, into a Chase: Moviemaking Remembered by the Guy at the Door* (Jefferson, NC: McFarland, 1996), 205.
2 Review of *The Great Alaskan Mystery*, *Exhibitor*, April 19, 1944, servisection 4.
3 Review of *S.O.S. Iceberg*, *Variety*, September 26, 1933, 15.
4 Witney, *In a Door*, 135–136.
5 David Bordwell, *Planet Hong Kong: Popular Cinema and the Art of Entertainment* (Cambridge, MA: Harvard University Press, 2000), 129, 130, 199.
6 William Cline, *In the Nick of Time: Motion Picture Sound Serials* (Jefferson, NC: McFarland, 1984), 162.
7 Jack Mathis, *Valley of the Cliffhangers* (Northbrook, IL: Jack Mathis Advertising, 1975), 111.
8 Howard Chudacoff, *Children at Play: An American History* (New York: NYU Press, 2007), 131–134.
9 Jennifer Barker, *The Tactile Eye: Touch and the Cinematic Experience* (Berkeley: University of California Press, 2009), 83.
10 Mathis, *Valley*, 112.
11 Ironically, because of this reordering of events Larry and Red actually lose ground, as it is now later in the ceremony. Our awareness of the parallel line of action is more important than the heroes' literal progress. Once the crosscutting commences, Nyoka's rescue is assured.
12 Edward Branigan, *Narrative Comprehension and Film* (New York: Routledge, 1992), 111–112, 138–140.
13 Jennifer Hayward, *Consuming Pleasures: Active Audiences and Serial Fictions from Dickens to Soap Opera* (Lexington: University Press of Kentucky, 1997), 110, 196.

Chapter 7: Cliffhanger Legacies

1 Properties like *Buck Rogers, The Lone Ranger*, and *Superman* migrated to broadcast television, which inherited radio's format of self-contained episodes rather than the serial's interrupted continuity. Columbia attempted to replicate their relationship with radio as a source of material when it produced the fifteen-chapter *Captain Video Master of the Stratosphere* in 1951 based on Dumont's successful live television show *Captain Video and His Video Rangers*, which aired between 1949 and 1951. The serial's competition with its new rival was short-lived. Columbia, the last remaining producer, admitted defeat with the release of its final chapterplay, *Blazing the Overland Trail*, in 1956.
2 Tino Balio, *United Artists*, vol. 2, *1951–1978: The Company That Changed the Film Industry* (Madison: University of Wisconsin Press, 1987), 263.
3 See Martin Rubin, *Thrillers* (Cambridge: Cambridge University Press, 1999), 129.
4 Tom Soter, "He Only Lived Twice," *Starlog* 169 (August 1991), reprinted on *The Tom Soter Blog*, http://www.tomsoter.com/?q=node/829. In both films, Bond (Sean Connery) investigates a source of interference with the American space program and infiltrates the villain's hidden lair. He is captured, escapes, and manages to

blow up the compound just before the villain can launch a final attack. Bond and his romantic partner watch the fiery explosion from a safe distance.

5 Ibid.

6 Blending self-aware comedy with adventure has a long history stemming from Douglas Fairbanks's inaugural cycle of films in the 1920s. In moving from modern comedies to historical adventures, Fairbanks cultivated his heroic image with a touch of irony. Jeanine Basinger sums it up well: through humor, Fairbanks "welcomed the grown-up masculine viewer into a world of games and exploits, but without asking him to surrender his dignity." Jeanine Basinger, *Silent Stars* (Middletown, CT: Wesleyan University Press, 2000), 100.

7 William Witney, *In a Door, into a Fight, out a Door, into a Chase: Moviemaking Remembered by the Guy at the Door* (Jefferson, NC: McFarland, 1996), 130.

8 Balio, *United Artists* 2:262.

9 Eric Greene, *Planet of the Apes as American Myth: Race and Politics in the Films and Television Series* (Middletown, CT: Wesleyan University Press, 1998), 166–168.

10 George Lucas, Steven Spielberg, and Lawrence Kasdan, "*Raiders of the Lost Ark* Story Conference Transcript," January 1978, http://maddogmovies.com/almost/scripts/raidersstoryconference1978.pdf. See also Patrick Radden Keefe, "Spitballing Indy," *New Yorker*, March 25, 2013, http://www.newyorker.com/culture/culture-desk/spitballing-indy.

11 Steven Spielberg, "Of Narrow Misses and Close Calls," *American Cinematographer* 62, no. 11 (November 1981): 1100, 1101.

12 Warren Buckland, "A Close Encounter with *Raiders of the Lost Ark*," in *Contemporary Hollywood Cinema*, ed. Steve Neale and Murray Smith (London: Routledge, 1998), 167, 171, 172–175.

13 Lucas, Spielberg, and Kasdan, "Story Conference Transcript."

14 Buckland, "A Close Encounter," 172–175.

15 David Bordwell, *The Way Hollywood Tells It: Story and Style in Modern Movies* (Berkeley: University of California Press, 2006), 28, 29, 34. The three-act structure is by far the most pervasive description of Hollywood plotting, but it may not be the most accurate. Kristen Thompson offers a compelling argument that most popular Hollywood films follow a five-part structure, with the "second act" split at a midpoint and an epilogue tacked onto the end. Still, the three-act-structure is the dominant way of teaching screenwriting, and it is a contemporary baseline that serves remarkably well for measuring Hollywood production. See Kristin Thompson, *Storytelling in the New Hollywood: Understanding Classical Narrative Technique* (Cambridge, MA: Harvard University Press, 1999).

16 *Raiders* also answers to Thompson's five-part structure, which she arrived at through empirical study of Hollywood feature films since the 1970s. The film has a clearly marked prologue (in South America), a complication (the introduction of the Ark as a goal), a development (the midpoint when Indy discovers and loses the Ark), a climax (the wrath of God), and an epilogue (in Washington, DC). In a sense, the five-part structure is Thompson's refinement of the more general three-act structure.

17 Bordwell, *Hollywood Tells It*, 105, 109.

18 Georges Polti, *The Thirty-six Dramatic Situations* (Boston: The Writer Inc., 1977), 116.

19 Rafael Vela pointed this out to me.

20 Bordwell, *Hollywood Tells It*, 29.

21 Ben Brewster and Lea Jacobs, *Theatre to Cinema* (New York: Oxford University Press, 1997), 21.

22 Polti, *Thirty-six Dramatic Situations*, 21, 114.

23 This incoherence appears to result from a cut scene. While translating the headpiece, the old man was to warn Indy and Sallah not to touch or look at the Ark.

24 Richard Schickel, "The Crisis in Movie Narrative," *Gannett Center Journal* 3 (Summer 1989): 2.

25 Murray Smith, "Theses on the Philosophy of Hollywood History," in Neale and Smith, *Contemporary Hollywood Cinema*, 13.

26 Todd McCarthy, review of *The Bourne Identity*, *Variety*, June 7, 2002, http://variety.com/2002/film/reviews/the-bourne-identity-1200549180/; David Edelstein, "Bourne to Run," *Slate.com*, July 23, 2004, http://www.slate.com/articles/arts/movies/2004/07/bourne_to_run.html; Carina Chocano, "The Pace Quickens," *Los Angeles Times*, August 3, 2007, http://articles.latimes.com/2007/aug/03/entertainment/et-bourne3.

Chapter 8: Conclusion

1 Elizabeth Cowie, "Storytelling: Classical Hollywood Cinema and Classical Narrative," in *Contemporary Hollywood Cinema*, ed. Steve Neale and Murray Smith (London: Routledge, 1998), 178.

2 William Cline, *In the Nick of Time: Motion Picture Sound Serials* (Jefferson, NC: McFarland, 1984), 199.

3 Henry Jenkins, "Game Design as Narrative Architecture," in *First Person: New Media as Story, Performance, and Game*, ed. Noah Wardrip-Fruin and Pat Harrigan (Cambridge, MA: MIT Press, 2004), 122.

4 Shane Denson and Andreas Jahn-Sudmann, "Digital Seriality: On the Serial Aesthetics and Practice of Digital Games," *Eludamos* 7, no. 1 (2013): 8.

5 Ibid., 6.

6 Jesper Juul, *Half-Real: Video Games between Real Rules and Fictional Worlds* (Cambridge, MA: MIT Press, 2005), 141–143.

7 For a parallel discussion of discontinuity in silent serials, see Shane Denson, "The Logic of the Line Segment: Continuity and Discontinuity in the Serial-Queen Melodrama," in *Serialization in Popular Culture*, ed. Thijs van den Berg and Rob Allen (London: Routledge, 2014), 65–79.

8 Denson and Jahn-Sudmann, "Digital Seriality," 4, 7.

9 Jason Mittell, "Playing for Plot in the *Lost* and *Portal* Franchises," *Eludamos* 6, no. 1 (2012): 5.

10 Johan Huizinga, *Homo Ludens: A Study of the Play-Element in Culture* (Boston: Beacon Press, 1950), 10.

Selected Bibliography

Archives

Academy of Motion Picture Arts and Sciences, Margaret Herrick Library, Los Angeles, CA
Autry National Research Center, Los Angeles, CA

Trade Periodicals

Daily Variety, 1930–1956
Motion Picture Exhibitor, 1934–1958

Books and Articles

Allen, Robert, and Thijs van den Berg, eds. *Serialization in Popular Culture.* London: Routledge, 2014.

Altman, Rick. "Dickens, Griffith, and Film Theory Today." In *Classical Hollywood Narrative: The Paradigm Wars*, ed. Jane Gaines, 39–41. Durham, NC: Duke University Press, 1992.

Backer, Ron. *Gripping Chapters: The Sound Movie Serials.* Albany, GA: BearManor Media, 2010.

Barker, Jennifer. *The Tactile Eye: Touch and the Cinematic Experience.* Berkeley: University of California Press, 2009.

Bifulco, Michael. *Heroes and Villains: Movie Serial Classics.* Woodland Hills, CA: Bifulco Books, 1989.

Blumer, Herbert. *Movies and Conduct.* New York: Macmillan, 1933.

Bordwell, David. *Poetics of Cinema.* New York: Routledge, 2008.

———. *The Way Hollywood Tells It: Story and Style in Modern Movies.* Berkeley: University of California Press, 2006.

Bordwell, David, Janet Staiger, and Kristin Thompson. *The Classical Hollywood Cinema: Film Style and Mode of Production to 1960.* New York: Columbia University Press, 1985.

Branigan, Edward. *Narrative Comprehension and Film.* New York: Routledge, 1992.

Brasch, Ilka. "Structuring Serial Worlds: New and Fiction Media in Film Serials of the 1910s." Paper presented at the annual meeting of the Society of Cinema and Media Studies, Seattle, WA, March 19–23, 2014.

Brewster, Ben, and Lea Jacobs. *Theatre to Cinema.* New York: Oxford University Press, 1997.

Brooks, Peter. *The Melodramatic Imagination: Balzac, Henry James, Melodrama, and the Mode of Excess*. New Haven, CT: Yale University Press, 1995.

Buckland, Warren. *Directed by Steven Spielberg: Poetics of the Contemporary Hollywood Blockbuster*. Continuum, 2006.

Chapman, James. *Licence to Thrill: A Cultural History of the James Bond Films*. London: I. B. Tauris, 2008.

Cline, William. *In the Nick of Time: Motion Picture Sound Serials*. Jefferson, NC: McFarland, 1984.

———. *Serials-ly Speaking: Essays on Cliffhangers*. Jefferson, NC: McFarland, 1994.

Connor, Steven. "I Believe That the World." In *Cultural Ways of Worldmaking: Media and Narratives*, ed. Vera Nünning, Ansgar Nünning, and Birgit Neumann. Berlin and New York: De Gruyter, 2010.

Cowie, Elizabeth. "Storytelling: Classical Hollywood Cinema and Classical Narrative." In *Contemporary Hollywood Cinema*, ed. Steve Neale and Murray Smith, 178–190. London: Routledge, 1998.

Denson, Shane, and Andreas Jahn-Sudmann. "Digital Seriality: On the Serial Aesthetics and Practice of Digital Games." *Eludamos* 7, no. 1 (2013).

Gerrig, Richard. *Experiencing Narrative Worlds*. New Haven, CT: Yale University Press, 1993.

Gunning, Tom. *D. W. Griffith and the Origins of the American Narrative Film*. Chicago: University of Illinois Press, 1991.

Hagedorn, Roger. "Doubtless to Be Continued: A Brief History of Serial Narrative." In *To Be Continued: Soap Operas around the World*, ed. Robert C. Allen. New York: Routledge, 1995.

Harmon, Jim, and Donald Glut. *The Great Movie Serials: Their Sound and Fury*. Garden City, NY: Doubleday, 1972.

Harris, Neil. *Humbug: The Art of P. T. Barnum*. Boston: Little, Brown, 1973.

Hays, R. M. *The Republic Chapterplays*. Jefferson, NC: McFarland, 1991.

Hayward, Jennifer. *Consuming Pleasures: Active Audiences and Serial Fictions from Dickens to Soap Opera*. Lexington: University Press of Kentucky, 1997.

How to Make Money with Serials: A Universal Text Book for Use of Motion Picture Exhibitors. New York: Universal Pictures Corporation, 1927.

Huizinga, Johan. *Homo Ludens: A Study of the Play-Element in Culture*. Boston: Beacon Press, 1950.

Hurst, Richard M. *Republic Studios: Between Poverty Row and the Majors*. Lanham, MD: Scarecrow Press, 2007.

Jenkins, Henry. "Game Design as Narrative Architecture." In *First Person: New Media as Story, Performance, and Game*, ed. Noah Wardrip-Fruin and Pat Harrigan. Cambridge, MA: MIT Press, 2004.

Jowett, Garth S., Ian C. Jarvie, and Kathryn H. Fuller. *Children and the Movies: Media Influence and the Payne Fund Controversy*. New York: Cambridge University Press, 1996.

Juul, Jesper. *Half-Real: Video Games between Real Rules and Fictional Worlds*. Cambridge, MA: MIT Press, 2005.

Keefe, Patrick Radden. "Spitballing Indy." *New Yorker*, March, 25, 2013, http://www.newyorker.com/culture/culture-desk/spitballing-indy.

Lauweart, Maaike. *The Place of Play: Toys and Digital Cultures*. Amsterdam: Amsterdam University Press, 2009.

Lucas, George, Steven Spielberg, and Lawrence Kasdan. "*Raiders of the Lost Ark* Story Conference Transcript," January 1978, http://maddogmovies.com/almost/scripts/raidersstoryconference1978.pdf.

Mathis, Jack. *Valley of the Cliffhangers*. Northbrook, IL: Jack Mathis Advertising, 1975.

———. *Valley of the Cliffhangers Supplement*. Barrington, IL: Jack Mathis Advertising, 1995.

Mayer, Jacob Peter. *Sociology of Film*. London: Faber and Faber, 1946.

Mayer, Ruth. *Serial Fu Manchu: The Chinese Supervillain and the Spread of Yellow Peril Ideology*. Philadelphia: Temple University Press, 2014.

Mitchell, Alice Miller. *Children and Movies*. Chicago: University of Chicago Press, 1929.

Murray, Janet. "From Game-Story to Cyberdrama." In *First Person: New Media as Story, Performance, and Game*, ed. Noah Wardrip-Fruin and Pat Harrigan. Cambridge, MA: MIT Press, 2004.

Neale, Steve. *Genre and Hollywood*. New York: Routledge, 2000.

Parnaby, Mary, and Maurice Woodhouse. *Children's Cinema Clubs Report*. London: British Film Institute, 1947.

Plantinga, Carl. *Moving Viewers: American Film and the Spectator's Experience*. Berkeley: University of California Press, 2009.

Purse, Lisa. *Contemporary Action Cinema*. Edinburgh: Edinburgh University Press, 2011.

Rubin, Martin. *Thrillers*. Cambridge: Cambridge University Press, 1999.

Shklovsky. Victor. "The Resurrection of the Word." *20th Century Studies* 7/8 (1972): 44.

Singer, Ben. *Melodrama and Modernity: Early Sensational Cinema and Its Contexts*. New York: Columbia University Press, 2001.

Sobchack, Vivian. *Carnal Thoughts: Embodiment and Moving Image Culture*. Berkeley: University of California Press, 2004.

Stedman, Raymond. *The Serials: Suspense and Drama by Installment*. Norman: University of Oklahoma Press, 1977.

Sternberg, Meir. *Expositional Modes and Temporal Ordering in Fiction*. Bloomington: Indiana University Press, 1993.

Sutton-Smith, Brian. *The Ambiguity of Play*. Cambridge, MA: Harvard University Press, 1997.

———. *Toys as Culture*. New York: Gardner Press, 1986.

Sutton-Smith, Brian, Jay Mechling, Thomas W. Johnson, and Felicia R. McMahon, eds. *Children's Folklore: A Sourcebook*. New York: Garland, 1995.

Taves, Brian. *The Romance of Adventure: The Genre of Historical Adventure Movies*. Jackson: University of Mississippi Press, 1993.

Thompson, Kristin. *Breaking the Glass Armor*. Princeton, NJ: Princeton University Press, 1988.

———. *Storytelling in the New Hollywood: Understanding Classical Narrative Technique*. Cambridge, MA: Harvard University Press, 1999.

Thorp, Margaret. *America at the Movies*. New Haven, CT: Yale University Press, 1939.

Tuska, Jon. *The Vanishing Legion: A History of Mascot Pictures, 1927–1935*. Jefferson, NC: McFarland, 1982.

Van Hise, James. *Serial Adventures*. Las Vegas: Pioneer Books, 1990.

Vela, Rafael. "With the Parents [*sic*] Consent: Film Serials, Consumerism and the Creation of a Youth Audience, 1913–1938." PhD diss., University of Wisconsin, Madison, 2000.

Vorderer, Peter, Hans Wulff, and Mike Friedrichsen, eds. *Suspense: Conceptualizations, Theoretical Analyses, and Empirical Explorations*. Mahwah, NJ: Lawrence Erlbaum Associates, 1996.

Wardrip-Fruin, Noah, and Pat Harrigan, eds. *First Person: New Media as Story, Performance, and Game*. Cambridge, MA: MIT Press, 2004.

Williams, Linda. *Playing the Race Card*. Princeton, NJ: Princeton University Press, 2001.

Witney, William. *In a Door, into a Fight, out a Door, into a Chase: Moviemaking Remembered by the Guy at the Door*. Jefferson, NC: McFarland, 1996.

Filmography, 1930–1956

1930

Finger Prints (Universal, 10 ch.)
The Indians Are Coming (Universal, 12 ch.)
The Jade Box (Universal, 10 ch.)
The Lightning Express (Universal, 10 ch.)
The Lone Defender (Mascot, 12 ch.)
Spell of the Circus (Universal, 10 ch.)
Terry of the Times (Universal, 10 ch.)
Voice from the Sky (Ben Wilson, 10 ch.)

1931

Battling with Buffalo Bill (Universal, 12 ch.)
Danger Island (Universal, 12 ch.)
Detective Lloyd (Universal, 12 ch.)
The Galloping Ghost (Mascot, 12 ch.)
Heroes of the Flames (Universal, 12 ch.)
King of the Wild (Mascot, 12 ch.)
The Lightning Warrior (Mascot, 12 ch.)
Mystery Trooper (Syndicate Pictures, 10 ch.)
The Phantom of the West (Mascot, 10 ch.)
Sign of the Wolf (Metropolitan, 10 ch.)
The Vanishing Legion (Mascot, 12 ch.)

1932

The Airmail Mystery (Universal, 12 ch.)
The Devil Horse (Mascot, 12 ch.)
Heroes of the West (Universal, 12 ch.)
The Hurricane Express (Mascot, 12 ch.)
The Jungle Mystery (Universal, 12 ch.)
The Last Frontier (RKO, 12 ch.)
The Last of the Mohicans (Mascot, 12 ch.)
The Lost Special (Universal, 12 ch.)
The Shadow of the Eagle (Mascot, 12 ch.)

1933

Clancy of the Mounted (Universal, 12 ch.)
Fighting with Kit Carson (Mascot, 12 ch.)
Gordon of Ghost City (Universal, 12 ch.)
Mystery Squadron (Mascot, 12 ch.)
Perils of Pauline (Universal, 12 ch.)
Phantom of the Air (Universal, 12 ch.)
Tarzan the Fearless (Principal Pictures, 12 ch.)
The Three Musketeers (Mascot, 12 ch.)
The Whispering Shadow (Mascot, 12 ch.)
The Wolf Dog (Mascot, 12 ch.)

1934

Burn 'Em Up Barnes (Mascot, 12 ch.)
The Law of the Wild (Mascot, 12 ch.)
The Lost Jungle (Mascot, 12 ch.)
Mystery Mountain (Mascot, 12 ch.)
Pirate Treasure (Universal, 12 ch.)
The Red Rider (Universal, 15 ch.)

The Return of Chandu (Principal Pictures, 12 ch.)
Tailspin Tommy (Universal, 12 ch.)
The Vanishing Shadow (Universal, 12 ch.)
Young Eagles (First Division, 12 ch.)

1935

The Adventures of Frank Merriwell (Universal, 12 ch.)
The Adventures of Rex and Rinty (Mascot, 12 ch.)
The Call of the Savage (Universal, 12 ch.)
Custer's Last Stand (Stage and Screen, 15 ch.)
Fighting Marines (Mascot, 12 ch.)
The Lost City (Krellberg/Regal, 12 ch.)

The Miracle Rider (Mascot, 15 ch.)
The New Adventures of Tarzan (BTE, 12 ch.)
The Phantom Empire (Mascot, 12 ch.)
Queen of the Jungle (Screen Attractions, 12 ch.)
The Roaring West (Universal, 15 ch.)
Rustlers of Red Dog (Universal, 12 ch.)
Tailspin Tommy in the Great Air Mystery (Universal, 12 ch.)

1936

Ace Drummond (Universal, 13 ch.)
The Black Coin (Stage and Screen, 15 ch.)
The Clutching Hand (Stage and Screen, 15 ch.)
Darkest Africa (Republic, 15 ch.)
Flash Gordon (Universal, 13 ch.)
Jungle Jim (Universal, 12 ch.)

The Phantom Rider (Universal, 15 ch.)
Robinson Crusoe of Clipper Island (Republic, 14 ch.)
The Shadow of Chinatown (Victory, 15 ch.)
Undersea Kingdom (Republic, 12 ch.)
The Vigilantes Are Coming (Republic, 12 ch.)

1937

Blake of Scotland Yard (Victory, 15 ch.)
Dick Tracy (Republic, 15 ch.)
Jungle Menace (Columbia, 15 ch.)
The Mysterious Pilot (Columbia, 15 ch.)
The Painted Stallion (Republic, 12 ch.)
Radio Patrol (Universal, 12 ch.)

Secret Agent X-9 (Universal, 12 ch.)
S O S Coast Guard (Republic, 12 ch.)
Tim Tyler's Luck (Universal, 12 ch.)
Wild West Days (Universal, 13 ch.)
Zorro Rides Again (Republic, 12 ch.)

1938

Dick Tracy Returns (Republic, 15 ch.)
The Fighting Devil Dogs (Republic, 12 ch.)
Flaming Frontiers (Universal, 15 ch.)
Flash Gordon's Trip to Mars (Universal, 15 ch.)
The Great Adventures of Wild Bill Hickok (Columbia, 15 ch.)

Hawk of the Wilderness (Republic, 12 ch.)
The Lone Ranger (Republic, 15 ch.)
Red Barry (Universal, 13 ch.)
Scouts to the Rescue (Universal, 12 ch.)
The Secret of Treasure Island (Columbia, 15 ch.)
The Spider's Web (Columbia, 15 ch.)

1939

Buck Rogers (Universal, 12 ch.)
Daredevils of the Red Circle (Republic, 12 ch.)
Dick Tracy's G-Men (Republic, 15 ch.)
Flying G-Men (Columbia, 15 ch.)
The Green Hornet (Universal, 13 ch.)
The Lone Ranger Rides Again (Republic, 15 ch.)

Mandrake, the Magician (Columbia, 12 ch.)
The Oregon Trail (Universal, 15 ch.)
Overland with Kit Carson (Columbia, 15 ch.)
The Phantom Creeps (Universal, 12 ch.)
Zorro's Fighting Legion (Republic, 12 ch.)

1940

Adventures of Red Ryder (Republic, 12 ch.)
Deadwood Dick (Columbia, 15 ch.)
Drums of Fu Manchu (Republic, 15 ch.)
Flash Gordon Conquers the Universe (Universal, 12 ch.)
The Green Archer (Columbia, 15 ch.)
The Green Hornet Strikes Again (Universal, 13 ch.)

Junior G-Men (Universal, 12 ch.)
King of the Royal Mounted (Republic, 12 ch.)
The Mysterious Doctor Satan (Republic, 15 ch.)
The Shadow (Columbia, 15 ch.)
Terry and the Pirates (Columbia, 15 ch.)
Winners of the West (Universal, 13 ch.)

1941

Adventures of Captain Marvel (Republic, 12 ch.)
Dick Tracy vs. Crime Inc. (Republic, 15 ch.)
Don Winslow of the Navy (Universal, 12 ch.)
Holt of the Secret Service (Columbia, 15 ch.)
The Iron Claw (Columbia, 15 ch.)
Jungle Girl (Republic, 15 ch.)

King of the Texas Rangers (Republic, 12 ch.)
Riders of Death Valley (Universal, 15 ch.)
Sea Raiders (Universal, 12 ch.)
Sky Raiders (Universal, 12 ch.)
The Spider Returns (Columbia, 15 ch.)
White Eagle (Columbia, 15 ch.)

1942

The Adventures of Smilin' Jack (Universal, 13 ch.)
Captain Midnight (Columbia, 15 ch.)
Don Winslow of the Coast Guard (Universal, 13 ch.)
Gang Busters (Universal, 13 ch.)
Junior G-Men of the Air (Universal, 12 ch.)

King of the Mounties (Republic, 12 ch.)
Overland Mail (Universal, 15 ch.)
Perils of Nyoka (Republic, 15 ch.)
Perils of the Royal Mounted (Columbia, 15 ch.)
The Secret Code (Columbia, 15 ch.)
Spy Smasher (Republic, 12 ch.)
The Valley of Vanishing Men (Columbia, 15 ch.)

1943

Adventures of the Flying Cadets (Universal, 13 ch.)
Batman (Columbia, 15 ch.)
Captain America (Republic, 15 ch.)
Daredevils of the West (Republic, 12 ch.)

G-Men vs. the Black Dragon (Republic, 15 ch.)
The Masked Marvel (Republic, 12 ch.)
The Phantom (Columbia, 15 ch.)
Secret Service in Darkest Africa (Republic, 15 ch.)

1944

Black Arrow (Columbia, 15 ch.)
The Desert Hawk (Columbia, 15 ch.)
The Great Alaskan Mystery (Universal, 13 ch.)
Haunted Harbor (Republic, 15 ch.)

Mystery of the River Boat (Universal, 13 ch.)
Raiders of Ghost City (Universal, 13 ch.)
The Tiger Woman (Republic, 12 ch.)
Zorro's Black Whip (Republic, 12 ch.)

1945

Brenda Starr, Reporter (Columbia, 13 ch.)
Federal Operator 99 (Republic, 12 ch.)
Jungle Queen (Universal, 13 ch.)
Jungle Raiders (Columbia, 15 ch.)
Manhunt of Mystery Island (Republic, 15 ch.)
The Master Key (Universal, 13 ch.)
The Monster and the Ape (Columbia, 15 ch.)

The Phantom Rider (Republic, 12 ch.)
The Purple Monster Strikes (Republic, 15 ch.)
The Royal Mounted Rides Again (Universal,
    13 ch.)
Secret Agent X-9 (Universal, 13 ch.)
Who's Guilty (Columbia, 15 ch.)

1946

Chick Carter, Detective (Columbia, 15 ch.)
The Crimson Ghost (Republic, 12 ch.)
Daughter of Don Q (Republic, 12 ch.)
Hop Harrigan (Columbia, 15 ch.)
King of the Forest Rangers (Republic, 12 ch.)

The Lost City of the Jungle (Universal, 13 ch.)
The Mysterious Mr. M (Universal, 13 ch.)
The Scarlet Horseman (Universal, 13 ch.)
The Son of the Guardsman (Columbia, 15 ch.)

1947

The Black Widow (Republic, 13 ch.)
G-Men Never Forget (Republic, 12 ch.)
Jack Armstrong (Columbia, 15 ch.)
Jesse James Rides Again (Republic, 13 ch.)

The Sea Hound (Columbia, 15 ch.)
Son of Zorro (Republic, 13 ch.)
The Vigilante (Columbia, 15 ch.)

1948

Adventures of Frank and Jesse James (Repub-
    lic, 13 ch.)
Brick Bradford (Columbia, 15 ch.)
Congo Bill (Columbia, 15 ch.)
Dangers of the Canadian Mounted (Republic,
    12 ch.)

Federal Agents vs. Underworld, Inc. (Repub-
    lic, 12 ch.)
Superman (Columbia, 15 ch.)
Tex Granger (Columbia, 15 ch.)

1949

The Adventures of Sir Galahad (Columbia,
    15 ch.)
Batman and Robin (Columbia, 15 ch.)
Bruce Gentry—Daredevil of the Skies (1949,
    15 ch.)

Ghost of Zorro (Republic, 12 ch.)
The James Brothers of Missouri (Republic,
    12 ch.)
King of the Rocket Men (Republic, 12 ch.)
Radar Patrol vs. Spy King (Republic, 12 ch.)

1950

Atom Man vs. Superman (Columbia, 15 ch.)
Cody of the Pony Express (Columbia, 15 ch.)
Desperadoes of the West (Republic, 12 ch.)

Flying Disc Man from Mars (Republic, 12 ch.)
The Invisible Monster (Republic, 12 ch.)
Pirates of the High Seas (Columbia, 15 ch.)

1951

Captain Video (Columbia, 15 ch.)
Don Daredevil Rides Again (Republic, 12 ch.)
Government Agents vs. the Phantom Legion (Republic, 12 ch.)

Mysterious Island (Columbia, 15 ch.)
Roar of the Iron Horse (Columbia, 15 ch.)

1952

Blackhawk (Columbia, 15 ch.)
Jungle Drums of Africa (Republic, 12 ch.)
King of the Congo (Columbia, 15 ch.)

Radar Men from the Moon (Republic, 12 ch.)
Son of Geronimo (Columbia, 15 ch.)
Zombies of the Stratosphere (Republic, 12 ch.)

1953

Canadian Mounties vs. Atomic Invaders (Republic, 12 ch.)
Commando Cody, Sky Marshal of the Universe (Republic, 12 ch.) [produced for television but released theatrically as well]

The Great Adventures of Captain Kidd (Columbia, 15 ch.)
The Lost Planet (Columbia, 15 ch.)

1954

Gunfighters of the Northwest (Columbia, 15 ch.)
Man with the Steel Whip (Republic, 12 ch.)

Riding with Buffalo Bill (Columbia, 15 ch.)
Trader Tom of the China Seas (Republic, 12 ch.)

1955

Adventures of Captain Africa (Columbia, 15 ch.)
King of the Carnival (Republic, 12 ch.)

Panther Girl of the Kongo (Republic, 12 ch.)

1956

Blazing the Overland Trail (Columbia, 15 ch.)

Perils of the Wilderness (Columbia, 15 ch.)

Index

action, 139, 147, 152; distribution, 116–120; and melodrama, 65, 177; plotting, 116; and problem solving, 143; and romance, 46; scenes and setups, 113; sequences, 125–141, 157. *See also* character action; chases; escapes; exposition and action; fights

action and adventure films, 156, 173, 174

action films, 21–22, 164, 170, 174; physical effect, 21; and serials, 25

action melodramas, 75, 174

action prologues, 167

act structure vs. episode structure, 164

adaptation, 161

adventure and comedy, 198n6

Adventures of Captain Marvel, 40, 57–58

Adventures of Frank and Jesse James, 93

Adventures of Robin Hood, 43–44, 45–46

"aesthetics of astonishment" (Gunning), 106

Aldridge, Kay, *118, 150, 153,* 196n11

alternate reality games (ARGs), 183

Altman, Rick, 11

amnesia, 121, 175

"anomalous suspense" (Gerrig), 81

appropriation, 127–132, 161

ARGs, 183

audiences, 7–9, 13, 16, 65, 111, 114, 155, 179

Backer, Ron, *Gripping Chapters,* 91, 189n4

Balio, Tino, 197n2 (ch. 7)

Barefoot, Guy, 4, 9

Barker, Jennifer, 21, 142–143

Basinger, Jeanine, 198n6

Batman, 99–100, 196n4

Batman [television series], 135, 180

Batman and Robin, 42, 55, 56, *56,* 61, 99, 100–101, *101,* 196n4

Benito Juarez, 40

Berkeley, Busby, 135

Bifulco, Michael, 189n4

Bitzer, Billy, 77

Blackhawk, 38, 50, 135

Blazing the Overland Trail, 197n1 (ch. 7)

blockbuster films, 159–161, 174

Blumer, Herbert, *Movies and Conduct,* 16–17, 84

Bond franchise. *See* James Bond films

Bordwell, David, 3, 36, 164, 170, 194n17, 198n15

Bordwell, David, Janet Staiger, and Kristin Thompson, *The Classical Hollywood Cinema,* 4, 11

The Bourne Identity, 174–175

The Bourne Supremacy, 174–176

The Bourne Ultimatum, 26, 174–176

Branigan, Edward, 83–84, 197n12

Brasch, Ilka, 51

Brenda Starr, Reporter, 9, 85

Brewster, Ben, and Lea Jacobs, *From Theater to Cinema,* 11, 12–13, 37, 164, 199n21

Brix, Herman, *112*
Broccoli, Albert, 157–159
Bronner, Simon, 54
Brooks, Peter, *The Melodramatic Imagination*, 14, 15, 22, 60–61, 103
Buckland, Warren, 160, 162
"bumps," 157
Burroughs, Edgar Rice, 196n11

Canutt, Yakima, 136
Captain Marvel, 103
Captain Midnight, 100, 134, *135*, 144–145, *144–145*
Captain Video Master of the Stratosphere, 197n1 (ch. 7)
Captain Video and His Video Rangers [television series], 197n1 (ch. 7)
capture-the-flag, 142
Carroll, Noel, 82–83, 90
Casablanca, 161
Casino Royale, 177
causality, 51, 54, 164, 173
Cerf, Norman, 129
chapter structure, 116–120
character: and action, 111–115, 130, 151; development, 165–166; and space, 142
characters, 60–63, 111–115; comic, 123–124; motivation, 114; and play, 142; psychological development, 175; symmetry, 111. *See also* heroes and villains
chases, 137
cheats, 154
China, 161
Chocano, Carina, 175
choreography, 137
Chudacoff, Howard, 142
cinema clubs, 8, 18
cinematic thinking, 176, 179
cinematography: and framing, 129, 138; and narrative comprehension, 134; and shooting style, 6, 135–136
Citizen Kane, 161
classicism, 4, 11, 160, 164
cliffhangers, 17, 19–20, 32, 72–97, 144–154, 167–173, 178, 182; conventions, 118; ellipses, 99–101; as games, 91; points of revision, 93–95; in television series, 180; viewing procedures, 95–96
"cliffover" (Backer), 91

climax, 170, 171–173. *See also* double climax
Cline, William, 44, 189n4, 196n5, 197n6, 199n2
close-up, 150–151, *151*
coincidence, 88
Cole, Royal, 190n14, 196n4
Collins, Lewis, 129
Collins, Suzanne, *The Hunger Games*, 182
Columbia, 98, 134, 189n10, 195n1, 197n1 (ch. 7); stunt team, 134–135
comedy, 51; and adventure, 198n6
comic books, 196n11
Commando Cody [television show], 192n5
composition, 138, 149, 150
Connor, Steven, 39
contest, 15
continuing narrative, 3
continuity, 129
convention and creativity, 120
Cowie, Elizabeth, 180
crisis and resolution, 93, 117–119
critics. *See* film critics
crosscutting/parallel editing, 14, 30, 78–80, 87, 147, 148, 152, 197n11
Crowley, Pat, 174
Custer's Last Stand, 65
cutting, 139, 149, 152. *See also* crosscutting/parallel editing
cyberdrama (Murray), 15

Dahl, Roald, 157, 158
Daredevils of the Red Circle, 24, 102–106, *104, 106*, 111–115, *112*, 117–118, 122–124, 135, 136–143, *138, 140, 143*, 146–148, *147*; plot, 114–115; score, 114
Daughter of Don Q, 92
Davidson, Ronald, 106
deathtrap, in plots, 104, 144–145
decline, of sound serials, 156
Demon Attack [game], 20
DeNormand, George, 136, *140*
Denson, Shane, 60, 199n7
Denson, Shane, and Andreas Jahn-Sudmann, "Digital Seriality" [article], 15, 181
Deutsche Universal-Film, 128
dialogue, 130
Dickey, Basil, 34
Dick Tracy vs. Crime Inc., 69–70, *70*

digital games, 181–183. *See also* videogames
directors, 6
discontinuity, 85, 169, 181, 199n7
Don Winslow of the Navy, 18, 58
double climax, 37
The Drums of Fu Manchu, 7, 58, 157, 164–165

economy episodes, 90, 122
Edelstein, David, 175
editing, 79, 126, 127–132, 148–154, 159;
    and cinematography, 134. *See also* cross-
    cutting/parallel editing; cutting
effects, 37, 105–106; on stage, 12–13
ellipses, 99–101
entrapment and escape, 146, 162, 169, 176
episodic series format, in television series,
    180
escapes, 120, 162, 176
Exhibitor [trade publication], 128
expectation of uniqueness (Gerrig), 82
Exploits of Elaine, 51
exposition, 30–31, 116–119, 146, 161, 166, 171;
    and action, 25, 34, 41

factory fights, 141, 143
Fairbanks, Douglas, 198n6
"fatal gesture" (Gunning), 79–80, 180
Fawcett, Jimmy, *112*, 136, 138, *140, 143*
feature films, adaptations of serials, 159–161
Field, Syd, *Screenplay*, 163
The Fighting Devil Dogs, 13, 159, 194n29,
    196n7
fights, 133–136, 141, 143
film combat. *See* fights
film critics, 7, 14
final chapters, of sound serials, 44
fistfights, 133
five-part format, 29–38, 43, 120, 179
flashback, 90, 100, 122–123, 195n22
Flash Gordon, 29–32, 40, 52, *52–53*, 102,
    127
flexibility vs. unity, in sound serials, 109
formal dominant (Thompson), 58
formula, 23, 29–38, 92, 98–124, 125–155, 179;
    in editing, 75; narrative economy, 41; in
    one-reelers, 75; in screenwriting, 163; for
    suspense, 82; and variation, 5, 120
frames of reference, 84
Frasca, Gonzalo, 15

Fraser, Harry L., 196n4
"functional fixedness" (Gerrig), 78

gag films, 51
games, 20, 54–55, 141–143, 180; and story-
    telling, 15, 20, 57, 141–143
Gang Busters, 92
Gerrig, Richard, 77–80, 81, 82
Ghost of Zorro, 6
Ghost Train, 71
Gilroy, Tony, 174
gimmicks, 104–105
Glickman, Mort, 119, 149
Glut, Donald, 93, 189n4, 196n5
G-Men Never Forget, 92
"golden age," of sound serials, 8, 98, 196n5
Goodgold, Ed, 190n27
Gray, Lorna, *126, 151*
The Great Adventures of Captain Kidd, 8
The Great Alaskan Mystery, 25, 55, 56, *56*, 63,
    127–132, *132*
The Great Train Robbery, 51
Greene, Eric, 198n9
Greengrass, Paul, 174–175
The Green Hornet, 133–134, *133*
Griffith, D. W., 76–80, *80–81*

Hansen, Miriam, 96
Harmon, Jim, 92, 189n4, 196n5
Harris, Neil, 23, 50
Hawk of the Wilderness, 136
Hayward, Jennifer, 154
Hazards of Helen, 75
Hennequin, Alfred, *The Art of Playwriting*, 37
heroes and villains, 60–63, 111, 162, 171, 175;
    origin stories, 40, 67, 111
hide-and-seek, 142
historical adventure films, 43, 62
historical poetics, 3, 5, 180
History Is Made at Night, 128
Hodgins, Earle, *112*
Hollywood: blockbusters, 159, 174, 179; clas-
    sicism, 4; plots, 198n15
Holt of the Secret Service, 9, 92
Horne, James, 134
hostage situations, 170–171
The House of Hate, 17
How to Make Money with Serials [manual],
    9, 38

Huizinga, Johan, *Homo Ludens*, 15, 48, 55, 183
humor, 158, 198n6
The Hunger Games, 182
The Hurricane Express, 64
Hurst, Richard M., 135, 196n5

illusions, 106
industrial settings, 141
infernal machines, 144, 145
innovation and formulas, 179
interactive narrative, 15
interpolations, 86
interruption and delay, 79
In the Balcony [online discussion], 195n28
The Invisible Monster, 7
irony, 198n6

Jack Armstrong, 135
Jacobs, Lea, 37, 164, 199n21
Jahn-Sudmann, Andreas, 15, 181
James Bond films, 156–159, 167, 177; formula, 157
Jason Bourne trilogy, 174–177
Jenkins, Henry, 18, 180–181
Jungle Girl, 196n11
Jungle Queen, 58
Junior G-Men, 9, 92
Just Imagine, 127
Juul, Jesper, 18, 19–20, 181–182, 191n50

Kalem Company, 75
Katzman, Sam, 102, 135, 195n1
Kimball, Russell, 126
King of the Mounties, 6
King of the Royal Mounted, 65
kung fu films, 136

labyrinths, 63
Landis, Carol, *147*
Lanning, Reggie, 149
Last of the Mohicans, 68
Lauwaert, Maaike, 54
Lava, William, 114
lighting, 150
Lively, William, 190n14
locations, 128, 141
The Lonely Villa, 14
The Lone Ranger, 40, 66–68, 90, 92, 100; pressbook, 6

The Lone Ranger [television series], 180
loss as theme, 64–68
Lost [ARG], 183
Lost in Space [television series], 180
The Lost Planet, 8
love interest, 42
Lucas, George, 159–160, 173
ludic space, 141–143
ludic tradition across media, 180
ludology, 15
Lydecker, Theodore, 146

machines, 52, 57, 144, 145
Maibaum, Richard, 158
Mandrake, the Magician, 55, *56*, 58, 61, 81
Manning, Knox, 85
Mapes, Ted, 136
Mark of Zorro, 42
Martinelli, Tony, 148
Marvel Studios, 174
masked figures, 61
The Masked Marvel, 93
The Master Key, 92
material culture, 54
Mathis, Jack, 7, 34, 190n12, 192n1, 196n5, 197n7; *The Valley of the Cliffhangers*, 102
Mayer, Jacob Peter, *Sociology of Film*, 18, 58
Mayer, Ruth, 48
McCarthy, Todd, 175
McLeod, Victor, 196n4
mechanisms, 50–57, 148–149
medical melodramas, 121
melodrama, 10–15, 75, 173; action elements, 65; and action films, 174; and classicism, 164, 179; conventions, 121, 174; and play, 10, 22, 60–65, 179; romantic, 121; and serials, 177; situations, 131; and storytelling, 182; theatrical, 11. *See also* action melodramas; medical melodramas
middle action, 31, 33
Miller, Seton, 43
miniatures, for effects, 146, 148
misdirection, 88, 152
Mitchell, Alice Miller, *Children and Movies*, 16
Mittell, Jason, 183
montage, 148
moral clarity, 179
motifs, 169

Motion Picture Exhibitor [trade publication], 7–8
movie theaters, 73
Moving Picture World [trade publication], 14
Murray, Janet, 15, 57
"muscular empathy" (Barker), 21, 142
Musser, Charles, 50–51

narration, 36, 154, 175; levels, 83–84, 90–91. *See also* storytelling
narrative: in early film, 77; experience of, 82; and play, 15, 19–20, 57, 141–143; and rules, 20; spatial, 116. *See also* continuing narrative; popular narrative
narrative architecture (Jenkins), 18–19, 43–44, 47, 142, 167, 175
narrative complexity, 122
narrative comprehension, 99, 101
narrative deception, 152
narrative economy, 115
narrative structures, 23, 173. *See also* plots
narrator and spectator, 90
Neale, Steve, 10
new media, 15
nickelodeon, 75
Nobles, William, 141
Nyoka and the Tiger Men, 196n11

obstacles, 176
one-reel films, 37, 75–80, 179
On Her Majesty's Secret Service, 177
opening episodes, of sound serials, 38–42
openings, of sound serial heirs, 159, 167, 169
operational aesthetic (Harris), 23, 50–52, 103, 113, 148, 176, 179; in stunts, 141
origin stories, 40, 67, 111
O'Sullivan, William, 196n11
Our Hospitality, 51
Overland Mail, 7

pacing, 166
The Painted Stallion, 59
parallel editing. *See* cross-cutting/parallel editing
Parnaby, Mary, 58, 84
participatory culture, 179
Pathé films, 79
pathos, 65–68, 114
Payne Fund Studies, 16

perils and escapes, 91–95, 120
Perils of Nyoka, 24, 106–111, *108*, 116–117, *118*, 118–122, 125–127, 148–154, *149*, *150*, *151*, *153*, 171; alternate versions, 196n11; plot, 116–117; score, 119, 149
Perils of Pauline, 11, 111, 168
The Phantom Empire, 1, *2*, 7, 62, 183, 194n9; opening episode, 49
phenomenology, in film studies, 21–22
Piaget, Jean, 55
Planet of the Apes, 159
plausibility, 174
play, 15–22, 60–71, 180–181; and melodrama, 10, 22, 64, 179; physical, 21, 141–143; and popular narrative, 15; vicarious, 142–143
playwriting, 12
plotting, 43, 164, 198n15; situational, 37
plots, 12–15, 43; multiple climax, 37; structural integrity, 109, 164; symmetry, 110. *See also* exposition; narration; weenie plots
Plympton, George, 128, 196n4
poetics, in film studies, 3, 180
point-of-view structure, 129
points of revision, in cliffhangers, 93–95
Poland, Joseph, 196n4
Polti, Georges, *The Thirty-six Dramatic Situations*, 12, 13, 164, 170, 172
Popular Mechanics [magazine], 54
popular narrative, 15
portability of character and situation, 62
postclassicism, 160
problem solving, 57, 77
"problem spaces" (Gerrig), 77–80, 168, 172, 175–176
procedures and operations, 50–60, *52–53*, 105–106, 131, 176, 178; in games, 54
production, 6, 179
production boards, 6
Production Code Administration, 18
production design, 127, 129
Purse, Lisa, 21, 91
puzzles, 15, 81

Quigley, Charles, *147*

race to the rescue, 14, 83, 87, 194n9
racism, 124

Radar Men from the Moon, 35

Radar Patrol vs. Spy King, 92

radio, 197n1 (ch. 7)

Raiders of the Lost Ark, 25, 159, 160, 161–174, 179

Raine, Norman Reilly, 43

Random Harvest, 121

Raymond, Alex, 31

recaps, 85, 169, 175

"recidivism," in suspense (Carroll), 83

redundancy, 36

reformers, 18

reframing, 153

reordering, 197n11

repetition, 36, 50

Republic, 5, 34, 98, 102, 119, 120, 127, 132–133, 141, 189n10, 195n1, 196n5; serial unit, 189–190n10; sets, 40; stunt team, 132–133, 136–143; television, 192n5

restaging, 153

revelation scenes, 61

revision, 127, 152–153, 197n11

Riders of Death Valley, 7, 102

romantic subplots, 46, 164

Rubin, Martin, 63, 197n3 (ch. 7)

rules, in gameplay and formula, 19–20, 70, 82

Saltzman, Harry, 157–159

Schickel, Richard, 113

Scouts to the Rescue, 9

screenwriters, 67, 85

Secret of the Incas, 161

"segment shooting," 136

sensation, 13, 173

seriality: and play, 181; studies, 3

serial media, 183

serial queens, 111

"service serials," 196n7

set design, 77, 137

sets, reused, 40, 50

setup, 99

The Seven Cities of Cibola, 168

sexuality, 158

Sharpe, David, 120, 136, *140*

Shipman, Barry, 103

Shklovsky, Viktor, 3

Shor, Sol, 190n14

shot scale, 134

Siegel, Moe, 158

Sign of the Wolf, 92

silent films, 51. *See also* silent serials

silent serials, 10, 51, 72, 179, 199n7; audience, 17

Singer, Ben, 10, 72, 193

situational dramaturgy, 11–12, 13, 37–38, 173, 174

situations: dramatic, 12; modular, 106; in sound serials, 38, 167

Sky Raiders, 193n15

Slocombe, Douglas, 168

Slocum, Cy, 136

Smith, Murray, 173

Snowflake (Fred Toones), 123–124

Sobchack, Vivian, 21

Soderberg, Charles, 112, *112*

S.O.S. Iceberg, 128–132, *130–131*

Soter, Tom, 197n4 (ch. 7)

sound and image, 150

"spatial stories" (Jenkins), 18–19

special effects. *See* effects

spectacle, 132, 166, 172

spectator and film, 90

Spielberg, Stephen, 160, 167–173

Spy Smasher, 58, 65, 101, 196nn4,7

Stagecoach, 166

stage melodrama, 11

Staiger, Janet, 192n6

standoffs, 171

Star Wars franchise, 159–160

Stedman, Raymond, 189n4

stereotypes, 123–124

Sternberg, Meir, 79–80, 81

stock footage, 127–132

stories and games, 15, 57

story and formula, 19

storyteller: and story world, 90; and viewer, 77–80

storytelling, 4, 36, 86, 90, 122, 161; elaboration, 101; in Hollywood films, 160; and melodrama, 182; physical, 140; and play, 15; in serials, 45–46, 159

story world of a film, 90

stuntmen, 134–137, *135, 138, 140–141, 143*. *See also by name*

stunts, 141, 166

Superman, 40, 42

suspense, 77, 79, 81–84, 148, 174, 194–195n17; and curiosity, 81–84; in genre films, 170; structures, 148

Sutton-Smith, Brian, *The Ambiguity of Play*, 22, 57
Swabacker, Leslie, 196n4
syndicated broadcast of serials, 156

tag [game], 142
Taves, Brian, 43, 62–63
Taylor, Ray, 129
technology, 51–52. *See also* machines; procedures and operations
television, 180, 197n1 (ch. 7)
theaters, 73
Thompson, Kristin, 58, 192n6, 198n15
Thorp, Margaret, 69
three-act structure, 163, 169, 171
"three-girl format," 158
The Three Musketeers, 24, 46, 58, 64, 73–74, *73–74*, 85, 86–88, *88–89*, 89, 92
thrillers, 63
The Tiger Woman, 93–95, *94–95*, *96*, 196n11
time frames, 182
Todd, Edward, 148
Tombragel, Maurice, 128
toys, 54, 57, 159
Trail of the Lonesome Pine, 196–197n15
transformations, 105–106
transitions, optical, 30
traps, 168
travel scenes, 59
The Treasure of the Sierra Madre, 161
tunnel traps, 146
Tuska, Jon, 189n4

Uncle Tom's Cabin [play], 12
undercranking, 134–135
Undersea Kingdom, 85
Under the Gaslight [play], 12

Universal, 5, 98, 127, 195n1; optical department, 30; studio unit, 189n10
The Unseen Enemy, 76–80, *80–81*

Van Hise, James, 189n4
The Vanishing Legion, 64, 85, 88
Variety [trade publication], 5, 131
Vela, Rafael, 4, 198n19
"vernacular modernism" (Hansen), 96
videogames, 15, 20. *See also* digital games
viewer: deception of, 101; engagement, 141–143; expectations, 171; experience, 170; participation, 90
viewing protocols, 169

Walker, Alexander, 157
Warner Bros., 43, 135
watching and playing, 143
weenie, 55–57; hunt, 161, 164–165; plots, 106–110
Weiss, Ken, 190n27
Weiss brothers, 195n1
White Eagle, 7, 65
Williams, Linda, 14, 22, 64, 84
Witney, William, 6, 67, 111, 114, 125, 126, 135, 158, 190n15, 193n13, 197n1 (ch. 6); *In a Door, into a Fight*, 102
Woodhouse, Maurice, 58, 84

You Only Live Twice, 157
youth club campaigns, 8

Zorro Rides Again, 42
Zorro's Black Whip, 34, 93
Zorro's Fighting Legion, 23, 28–29, 32–33, *33*, 39–42, 44–45, 46, 50, 59, 166

About the Author

SCOTT HIGGINS lives in Middletown, Connecticut, where he chairs the College of Film and the Moving Image at Wesleyan University. His previous books include *Harnessing the Technicolor Rainbow: Color Design in the 1930s* (2007) and the edited volume *Arnheim for Film and Media Studies* (2011). He maintains a blog at http://shiggins.blogs.wesleyan.edu/.